Praise for *Stirring Into Flame*

"Deacon Knuth masterfully has assembled an ensemble of scriptures, readings and reflections on the Holy Spirit. A must read for both beginner and seasoned Holy Spirit seekers! As the Holy Spirit gives us one step at a time, so these beautiful presentations from the Holy Spirit are given to us one day at a time! Personally, I have found the book very enriching and helpful."

~ Bishop Daniel Felton, Diocese of Duluth

"*Stirring Into Flame's* invitation to get to know and to love the self-effacing member of the Trinity, the Holy Spirit, is timely. Fifty years ago, St. Paul VI called for a new devotion to the Holy Spirit, fueled by a new study of his role in the mystery of Christ and in the mystery of the Church, 'as an inevitable complement to the teaching of Vatican II.' *Stirring into Flame's* method, lectio divina, facilitates the movement from mind to heart, from reading (lectio) to reflection (meditatio) to devotion (oratio-contemplatio), so that the revealed truth about the Holy Spirit becomes light for one's life (actio)."

~ Douglas Bushman, S.T.L. Retired Prof. of Theology

"Deacon Knuth has created a valuable resource for anyone looking for a compendium of rich references to the Holy Spirit, but *Stirring Into Flame* is much more because he puts each reference into a context of spiritual reflection and practical application. In this new pentecostal age, it is a gift meant to foster our personal renewal and pastoral renewal in the Church and world."

~ Thomas Quinlan, Ministry Director
St. Joseph Evangelization Center

"By carefully collecting hundreds of pieces of spiritual wisdom, Deacon Knuth diligently crafts a masterful mosaic of meditations that carefully craft a tangible portrait of the Holy Spirit. This is a manageable 'Holy Minute' daily devotion for busy mamas."

~ Danielle Rose Hesley, wife, mother, and music missionary

"Deacon Knuth has provided us an abundance of wonderful quotes from the saints, renowned authors, and documents of the Catholic Church on the workings of the Spirit of God. What a wonderful way to begin the day with a reflection on the Holy Spirit. *Stirring Into Flame* is a treasure that can inspire us all to do our part in sharing Jesus with others and to have a way to fan the flame of God's love working powerfully through the Holy Spirit. My prayer is this book will be read by all people. May Jesus be praised!"

~ Mother Lucy Lukasiewicz, DLJC, Superior General

Stirring Into Flame:

A YEAR WITH THE

HOLY SPIRIT

By Deacon Mike Knuth

"… the Lord said: 'I came to cast fire upon the earth; and would that it were already kindled!'"

Lk. 12:42, 49

"King of Mercy, I beg You, by all the love with which Your Heart burns, to destroy completely within me my self-love and, on the other hand, to enkindle in my heart the fire of Your purest love."

St. Faustina – Diary #371

ISBN: 979-8-9904557-0-2 Paperback edition
ISBN: 979-8-9904557-1-9 eBook edition

Excerpts used throughout the book have their sources noted with an extensive bibliography found in the back of the book. These quotes have not been edited and have been printed as they were written. Excerpts from the Holy Ghost Father's Novena to the Holy Spirit (1989 Edition) have used updated language with their permission. Tan Publishing has reprinted and made available, the original novena since 2010.

Cover art by Julie Clark.
Book design by Cathy Behrens.

Contents

I dedicate this book to my wife Lori and all other open vessels of the Holy Spirit who have brought me to Him. *Vene Sancte Spiritus!*

Foreword

"For this reason, I remind you to stir into flame the gift of God that you have through the imposition of my hands. For God did not give us a spirit of cowardice but rather of power and love and self-control. So do not be ashamed of your testimony to our Lord, nor of me, a prisoner for his sake; but bear your share of hardship for the gospel with the strength that comes from God." (2 Timothy 1: 6–8)

There are times in our lives whereby some people may see odd coincidences, but where we who believe, see the hand of God working. I had preached at a daily Mass on this particular passage from St. Paul's letter. After I had finished Mass, I had a visit from Deacon Mike Knuth (and his lovely wife Lori), who had been at that particular Mass. Deacon Mike let me know he was writing a book, and my short homily was right in line with the themes in his writings. I jokingly offered to write the preface. To my surprise, he said yes.

We have known and worked with each other for many years. He and his wife, Lori, have always been great examples to me of true and faithful disciples of Jesus Christ, well in tune with the Spirit's working in and through their lives. So it's no surprise that Mike has taken those many years of teaching, preaching, spiritual direction, and prayer, and compiled them into a book that will help you to know better the Third Person of the Holy Trinity. On day 146 of this book, Deacon Mike quotes Fr. Michael Scanlan, TOR: "The graces and gifts that come with being baptized in the Spirit are not necessarily new gifts that come from the outside. They are also the release of graces we have always had, the fruition of a work the Lord began in us when we were baptized."

In the homily I referred to above, I mentioned a YouTube video I had recently seen. I had discovered a series of videos that demonstrate cooking in the early 1800's. What fascinated me was how there might be slow burning embers or coals in the fireplace, but when breathed on through a pipe, they were easily stirred into flame, and became the means for cooking all sorts of dishes. In a similar way, St. Paul tells St. Timothy to stir into flame the gift of God. If Fr. Scanlan is right, then all of us who have been baptized have hot little coals, embers of the Spirit, already burning deep within. But if those embers aren't stirred and given oxygen, then they remain little coals that only warm our own insides. If they are to become flames that set the whole world on fire with God's Holy Spirit, they need to be stirred into flame! We have not been given the Spirit's gifts and power only for ourselves, but to be used to glorify God and bring others to know Him.

By using this series of reflections, questions and prayers over the next year, you will be giving oxygen to the embers of the Holy Spirit that already burn deep within you. The world needs more disciples of Jesus Christ, who have stirred into flame the gift of God within. The world needs you! The world needs God's servants who both know the Holy Spirit, and are aflame with the Spirit's power.

Fr. Anthony Wroblewski
Pastor of Our Lady of the Lakes Parish
Diocese of Duluth Director of Ministry to Priests

Preface

As I moved down the line of retreatants gathered at the base of the sanctuary, who were waiting to be prayed over, I stepped up to one of our parishioners. Her demeanor told it all. Fear and uncertainty filled her eyes. There was concern written all over her face. Tension and hesitation filled her body with an unnatural stiffness resembling a board. When she saw it was me, the muscles in her face relaxed. As I began to pray over her, the tension and stiffness drained from her and it was a beautiful prayer experience for the two of us. When I moved on to the next person, her eyes were peaceful and a smile was on her lips. But that initial fear in her eyes has haunted me ever since, driving me to ask, why do we fear the Holy Spirit?

Forty years earlier, on Pentecost Sunday, in May of 1978, my wife and I had invited some neighborhood friends that were a part of our ecumenical prayer group to our home for a potluck picnic supper on the beach and a time of worship and praise afterwards. It was a perfect late May evening in Minnesota: cool, blue sky, no bugs, and no breeze or wind. The lake was like glass. Not a ripple could be seen. After a delightful meal, we brought out the guitars and began to praise and worship the Lord, asking for a new outpouring of the Holy Spirit.

In the midst of our prayer, a slight breeze dropped down upon us from above, moved among us for a few seconds, and then headed out across the glass-like surface of the lake, leaving slight ripples in Its wake. As mysteriously as it had come, it was swiftly gone. We all looked at each other and asked at the same time: "What was that?" We recalled the Scripture where Jesus tells us that our Father will give the Holy Spirit to those who ask, and like the wind, we won't know where the Spirit comes from or where He goes. We had been visited by the Holy Spirit.

In both of these experiences, the same Holy Spirit was encountered. In one situation, there was a fear of the unknown

Person. In the second, there was an anticipation and an invoking of a coming of a known Person. Different expressions of anticipation, but the same Spirit, and the same Spirit moving in the midst of His people.

It can be in our fears, in our expectations, in our needs or in our desires that we encounter the Holy Spirit. But how can we relate to the most unknown Member of the Blessed Trinity? How can we come to know this Invisible Person? What can we expect with our encounter with Him? How do we find Him and how do we know it is He and not something or someone else?

An experience of one of my grandchildren can give us some insight. Our 2 year-old grandson was having his diaper changed, and he asked his mother (our daughter) why the bible says the Holy Spirit is a dove. How do you respond to such a theologically rich question in an age appropriate manner to a captive audience lying on a changing table? She told him that the Holy Spirit was invisible and we can't see Him, and that is why the Bible uses images for Him like a dove, fire, and water. After a pause he stated: "I am going to get my 'flash-shlight' and go to look for the Holy Spirit to see if I can find Him."

Looking to find the Holy Spirit is key to answering the questions I posed and to our spiritual lives. It makes sense to me. I have been looking for Him my whole adult life and have experienced Him in countless ways. I have come to find the Holy Spirit to be alive and active, personal and patient. I have felt His gentle presence, His tender whisper, His inspiration and nudges, His profound and simple revealing of truths and mysteries to me. I have experienced His power and might and have seen amazing healings and transformation of people's lives. But who is this Holy Spirit?

There is a need to theologically know who and what the Holy Spirit is and does, but there is a deeper need to go beyond our knowledge about Him, to knowing Him personally and intimately. Knowledge and experience of Him need to go hand-in-hand. In order to understand His role in our lives and the gifts and fruits He bestows, we need to overcome our fears of Him and to come to know Him personally as our closest of friends. This is the One the Father and Son sends, pouring Him into our hearts. This is the One who is to clothe us with power from on high. This is the One who is love Itself.

The Holy Spirit is present to us, but we are often not present to Him. When dealing with the invisible Holy Spirit we can risk seeing Him simply as a symbol or some impersonal power, a dove, a tongue of fire, a mighty wind. These can be of little use to us if they leave us unchanged, slaves to our passions, fears, and sins. Many feel this unknown invisible Person of the Trinity should remain a mystery and kept at arm's length, put on the history shelf, delegated to a non-necessary status. Many don't think He is important or that there is a personal need for Him in their lives and in the life of the Church. In doing so, we have turned off the switch to our "supernatural power source." We have turned our back to Love itself. We are, in fact, denying the way God desires to love us.

The Kingdom of God does not consist in words, but in works of charity and in signs and wonders; the mighty works of God. These are the works of the Holy Spirit, who transforms words into works and sinners into saints. Disciples are made and not born. They are made through the workings of the Holy Spirit, who desires to be present in our life at every moment, and who wishes to fill us with the fullness of God.

My quest to find Him has been very insightful and fruitful, but the most fascinating adventure has been the putting together of this devotional. Everything behind its conception and content was focused around a question that I posed daily and directly to my closest friend, the Holy Spirit: 'Who are You O Holy Spirit?' The answers He has given me have been a real blessing and I hope the fruit of them, this book, will aid you on your search and quest for Him.

So if your heart is willing to encounter and work with the Holy Spirit, it's time to grab your spiritual "flash-shlights" as you spend this next year looking for the Holy Spirit, coming to know Him through the things He has done and continues to do. Do not be afraid. May He renew your faith, making it alive. May He become your closest friend. May this devotional help you to "go and look for the Holy Spirit to see if you can find Him." He is well worth your searching for, and definitely well worth finding. Veni, Sanctus Spiritus, Come, Holy Spirit.

How to Use This Book

Though this is not a book about prayer, it is written to be used in personal prayer. Prayer is the filial relationship between God and you. God seeks to meet His children with great love and to speak to them. His children in turn respond in a conversation. Jesus Himself spent time alone with His Father in prayer in secluded quiet places. Silence, pondering, listening to God speak, and having a filial conversation are the means He used to draw closer to His Father. This book's format has been written to help facilitate this kind of conversation with God and you. Following His model of prayer can bring about maturity in your spiritual life. This is basically the method of prayer known as lectio divina or "divine reading."*

In using lectio divina you read the text slowly, listening for what God has to say to you. You then ponder (meditate) on what you have read, asking God to show you how the sacred text you are praying with applies to your life. Often this leads you to entering into a conversation, a dialogue with God (prayer). Then you sit in silence for a while, just resting in God's presence. Draw your time of prayer to a close by making a resolution or commitment on how you are going to live out the truth God spoke to you. End with a prayer of thanksgiving.

Stirring Into Flame provides you each day a brief reading taken from theological documents, Council documents, the *Catechism of the Catholic Church*, writings of Church Fathers, Saints of both East and West traditions, modern day spiritual writers, and the Bible. The effort is to present the information about the Person of the Holy Spirit both from a scholastic and experiential side. As Church, our theology and lived experience of the Holy Spirit has a deep and rich history as our understanding of Him has evolved over the centuries.

There might be times in your readings that you may think you have heard this elsewhere in the meditations. I have sought to allow similar slants on various themes to be included throughout the book to show the universality of the Church's comprehension of the Holy Spirit.

Each day will have an overview, a citation, questions for your own reflection, and a Closing Prayer. There may be some meditative questions that are similar. This has been done in light of your anticipated spiritual growth throughout the year and the probability of being in a different place and needing to relook at those particular questions as they apply to the given meditation. A sequel to this book of a 33–day preparation to consecrate your life to the Holy Spirit is already in the process.

Readers will note the interchange and use of the title of the Third Person of the Blessed Trinity as Holy Ghost or as Holy Spirit. Quotes cited in this book will reflect the common title used at the time of the author's writing. Because of this interchange of titles, it would be helpful if we took a brief moment to look at the two titles and how to properly understand and use them.

During the great international biblical movement prior to Vatican II, the words Holy Ghost and Holy Spirit were seriously looked at. In an article written for ZENIT NEWS, in May 8, 2012, Father Edward McNamara, LC, gives us insight into these two titles. Both titles can be used.

"The word ghost is of Germanic origin and comes from Old English *gast*, meaning soul, life, breath, good or bad spirit, angel or demon. Christian texts in Old English use *gast* to translate the Latin *Spiritus* from where we get Holy Ghost. The more modern sense of a disembodied dead person is first attested in the late 14th century but remained quite rare. In modern English, the word *gast* sneaked into the word *aghast*, which means "to be terrified, shocked, or rendered breathless." The related German word *Geist*, which means both spirit and ghost, has occasionally found its way into English in words such as *poltergeist*."

In regards to the use of the word Spirit, he says, "*Spirit* comes to English from Latin through French and also means souls, courage, vigor, breath. The original uses in English are mainly translations from the Vulgate Latin Bible that translate the Greek *Pneuma* and Hebrew *Ruah*. Christians also made a distinction between soul and spirit. *Spirit*, in the sense of a supernatural being, is found from the 13th century on."

In the article he makes the point that almost all modern day biblical translations, both Protestant and Catholic, have preferred Holy *Spirit* in most instances. The probable reason he gives is because the meaning of the word *ghost* has gradually shifted over the last 300 years and now predominantly refers to the vision of the specter of a deceased person or a demonic apparition. The title Holy Spirit is now universally used in all official texts, and over the last 50 years has become common usage. The expression *Holy Ghost*, when properly understood, retains its validity in the context of personal prayer for those who wish to continue using it.

I would encourage you to begin each day of meditation invoking the Holy Spirit to aid you in your reflecting. It can be as simple as this: *"Come, Holy Spirit, enkindle in my heart the fire of Your love. Lead me in this time of prayer and meditation. Amen."*

May you come to truly know more personally the Holy Spirit who abides in you.

*An excellent book I use as a text book when teaching lectio divina is Dr. Tim Gray's *Praying Scripture for a Change.* It gives a great step-by-step explanation how to use this method of prayer. Information on his book is found in this book's bibliography. When you do lectio divina, you are not concerned with study and acquiring knowledge, rather you are seeking to grow closer to God by learning to listen and allow the Holy Spirit to lead you.

Breathe in me, O Holy Spirit, that my thoughts may all be holy.
Act in me, O Holy Spirit, that my work too may be holy.
Draw my heart, O Holy Spirit, that I love but what is holy.
Strengthen me, O Holy Spirit, to defend all that is holy.
Guard me then, O Holy Spirit, that I always may be holy.
~ *St. Augustine*

Holy Spirit as Least Known Person of the Trinity

As important as the Holy Spirit is in the Christian life, many have little to no understanding, a vague knowledge, and even more have no real grasp of what the Holy Spirit has done for them or is ready to do if only allowed to.

"The doctrine of the Holy Ghost is without doubt the most important of all the Church's teachings because; if we do not know and love the Holy Ghost we cannot possibly understand the other great truths of our Holy Religion.... Without the Holy Ghost we are blind.

"Not only is this doctrine the most important, it is the most wonderful, the most consoling, the most sublime of all doctrines, for with the Holy Ghost we can do all things easily and well. He is the Spirit of Love, of Peace, of Joy, the Spirit of Divine Consolation. He is the Light of our Souls and Strength of Our Wills.... Yet, strange to say, this doctrine is little understood by great numbers of Christians."

Fr. Paul O'Sullivan, O.P. – *The Holy Ghost Our Greatest Friend*

In God's Presence Consider ...

Could it be possible that my lack of understanding the truths of our faith is directly related to my not knowing and loving the Holy Spirit? Have I been blind to the Holy Spirit's presence in my life?

Closing Prayer

O Holy Spirit, Light of my soul, open the eyes of my heart, that I may see You. Help me to know and love You so that I will never be blind to Your presence in my life.

Flowing from the Pierced Side **Day 2**

The Father sends the Son and in turn, they both send the Holy Spirit with His many gifts to work among us. His work, the extension of the Father and Son, gives us life and is compared to water that is needed for life.

"By the same right as the Son, the Holy Spirit in St. John's writings possesses a divine activity. But what the Son is to the Father, the Holy Spirit is to the Son. The Son has exalted the Father's glory (Jn. 17:4), the Holy Spirit will bring honor to the Son (Jn. 16:14). The Son has made the Father known (Jn. 17:6), the Holy Spirit will make known the Son. In other words he will make us understand the revelation which we have been given (Jn. 14:26; 15:26; 16:14–15). "Finally, the Holy Spirit is the soul of the Church. Now that Jesus is risen and glorified he gives her life: '… If any man is thirsty let him come to me and drink.… Fountains of living water shall flow from his bosom. He was speaking here of the Spirit which was to be received by those who learned to believe in him …' (Jn. 7:37–39).

"So the Spirit is that living water that flows from the pierced side of Jesus, and it is given to the Church now that Jesus is in glory.… Sacramental theology draws some of its most important conclusions from this symbolism, by relating Christian rites to the pierced side of Christ, to the Lord in glory and to the Holy Spirit, the source of living water.

Bernard Piault - *What is the Trinity?*

In God's Presence Consider …

Do I go to God and ask for the "Living Water"? Are there blockages in my life that prevent the "Living Water" from welling up as a fountain? Do I ponder how the Holy Spirit is the source of the "Living Water" flowing forth from the pierced side of Jesus?

Closing Prayer

Come, Holy Spirit, Living Water flowing from the pierced side of our Lord, cleanse me of all self-centeredness and sin. Refresh my tired and weary heart. Quench my parched thirst. Bring me to an understanding of Your revelations as I bathe in the waters of mercy.

God loves us personally and intimately; He cares. It is the Holy Spirit who calls us to believe in this great love and to respond in expectant faith.

"Faith is so crucial. The Spirit calls us to the Gospel dimension of faith. This is not just doctrinal faith which accepts propositions and formulations of beliefs as true. It is not just providential faith which believes in the overall providence of God that he sees that everything will work out in the end. It is expectant faith which expects God's saving love to operate in my life here and now. This is the faith which releases God's power. This is the faith that pulsates in the writings of the New Testament Church. The Spirit is not so concerned whether we believe that the wonders of the Apostolic Church are happening anew today as he is that we expect the saving Lord to be involved powerfully and lovingly in our lives. The Spirit is ever the same and yet ever new. We cannot understand this mystery, but we can understand that this means that what God is doing today is at once the same thing as he did before and a new work which we have never seen before. We are not to dwell on the work itself be it yesterday's or today's. We are to look to the Lord and expect him to be present."

Fr. Michael Scanlan, T.O.R. – *Inner Healing*

In God's Presence Consider …

Do I expect God to love me and be involved in my life here and now? Do I believe that what God has done through His Spirit in the past can be ever new and happen to me today?

Closing Prayer

O Holy Spirit, You are the same yesterday, today, and forever. Dwell in me, giving me an expectant faith; a faith which releases God's power to love and heal me as He so desires to love and heal me; and through me, others.

Vatican II's Dogmatic Constitution on Divine Revelation (Dei Verbum) *speaks of the Holy Spirit as the inspiration, teacher, and helper in regards to the Scriptures, Tradition, and Magisterium; which makes the voice of the Holy Spirit ring out to the world and leads believers to truth.*

"The obedience of faith' (Rom. 16:26; cf. Rom. 1:5; 2 Cor. 10:5–6) must be given to God as he reveals himself. By faith man freely commits his entire self to God, making 'the full submission of his intellect and will to God who reveals,' and willingly assenting to the Revelation given by him. Before this faith can be exercised, man must have the grace of God to move and assist him; he must have the interior helps of the Holy Spirit, who moves the heart and converts it to God, who opens the eyes of the mind and 'makes it easy for all to accept and believe the truth.' The same Holy Spirit constantly perfects faith by his gifts, so that Revelation may be more and more profoundly understood....

"Sacred Scripture is the speech of God as it is put down in writing under the breath of the Holy Spirit. And Tradition transmits in its entirety the Word of God which has been entrusted to the apostles by Christ the Lord and the Holy Spirit ... And the Holy Spirit, through whom the living voice of the Gospel rings out in the Church—and through her in the world—leads believers to the full truth, and makes the Word of Christ dwell in them in all its riches (CF. Col. 3:16)."

Vatican II - *Dei Verbum* #5, 9, 8c

In God's Presence Consider ...

Man must have the interior helps of the Holy Spirit. Do I allow the Holy Spirit to move and assist me to accept and obey truth as God, through His Church, reveals and teaches? Do I meditate and contemplate the living voice of the Holy Spirit in the Scriptures?

Closing Prayer

May God, who has been pleased to unite many tongues in the profession of one faith, give you perseverance in that same faith and, by believing, may you journey from hope to clear vision.

Solemn Blessing of Vigil Mass for Pentecost

To be in the rhythm of divine life, I am to be caught up in-between the love the Father showers on His Son, and the Son's love showered on the Father.

"The Spirit places us in the very rhythm of divine life, which is a life of love, making us participate personally in the relations that exist between the Father and the Son. It is highly significant that Paul, when he enumerates the different elements of the fruits of the Spirit, mentions love first: 'the fruit of the Spirit is love, joy, peace,' etc. (cf. Gal. 5:22) And, given that by definition love unifies, the Spirit is above all creator of communion within the Christian community....

"However, moreover, it is also true that the Spirit stimulates us to engage in relationship of charity with all people. In this way, when we love we make room for the Spirit, we allow him to express himself in fullness....

"Finally, according to St. Paul, the Spirit is a generous pledge which God himself has given us ahead of time and at the same time is a guarantee of our future inheritance (cf. 2 Cor. 1:22; 5:5; Eph. 1:13–14). Thus let us learn from Paul that the action of the Spirit orients our life toward the great values of love, joy, communion, and hope. It is for us to experience this every day, seconding the interior suggestions of the Spirit, helped in discernment by the illuminating guidance of the Apostle."

Pope Benedict XVI - *Paul's Teaching on the Holy Sp*irit

In God's Presence Consider ...

Am I participating in the rhythm of divine life? Do I see loving others as making more room for the Holy Spirit within my heart?

Closing Prayer

Holy Spirit, help me to make room in my heart for You; that together we may love the people around me and may grow in our communion with each other and You.

The Paschal Mystery is the passion, crucifixion, death, burial, resurrection, and ascension of Jesus. It is through these events that the work of salvation is accomplished and it is through the Holy Spirit that this economy of salvation is made present, manifested, and re-presented for us to participate in, through and within the liturgy of the Church.

"The Church was made manifest to the world on the day of Pentecost by the outpouring of the Holy Spirit. The gift of the Spirit ushers in a new era in the dispensation of the mystery—the age of the Church, during which Christ manifests, makes present, and communicates his work of salvation through the liturgy of his Church … it is principally his own Pascal mystery that Christ signifies and makes present.… Christ now lives and acts in and with his Church, in a new way appropriate to this new age. He acts through the sacraments and all that Christ is—all that he did and suffered for all men—participates in the divine eternity, and so transcends all times while being made present in them all."

Catechism of the Catholic Church (CCC) #1076, 1085

In God's Presence Consider …

Do I believe that Jesus is here present, alive and well working in and through the Church today, despite the scandals and sinfulness of her members? Do I believe in the power of Jesus' resurrection and the sending of His power, the Holy Spirit, which continues to make present the work of my salvation through the sacraments?

Closing Prayer

Come, Holy Spirit and make present to me the Paschal mystery. That I may also transcend time and participate in the divine eternity with Jesus my Lord.

Our soul is either a sponge or a stone, filled or not inhabited.

"Those who are led by the Holy Ghost experience all sorts of happiness in themselves, while bad Christians roll themselves on thorns and flints. A soul in which the Holy Ghost dwells is never weary in the presence of God; his heart gives forth a breath of love. Without the Holy Ghost we are stones on the road.... Take in one hand a sponge full of water, and in the other a little pebble; press them equally. Nothing will come out of the pebble, but out of the sponge will come abundance of water. The sponge is the soul filled with the Holy Ghost, and the stone is the cold and hard heart which is not inhabited by the Holy Ghost."

St. John Vianney - *Catechism on the Holy Spirit,* Chapter 3

In God's Presence Consider ...

Does the Holy Spirit dwell in me? Is my soul filled with the Holy Spirit as a sponge with water? Do I weary in the presence of God or avoid extended periods of time with my prayer and meditation?

Closing Prayer

Come, Holy Spirit, Living Water of God; come fill my soul with Your abundant presence. St. John Vianney, pray for me.

I'm All In; I'm All Yours **Day 8**

During Vespers the evening before his ordination and installation as the 10th Bishop of the Diocese of Duluth, the Most Reverend Daniel J. Felton gave a homily in which he shared how in prayer, after receiving a call from the Nuncio inviting him, on behalf of Pope Francis to become the bishop of Duluth, that he stood before the Holy Spirit and said, "Holy Spirit, I am surrendering all of this to You. I'm all in. I'm all yours." Now he is inviting the diocese to join him in a renewing of our surrender to the Holy Spirit.

"So in this moment; tonight; I'm going to ask you to do something. In this moment tonight, I'm asking you to join me. And I'm asking you to join me in reaching out and grabbing on to the wings of the Holy Spirit. Let's grab on to the wings of the Holy Spirit as we shout in this moment and in this time: 'I'm all yours. I am all in.' And as we grab onto the wings of the Holy Spirit, the Spirit is going to lift us up and we are going to take flight. I have no idea where we are going. I have no idea where we are going to land. But I know this much; that wherever the Holy Spirit takes us as we are clinging to the wings of that Spirit, and where ever that Spirit lands in the days, the weeks, the years that are ahead, in that moment, and in that place, that will be the beginning of the next chapter in the Acts of the Holy Spirit in our diocese of Duluth."

Bishop Daniel J. Felton - *Homily*

In God's Presence Consider …

Am I willing to grab onto the wings of the Holy Spirit and let Him take me where ever He desires? Am I willing to stand before the Holy Spirit and declare: I'm all Yours. I am all in? What might cause my hesitancy?

Closing Prayer

May your people exult forever, O God, in renewed youthfulness of spirit, so that rejoicing now in the restored glory of our adoption, we may look forward in confident hope to the rejoicing of the day of resurrection.

Collect from the 3rd reading of the Vigil Mass for Pentecost

Paraclete Not Parakeet **Day 9**

I will ask the Father and he will give you another Paraclete that he may abide with you forever, the Spirit of Truth whom the world cannot receive since it neither sees nor knows him; you know him because he dwells with you and remains with you. (Jn. 14:17)

"Paraclete is really new, the very word is new, found nowhere else in Greek. It is a noun derived from the verb *para-kalein—para* meaning "alongside," *kalein* meaning "to summon." The whole verb means to summon to one's side, to call to one's aid, especially as an advocate either pleading one's cause or defending one against an enemy, or even as a comforter in one's affliction.

"In the Old Testament, the Spirit could aid or enlighten or rebuke. But to act upon men and within, to remain with them permanently —with this we have "indwelling" and practically a definition of sanctifying grace.

Frank Sheed - *The Holy Spirit in Action*

In God's Presence Consider …

Have I ever used the Holy Spirit as the Paraclete? Do I see the Holy Spirit beside me acting upon and within me?

Closing Prayer

Thank You Father and Jesus for giving me the Holy Spirit as my Paraclete and for His permanent indwelling. Remove any fear that I have of Him or any obstacle that prevents Him from freely acting in or upon me.

"The Paraclete, the Holy Spirit, whom the Father will send in my name, he will teach you all things, and bring all things to your mind whatever I shall have said to you." (Jn. 14:26)

"As the words came from the Lord's mouth the apostles may not have caught the significance of the word 'he.' '*He* will teach you all things.' 'He' occurs a dozen times in the discourse, all the more surprisingly because the word for 'spirit,' *pneuma*, is neuter. So, the Spirit is a person: someone not some divine action or attribute or by a divine influence, but by another *someone*. Jesus, the first Paraclete (1Jn. 2:11), was divine. Was the second?

"It would be difficult to be certain from the four Gospels that he was divine.... At the end of Matthew's Gospel, we read how Jesus instructs the apostles. 'Go teach all nations baptizing them in the name [the Greek means 'into the name'] of the Father and of the Son and of the Holy Spirit.'.... And for a reader of scripture, the word *name* in the singular is decisive—if the third member of the group shares the name, he shares the nature. If the first two are divine, so is the third."

Frank Sheed - *The Holy Spirit in Action*

In God's Presence Consider ...

Do I see the Holy Spirit as a person or a divine action, attribute or divine influence? What does the significance of the word "he" in reference to the Holy Spirit have for me?

Closing Prayer

Dear Holy Spirit, the Paraclete that was sent to dwell in me, teach me to see You as a divine person and not some impersonal force or action of God.

All those who have been baptized and confirmed have the fullness of the Holy Spirit living in them. Sadly, many often don't acknowledge or know the Holy Spirit as God's great Gift to us and He goes unrecognizable. We often cheat the world with our ignorance in not accepting the Holy Spirit in our lives.

"One of God's greatest gifts to us is one He Himself calls 'the Gift of God' (Jn. 4:10). It is a reference to the Holy Spirit, Whom He in His great love has bestowed so generously upon us! One would think that because we have received such a priceless Gift from God, we would esteem and treasure it above all His other gifts—acknowledging it, expressing gratitude for it, and using it as God intended us to! Yet, the sad fact is that God's most precious Gift to us, the Holy Spirit, is often not acknowledged; indeed, He is often unknown. He has, for this reason, so frequently been referred to as the 'Forgotten God' among the Three Divine Persons of the Blessed Trinity!

"How many Catholics, even today, despite receiving the Holy Spirit both at their Baptism and Confirmation, fully realize or appreciate this priceless treasure? Might not Our Lord's words to the Samaritan woman—'If only you recognized the Gift of God'—also apply to us? What a difference it would make if only we appreciated the Holy Spirit in our daily Christian lives! How much more alive our own faith in Jesus would become."

Fr. Andrew Apostoli, C.F.R. - *The Gift of God: The Holy Spirit*

In God's Presence Consider …

God's greatest gift that He generously bestows upon us is the Holy Spirit. Do I recognize the Holy Spirit dwelling in me? Do I acknowledge and treasure the Holy Spirit as God's gift to me? Do I express thanks for the Holy Spirit?

Closing Prayer

Come Gift of God and fill my heart that I may receive You as generously as God has given You to me. Help me to recognize You as Gift and to make You known to others.

The Holy Spirit proceeds from the Father and the Son by their shared nature and the unity of love that they share with Each other. They are a communion of Persons, sharing in the same Godhood, united in love, that our Creeds profess, teach, and that we subscribe to.

"Why is he called the Holy Spirit? St. Thomas Aquinas explains that he is called the Spirit because he proceeds from the Father and the Son by a sort of shared and uniting breath (the theologians call it a 'spiration'). And he is called 'Holy' because all things are called holy which are consecrated to God. Love proceeds from Father and Son joined together in the unity of love, forming in their two selves but one single principle, so the Holy Spirit proceeds from both Father and Son. In this way faith of the Creed is explained and reason is satisfied: 'The father and the Son', says St. Thomas, 'have but one single power of spiration, identical in number; that is why the Holy Spirit proceeds equally from both of them' (Summa Theologica, 1. 36, 2, solution 2) …. Faith teaches it, reason subscribes to it."

Bernard Piault - *What is the Trinity*

In God's Presence Consider …

The Holy Spirit shares a united breath with the Father and the Son. Is this uniting breath found in my spiritual life? Have I consecrated or reconsecrated myself to God lately? Faith and reason go hand in hand. Does my experience of the Holy Spirit line up with what faith teaches and reason subscribes to?

Closing Prayer

Come "Uniting Breath of God." Come and bring me into the communion of love with the Blessed Trinity. Help me accept that which faith teaches about You. Help my reason to accept and follow You.

He Remains **Day 13**

The Commission says that it is not easy to speak of the Holy Spirit. While referring to the Father and to the Son recalls something personal and familiar, the word Spirit alludes to someone who is present and working yet remains hidden and unknown. We tend to speak of Him only indirectly based on His actions and our experiences of His effects. Yet He is not a force but a Person.

"The Holy Spirit unveils the profundity of God, but his nature remains hidden. He reveals, yet remains in the shadows; he makes the Word concrete, but remains absolutely otherworldly. He turns the plan of God into history, but does not himself become history; he makes possible the incarnation of the Word but remains 'Lord' in the absolute. He is in every heart of every creature and gives life to every living thing, but remains 'Spirit.' His nature is so hidden that we can speak of him only indirectly, based on his actions and in the measure by which we experience him in his effects. Indeed, we can say that it is impossible to speak of the Holy Spirit except in the Holy Spirit himself. Otherwise, we run the risk of considering him as a simple 'force' of God. He is a 'person' distinct from the Father and the Son."

Theological Historical Commission (THC) -
The Holy Spirit, Lord and Giver of Life

In God's Presence Consider …

Do I have a hard time putting my mind around who the Holy Spirit is and in trying to see Him as a Person? Do I find it extremely challenging to embrace His hidden nature, His mystery, His aloofness, amidst His actions and presence?

Closing Prayer

Breathe in me Your life O Holy Spirit that I may walk in Your ways and come to experience and know, love, and to serve the Triune God in this life, preparing to live with Him in the life to come.

Bathing in Divine Love **Day 14**

If we tire of religious things and find a reluctance to pray, we don't have the Holy Spirit residing in us.

"A soul that possesses the Holy Ghost tastes such sweetness in prayer, that it finds the time always too short; it never loses the holy presence of God. Such a heart, before our good Savior in the Holy Sacrament of the Altar, is a bunch of grapes under the wine press. The Holy Ghost forms thoughts and suggests words in the hearts of the just.... Those who have the Holy Ghost produce nothing bad; all the fruits of the Holy Ghost are good. Without the Holy Ghost all is cold; therefore, when we feel we are losing our fervor, we must instantly make a novena to the Holy Ghost to ask for faith and love.... See, when we have made a retreat or a jubilee, we are full of good desires: these good desires are the breath of the Holy Ghost, which has passed over our souls, and has renewed everything, like the warm wind which melts the ice and brings back the spring.... You who are not great saints, you still have many moments when you taste the sweetness of prayer and of the presence of God: these are visits of the Holy Ghost. When we have the Holy Ghost, the heart expands—bathes itself in divine love. A fish never complains of having too much water, neither does a good Christian ever complain of being too lone with the good God. There are some people who find religion wearisome, and it is because they have not the Holy Ghost."

St. John Vianney - *Catechism on the Holy Spirit,* Chapter 3

In God's Presence Consider ...

In my prayer, do I lose the holy presence of God? Do I complain about the time with God being too long? Do I find spiritual or religious things to be wearisome?

Closing Prayer

St. John Vianney, pray that the Holy Spirit would breathe on me the warmth of His breath to melt the ice and coldness of my soul. Bathe me in Your Divine Love, O Holy Spirit, that I may never weary of God, prayer, and religious things.

Throughout the Old Testament the Holy Spirit is seen as a power, a force, which comes forth from God to carry out in the world the work He wished to accomplish. Often times the Spirit would come and then leave. In the New Testament, the Holy Spirit is presented as a Person with a role to play in the lives of God's people, and is sent, coming to abide, to stay in the heart of a believer as in a temple.

"And I will ask the Father, and he will give you another Counselor, to be with you forever, even the Spirit of truth, whom the world cannot receive, because it neither sees him nor knows him; you know him, for he dwells with you, and will be in you." Jn. 14:16–17

"Do you not know that you are God's temple and that God's Spirit dwells in you?" 1 Cor. 3:16

"Do you not know that your body is a temple of the Holy Spirit within you, which you have from God?" 1 Cor. 6:19

In God's Presence Consider …

Does my spiritual life and my living in the world reflect the fact that the Holy Spirit dwells in me? What kind of care and attention do I give to God's temple that I am? How can I come to know intimately the Holy Spirit who has been sent to me and abides in me?

Closing Prayer

You, O Holy Spirit, are the Creative Power and Love of God. Sanctify me with Your presence, making me holy and a fit dwelling place, a temple, for You to abide within.

A Silent Soul **Day 16**

Silence plays a key part in our ability to sense the Holy Spirit's movements and inspirations.

"Silence is a sword in the spiritual struggle. A talkative soul will never attain sanctity. The sword of silence will cut off everything that would like to cling to the soul. We are sensitive to words, quickly want to answer back, without taking any regard as to whether it is God's will that we should speak. A silent soul is strong; no adversities will harm it if it perseveres in silence. The silent soul is capable of attaining the closest union with God. It lives almost always under the inspirations of the Holy Spirit. God works in a silent soul without hindrance.

"Oh, if souls would only be willing to listen, at least a little, to the voice of conscience and the voice—that is, the inspirations—of the Holy Spirit! I say at least a little, because once we open ourselves to the influence of the Holy Spirit, He Himself will fulfill what is lacking in us.... The shortest road is faithfulness to the inspirations of the Holy Spirit...."

St. Maria Faustina Kowalska - *Diary: Divine Mercy in My Soul*

In God's Presence Consider ...

Do I ever address and listen to the voice of my conscience? Is silence a part of my prayer life? Why is silence difficult for me?

Closing Prayer

O Divine Spirit, pervade my whole being. Lead me to embrace silence that I may be initiated into Your Divine Essence, and capable of attaining the closest union with God. St. Faustina, pray for me.

The Holy Spirit is the living voice of the Gospel given to the Church. It is through her, in the Holy Spirit, that the Word of Christ is proclaimed and taught. Thus, dwelling richly in the lives of believers, they in turn join in and share in the mission of the Church of bringing others to faith in Christ.

"Sacred Scripture is the word of God, written by men under the inspiration of the Holy Spirit. It is the divine Paraclete who speaks to us therein, enlightening our intellects with His light and spurring our wills by His motions; hence, meditation of the sacred texts is somewhat like 'attending the school' of the Holy Spirit. Furthermore, the Holy Spirit continually teaches us and stimulates us to do good by the living word of the Church, since all those in the Church who have the mission to teach are under His influence when they expound sacred doctrine to the faithful. If we listen to the inspirations of the divine Paraclete, and accept His invitations, He unites Himself to us, abiding us by actual graces, so that we are able to perform virtuous acts."

Fr. Gabriel of St. Mary Magdalen, O.C.D. - *Divine Intimacy*

In God's Presence Consider ...

Is reading and meditating on Scripture a daily part of my prayer? Do I seek the inspiration, the movement of the Holy Spirit, when I read and study the Scripture? St. Jerome says that ignorance of Scripture is ignorance of Christ. Do I place myself in the school of the Holy Spirit in order to come to know Christ more intimately through the Scriptures?

Closing Prayer

O Holy Spirit, grant me a penetrating mind to understand Your inspired word that comes to me through the Holy Scriptures. Give me a lucidity to comprehend the divine truths, accepting Your invitation, that You will unite me to You and I may abide in Your graces.

Not Magic but a Synergy

"Baptism of the Spirit" is often not understood. Fr. Cantalamessa, reminds us that this 'baptism' is not a sacrament but it is an outpouring of grace, a re-stirring of the graces already present but unreleased, that actualizes, or renews Christian initiation and revives our baptism.

"A sacrament can be valid and legal but 'unreleased.' A sacrament is called 'unreleased' if its fruit remains bound, or unused, because of the absence of certain conditions that further its efficacy … there are other cases in which a sacrament, while not being completely ineffective, is nevertheless not entirely released; it is not free to works its effects.

"Sacraments are not magic rites that act mechanically, without people's knowledge or collaboration. Their efficacy is the result of a synergy, or collaboration, between divine omnipotence (that is, the grace of Christ and of the Holy Spirit) and free will. As St. Augustine said, 'He who created you without your consent will not save you without your consent.'

"… the fruit of the sacrament depends wholly on divine grace; however, this divine grace does not act without the 'yes'—the consent and affirmation—of the person…. One thing is certain. It is not the brothers and sisters who confer the Holy Spirit. Rather, they invite the Holy Spirit to come upon a person. No one can give the Spirit, not even the pope or bishop, because no one possesses the Holy Spirit. Only Jesus can actually give the Holy Spirit. People do not possess the Holy Spirit, but, rather, are possessed by Him."

Fr. Raniero Cantalamessa, O.F.M. Cap. - *Sober Intoxication of the Spirit*

In God's Presence Consider …

Am I aware of unreleased graces from the sacraments residing within me? Do I sometimes view sacraments as magical and mechanical rather than a synergy between God's divine omnipotence and my free will? Do I allow myself to be possessed by the Holy Spirit?

Closing Prayer

Grant, we pray, almighty God, that the splendor of your glory may shine forth upon us and that, by the bright rays of the Holy Spirit, the light of your light may confirm the hearts of those born again by your grace.

Collect from the Vigil Mass for Pentecost

The Holy Spirit supports and sustains us seeking nothing other than taking us to heaven.

"If the damned were asked: Why are you in Hell? They would answer: 'For having resisted the Holy Ghost.' And if the saints were asked: Why are you in Heaven? They would answer: 'For having listened to the Holy Ghost.' When good thoughts come into our minds, it is the Holy Ghost who is visiting us. The Holy Ghost is a power. The Holy Ghost supported Saint Simeon on this column; He sustained the martyrs. Without the Holy Ghost, the martyrs would have fallen like the leaves from the trees. When the fires were lighted under them, the Holy Ghost extinguished the heat of the fire by the heat of divine love. The good God, in sending us the Holy Ghost, has treated us like a great king who should send his minister to guide one of his subjects, saying 'You will accompany this man everywhere, and you will bring him back to me safe and sound.'

"How beautiful it is, my children, to be accompanied by the Holy Ghost! He is indeed a good Guide; and to think that there are some who will not follow Him. The Holy Ghost is like a man with a carriage and horse, who should want to take us to Pans. We should only have to say 'yes', and to get into it. It is indeed an easy matter to say 'yes!'.... Well, the Holy Ghost wants to take us to Heaven; we have only to say 'yes', and to let Him take us there."

St. John Vianney - *Catechism on the Holy Spirit,* Chapter 3

In God's Presence Consider …

Do I resist the Holy Spirit working in my soul? Have I ever thought of God sending His Spirit to accompany me in life and guiding me to heaven?

Closing Prayer

Blessed Mary my Mother, help me to be like you, to say "yes" and not to resist the Holy Spirit, so that He may take me to be with you to Heaven. St. John Vianney, pray for me.

The One Who Paints **Day 20**

Humanity has been called to communion since creation. This communion means that we are made images of God through Jesus Christ in the Holy Spirit. "The dignity of man rests above all on the fact that he is called to communion with God." CCC #27

"The Eastern and Western traditions of the Church are unanimous in affirming that the Holy Spirit stamps the image of God in each individual. He is considered the 'iconographer' (the one who paints the sacred icon) of the image of God in each human because, with Christ as a model, he paints the living image of the Redeemer in each person and in this manner increasingly Christifies the faithful. The principle is always the same: God becomes present in each individual through Jesus Christ in the Holy Spirit; each human is the image of God because each is called to communion with God, and the Spirit is the one who causes the communion. This tie is not an external or psychological event, but transforms the very being of the person."

THC - *The Holy Spirit, Lord and Give of Life*

In God's Presence Consider …

I have been created in the image and likeness of God. Do I ever reflect that it is the Holy Spirit who stamps this image into me being? Do I see myself as a sacred icon painted by the Holy Spirit? Do I take time to reflect on what it means to be in communion with God?

Closing Prayer

O Great Artisan of my soul, paint the sacred icon of Jesus in the depths of my being, that I may be drawn into communion with God and be transformed, Christified, and pleasing to the Father.

God has no need to use men and women to accomplish His work, but He shows us time and time again in the Scriptures and in our Tradition, that He uses human vessels joined with Him to do His work. The Blessed Virgin Mary is a key example of this grace.

"Mary, the all-holy ever-virgin Mother of God, is the masterwork of the mission of the Son and the Spirit in the fullness of time.... The Holy Spirit prepared Mary by his grace. In Mary, the Holy Spirit fulfills the plan of the Father's loving goodness. Through the Holy Spirit, the Virgin conceives and gives birth to the Son of God.... In Mary, the Holy Spirit manifests the Son of the Father, now become the Son of the Virgin.... Filled with the Holy Spirit she makes the Word visible in the humanity of his flesh.... At the end of this mission of the Spirit, Mary became the Woman, the new 'Eve' (mother of the living), the mother of the whole Christ."

Cf. CCC #721–726

In God's Presence Consider ...

Mary is like the burning bush in the desert before Moses: totally engulfed in fire but not consumed. Do I give the Holy Spirit my consent to set me on fire and be used by God as a channel of grace? Do I ever ask Mary to bring me into deep communion with her Son?

Closing Prayer

Hail Mary, full of grace and the Holy Spirit, please pray for me, that I may fully accept and be filled with your Spouse so that I may be brought into deeper communion with your Son.

Helmsman and Guide **Day 22**

The Holy Spirit not only defends and sanctifies the Church, but is her guide, light, and judge over which He presides.

"The Holy One who sanctifies, helps, and teaches the Church is, in fact, the Holy Spirit, the Paraclete.... He has come down from heaven to defend and sanctify the Church, as a guide for souls and a helmsman for storm-tossed humankind, a light to guide the wayfarers, a judge who presides over the contest and the crowning of the victorious."

St. Cyril of Jerusalem - *Catechesis* XVI

In God's Presence Consider …

Do I seek the Holy Spirit as a defender of my sanctity? Do I turn to the Holy Spirit when I feel storm-tossed? Do I see Him as a judge who awaits to crown me with victory?

Closing Prayer

O Helmsman of my storm-tossed humanity, guide me by the light of Your presence, helping me to avoid the rocks that will destroy me and bring me to the safety of Your harbor. St. Cyril of Jerusalem, pray for me.

God loves us and desires to help us to go beyond our limited selves to be lifted up to the supernatural life of grace; not only to have access to Him, but to share in His Divine Life.

"The Holy Spirit is the master of the interior life … the artisan of God's works, the master of prayer…. To be sure, there are as many paths of prayer as there are persons who pray, but it is the same Spirit acting in all and with all. It is in the communion of the Holy Spirit that Christian prayer is prayer in the Church. (He is) a gentle quest and friend who inspires, guides, corrects, and strengthens this life."

Cf. CCC #1995, 2672, 741, 1696

In God's Presence Consider …

Through the Holy Spirit's anointing, He permeates our whole being. Do I give Him permission to form me in prayer? Do I allow Him to take me into the deeper depths of prayer? Do I allow Him to be my guest, friend, artisan of God's work within me?

Closing Prayer

O come Master, of the Interior Life, Artisan of God's Works, Master of Prayer. Inspire me. Guide me. Help me to be open to and to say "yes" to Your corrections; that strengthened by Your grace, the work of my hands may bear fruit for eternal life.

The Spirit is Essential **Day 24**

The Holy Spirit is real and not a feeling. He can easily be shut off by our pride. The reason the Holy Spirit has been given to us is for the good of and building up of the Body of Christ.

"… sometimes the working of the Holy Spirit is accompanied by strong feelings of fervor or consolation. On the other hand, it may be accompanied by no feelings at all; in fact, a person may experience dryness and even spiritual darkness. In either case, the authentic working of the Holy Spirit can only be known through the results or 'fruits' that His graces produce in our lives. It would certainly hinder our spiritual growth and it might even do serious harm to our spiritual life if we were to insist on enjoying emotional consolations or 'feelings' of the presence of the Holy Spirit, rather than on being open to His presence and His Will for us, even if it means dryness or emptiness of feelings.

"The danger of pride is always present in the spiritual life. A humble person is clearly aware that every gift he or she possesses has been given by God. Accordingly, we must use them not for our own vainglory, but rather for the good of others, as well as for our own growth in holiness. The Spirit's Gifts are essential for carrying out God's will, to promote God's glory, to grow in holiness, to help us spread the Kingdom of God, and to assist our brothers and sisters in their physical and spiritual needs.

"We must never let the gifts that the Holy Spirit has given us ever become opportunities for our own pride, vanity, or boasting. Rather, we must grow in the virtue of humility and learn to give over to God the glory that is His from the Spirit's working in us."

Fr. Andrew Apostoli, C.F.R. - *The Gift of God: The Holy Spirit*

In God's Presence Consider …

How well do I identify and use the gifts God has given me? Do I use the gifts God gives me for personal opportunities or the good of others? What fruits of the Holy Spirit can I identify in my life?

Closing Prayer

Holy Ghost, Divine Consoler, I give You my heart and I offer my ardent thanksgiving for all the grace which You never cease to bestow on me.

Prayer of St. Alphonsus Liguori

The Holy Spirit, who comprehends the thoughts of God, does not speak or do anything on His own, but only what He receives from the Father and the Son.

"… Now God's Spirit, who reveals God, makes known to us Christ, his Word, his living Utterance, but the Spirit does not speak of himself. The Spirit who 'has spoken through the prophets' makes us hear the Father's Word. We know him only in the movement by which he reveals the Word to us and disposes us to welcome him in faith. The Spirit of truth who unveils Christ to us 'will not speak on his own' (cf. Jn. 16:13) … those who believe in Christ know the Spirit because he dwells with them." (cf. Jn. 14:17).

CCC #687

In God's Presence Consider …

Do I feel comfortable in inviting the Holy Spirit to help me in hearing the Father's Word? Am I sensitive to the movements of the Holy Spirit that dispose me to faith and to how Christ unveils Himself to me? How do I act by knowing the Holy Spirit dwells in me?

Closing Prayer

Come, Holy Spirit, Breath of God, You who continue to speak to the Church today, help me to recognize Your movement and Your utterance of Jesus in my heart.

He Is Everywhere Superabundant **Day 26**

A true Christian worships God, who is Spirit, in spirit and in truth. God wants to have our hearts as temples of prayer, where He is adored and worshiped. The Holy Spirit is the means for this worship.

"Because God is invisible, incomprehensible, and immense, the Lord said that the time has come in which God will no longer be worshiped on a mountain or in a temple, 'for God is Spirit.' The Spirit cannot be circumscribed nor enclosed because by the power of his nature he is everywhere, absent from no place, and his fullness is superabundant in everything. Those who worship in the Spirit and truth are the true worshipers. Those who worship God—who is Spirit—in the Spirit will have God as an end and the Spirit as a means for their reverence, because each person has a different relationship toward the one to be worshiped. Saying 'God is Spirit' does not do away with the name and gift of the Holy Spirit.... The nature of the gift and honor is indicated when it is taught that it is necessary to worship God who is Spirit, in the Spirit. This reveals the type of freedom and consciousness reserved for those who worship. It also reveals the immense goal of worship because God, who is Spirit, is worshiped in the Spirit.

St. Hilary - *On the Trinity*, II, 31

In God's Presence Consider ...

Do I see my heart as a temple of prayer where God desires to reign and to be worshiped and adored? Do I worship God in spirit and in truth? Do I seek the Holy Spirit to lead me in reverence and prayer?

Closing Prayer

Jesus, You tell me, that "if I only knew the gift" that You offer me, I would ask for the "living water." Fill me with the superabundant fullness of Your Holy Spirit, the Living Water, that I may truly worship the Father in spirit and in truth. St. Hilary, pray for me.

Unappreciated and Unrecognized **Day 27**

The Holy Spirit is active in us at all times but He does not control our responses. Even though He is present and active, He is often unappreciated, not recognized, and we have a false sense of who He is and fear what He does.

"In all Christian traditions the Holy Spirit is clearly presented as sanctifier. Since Jesus' resurrection the task of bringing the world to the Father has been entrusted to the Spirit. Even the word we use, spirituality, reflects the centrality of the Spirit in beginning both individuals and the world as a whole under the reign of the Father.

"If there is any Christian truth that has gone unappreciated, it is the presence of the Holy Spirit in our activities. The fact of the presence is clear; the problem is that we don't recognize it. There are many reasons for this. The main reason, I believe, is that we live in a secular society which explains all truth, including its understanding of human behaviors, in secular terms.

"Another reason we don't recognize the Holy Spirit in our daily activities is that much of our spirituality has been dominated by a self-outside-God model. God is in heaven; we are in our world.... The Holy Spirit is active in us at all times drawing us toward greater love and service of God and others, but the Spirit does not control our response."

Fr. Richard Hauser, S.J.—*In His Spirit*

In God's Presence Consider ...

Do I have a sense of being unappreciative of the Holy Spirit's activities in my life? Do I have problems recognizing the Holy Spirit? Do I see God as in heaven verses dwelling within me?

Closing Prayer

Father, You have entrusted bringing the world to You to the Holy Spirit. Through His sanctifying presence, may He become central in my life. May I recognize and appreciate the love and work He desires to do within me. Draw me to a greater love and service of You and others.

In the Night of Trial **Day 28**

Cardinal Nguyen Van Thuan, suffered imprisonment by the Vietnamese government from 1975-1988, during which he secretly sent prayers and spiritual writings to his flock. The Cardinal shows us God's love and power through sending the Holy Spirit to comfort us in the darkest of places in our lives and give us courage and hope.

"Infinitely good Lord, you know my heart and my weaknesses. Do not abandon me. You are infinitely just and ask nothing of me that is beyond my strength. My happiness knows no limit when I contemplate your infinite righteousness and put all things in your hands. From experience I know that on my path, covered with innumerable obstacles, in the night of trial without exit, you, the infinitely righteous One, have never abandoned me.

"At those moments when I nearly fainted under the weight of evil, you did not abandon me. When I felt tempted to despair and to give up everything, when the storm raged without and within, when the winds of calumny buffeted against my good intentions and actions, Lord, you did not abandon me.

"It was at such moments that the Holy Spirit taught me what I should do and how I should speak. At such moments the Holy Spirit poured courage and hope into my weakened soul and comforted me. The Lord will never abandon me to my limitations!"

Venerable Francis Xavier Nguyen Van Thuan -
Prayers of Hope, Words of Courage

In God's Presence Consider …

What do I do when my heart knows weakness, temptations leading to despair, and the darkness of trial without exit? Do I place my confidence in the Holy Spirit and trust His provisions? Do I seek the Holy Spirit in my moments of having a weakened soul?

Closing Prayer

Venerable Nguyen Van Thuan, when you were imprisoned and experienced the night of trial without exit, you turned to the Holy Spirit for courage, hope, and comfort. Through your intercession, help me to turn also to Him for help.

Because the Holy Spirit is the silence of God, we often have a great misunderstanding of Him. It is through His silent presence that He leads us to Christ. Because Christ is the truth and has the words of eternal life, the Holy Spirit repeats His Words and His silent force sets our hearts ablaze.

"The Holy Spirit has no face and no speech. He is silent by his divine nature. The Spirit acts in silence from all eternity. God speaks, Christ speaks, but the Holy Spirit is always expressed through the prophets, saints, and men of God.

"The Holy Spirit never makes noise. He leads to the truth by remaining the great intermediary. In silence, he leads mankind toward Christ by repeating his teaching. The only time where the Holy Spirit came with noise was at Pentecost, in order to reawaken sleeping mankind and to draw it from its torpor and sin ….

"The Spirit dwells in the interior of man by regenerating him without manifest noise. The Spirit is a silent force. Free as the wind, the Spirit blows unpredictably. If we do not drive away his Fire, he sets the world ablaze."

Robert Cardinal Sarah - *The Power of Silence*

In God's Presence Consider …

Do I have difficulty fostering a relationship with the Holy Spirit because He doesn't speak? Am I growing closer to Christ through my learning more of Jesus' teaching? Do I drive the Holy Spirit away or do I encourage Him to set the world ablaze including me?

Closing Prayer

Come, Holy Spirit, let Your Fire fall. Set the world ablaze with the Fire of Your love. May my heart be like dry tinder. Fan the flames of Your eternal Fire as the wind freely stirs creation. Let Your presence be the silent force for my regeneration.

To inflame our hearts with love, God sends and infuses us with the Holy Spirit. There needs to be a yielding on our part to the Holy Spirit allowing Him to work transformation in our hearts.

"In God, love is always perfect and therefore it is sustained, eternal … and this love is the Holy Spirit, who works all miracles of charity …. The beautiful work of inflaming hearts with love of God belongs to this same Love. Love came and man loved…. He sent them the Holy Spirit, that is, the substantial and personal Love of God himself…. One does not rely on the will but rather on yielding which allows the Holy Spirit to work and to transform.

"All the benefits of redemption are of infinite excellence, but what fulfills and crowns them all is the infusion of God's Spirit in his creatures. The Spirit of God descends in the Son to pour himself out on humanity. The Consoler liberates human beings from the spirit of the world by drawing them to himself, providing for their every need with care and tenderness When I had barely emerged from my mother's womb, you, Lord, embraced me and washed me with the water of Baptism, making me your daughter…. Reborn through water, we must be reborn in the Holy Spirit. You alone, Lord, can make me understand and put into practice this blessed rebirth … so that my life may be a continuous communion, an uninterrupted rebirth and growth in the Holy Spirit."

Blessed Elena Guerra - *Home Web Site of Her Cause*

In God's Presence Consider …

Am I asking for the infusion of the Holy Spirit into my whole being? Am I allowing the Holy Spirit to work inner transformation in my heart that it is inflamed with divine love? Does my spiritual life reflect an uninterrupted rebirth and growth in the Holy Spirit?

Closing Prayer

O Lord, You have given me new life through the waters of my baptism. I ask to be reborn in the Holy Spirit. You alone, Lord, can make me understand and put into practice this blessed rebirth so that my life may be a continuous communion, an uninterrupted rebirth and growth in the Holy Spirit. Blessed Elena Guerra, pray for me.

The Holy Spirit is the power that allows the Church to continue to make the Eucharist present, continues to dispose us to receive Jesus in the Eucharist, and will not abandon us but will dwell with us forever in the Church.

"Christ ordered the apostles, and through them the Church, to do thusly: 'Do this in memory of me.' He could not have given such an order if he had not, at the same time, put at our disposition the only power capable of executing it. What is this power? It is the Holy Spirit, strength which from on high fortified the apostles, according to the word of the Lord: 'Stay here in the city until you have been clothed with power from on high' (Lk. 24:49, Acts 1:8). Here is the action of this divine presence: once descended, the Holy Spirit does not abandon us but remains with us to the end. The Savior sent him precisely so he would dwell in us forever.... But the Lord did more than send the Holy Spirit to dwell in us; he himself promised to live with us 'to the end of the age' (Mt. 28:20). The Paraclete is invisibly present, lacking human form...."

Nicholas Cabasilas - *Commentary on the Divine Liturgy*, 28

In God's Presence Consider ...

Have I come to see the Lord putting at my disposition the power of the Holy Spirit? Am I clothed in the power from on high? Have I ever thought that it is the Holy Spirit that makes Jesus live with me to the end of the age?

Closing Prayer

Come, Holy Spirit and clothe me with Your power. Do not abandon me or allow me to walk in the ways of my own council, but dwell in me and lead me to Jesus who promised to live with me forever.

Ted Cole spent the majority of his life incarcerated. He had become Catholic and a lay Carmelite as he was on Death Row in a Texas prison awaiting execution.

"(St.) Father Titus Brandsma, O. Carm. confirms for me the fact that I will find God where I am, and not necessarily where I expect Him to be. We, on Death Row in Texas, are no longer allowed to have religious services. The last Mass I had the privilege of attending—actually a very hurried and haphazard Communion service—was more than a year ago. But Titus' own life in prison is a poignant reminder that, regardless of how our actions may seem to prove otherwise, God is not confined to a church or a chapel or to any other physical place, nor is He confined to any rite or ritual, even one as sacred as the Holy Mass. Even as he lay dying at Dachau, Titus was, himself, a chapel where God was alive and well and still reaching out to others. Titus assures me that I can also be a chapel dedicated to God, and that one's duty to serve others and to influence others to do good does not stop simply because "home" is now a prison cell.

"Solitude, loneliness, and time alone with God is so very precious and can be an asset in one's spiritual life. Titus wrote, 'I am here alone, but never was our Lord so close to me.' I firmly believe that what was accomplished in one man can, with the grace of God, be accomplished in me."

Ted Colins - *"Titus as Role Model on Death Role"*

In God's Presence Consider ...

Where do I find God? Do I make time to be alone with God? How does the Holy Spirit help me sit at the feet of Jesus?

Closing Prayer

Holy Spirit, You who bring new life to those held captive in darkness, help me to choose the better part and make time to be alone with God. St. Titus Brandsma, pray for me.

The Holy Spirit, St. Cyril says, comes gently and with tenderness, as light helping us to see and discern the things that are of God. He helps us to see everything in a new way that enables us to interpret human history.

"The Spirit comes gently and makes himself known by his fragrance. He is not felt as a burden, for he is light, very light. Rays of light and knowledge stream before him as he approaches. The Spirit comes with the tenderness of a true friend and protector to save, to heal, to teach, to counsel, to strengthen, to console. The Spirit comes to enlighten the mind first of the one who receives him, and then, through him, the minds of others as well.

"As light strikes the eyes of a man who comes out of darkness into the sunshine and enables him to see clearly things he could not discern before, so light floods the soul of the man counted worthy of receiving the Holy Spirit and enables him to see things beyond the range of human vision, things hitherto undreamed of.

"Thus, those who have become worthy to receive the Holy Spirit have their souls illuminated and see in a superhuman way that which was not seen before. The body is on earth and the soul contemplates the heavens as if in a mirror.... Each human, so small, extends his glance over the universe, from the beginning to the end, over the time in between and over the successive kingdoms. He comes to know that which no one has taught him because he is side by side with the person who illuminates him."

St. Cyril of Jerusalem - *Instructions to Catechumen*s

In God's Presence Consider ...

Do I experience the gentleness and tenderness of the Holy Spirit in my life? Can I see clearly spiritual things? Do I seek the light of the Holy Spirit to see beyond the range of my human vision?

Closing Prayer

Come, Holy Spirit, enlighten my mind helping me to see clearly and discern those realities that are beyond my range of human vision. Come O Light Divine, dispel my darkness and help me to walk in Your light as in the sunshine. St. Cyril of Jerusalem, pray for me.

A Fool **Day 34**

"All who are led by the Spirit of God are sons of God." Rom. 8:14

"While the firm and clear foundations of the Christian truth and the empowering of the Holy Spirit are essential to any adequate vision of Christianity, the guiding action of the Holy Spirit is uniquely important. Only the Spirit of God knows the depths of God, the depths of our own soul, and the real situation of the world and guides us along the only truly wise course for individuals, the family, the parish, the diocese, the religious order, and the universal Church. Seeking God directly for his guidance and developing a sensitivity to the leading of the Holy Spirit is crucial for adequate Christian life and action today. Scripture calls the person 'foolish' who doesn't seek God—and it is a very bad thing to be called a 'fool' by the inspired Word of God."

Ralph Martin - *A Church in Crisis*

In God's Presence Consider …

Do I seek God directly for His guidance and the leading of the Holy Spirit? Do I try to nurture and develop a sensitivity to the presence of the Holy Spirit?

Closing Prayer

Father, send forth Your Spirit to renew me and the face of the earth. Help me to be more sensitive to seeking Your guidance and the leading of Your Spirit.

Father Victor Dillard, a Jesuit priest who died in Dachau on January 12, 1945, prayer expresses the believer's difficulty in picturing the uniqueness of the Divine Person named the Holy Spirit:

"'Lord, make me see … I do not even know how to call on you, what to say: Holy Spirit, O Holy Ghost … I try to understand you, to isolate you in the divine sea into which I plunge. But my outstretched hand brings me nothing, and imperceptibly I drift away and kneel before the Father or lean over my more familiar interior Christ. My body stops. The senses want their ration of images so as to enable the soul to fly toward you. And you give them only strange material foods: a dove, tongues of fire, breath. Nothing that allows the warm intimacy of a familial human prayer for two. The trouble is that you are too close to me. I would need a bit of distance in order to look at you, to demarcate you, and to demarcate me, too, with respect to you, to satisfy my need for precise contours in order to understand our union.'

"… Christ gave us the great silence of the Holy Spirit. If people wander away from the devouring fire of the Spirit's silence, they always end up adoring idols. Without the Spirit's silence, men are empty husks. Silence is not the exile of speech. It is the love of the one Word.… Without silence, God disappears in the noise. And this noise becomes all the more obsessive because God is absent. Unless the world rediscovers silence, it is lost. The earth then rushes into nothingness."

Robert Cardinal Sarah - *The Power of Silence*

In God's Presence Consider …

Have I ever felt a similar longing as Fr. Dillard for the Holy Spirit to be more tangible to me? Do I harbor difficulty in picturing the Holy Spirit? Does it seem that God has disappeared because of my noisy life? Do I accept the Spirit's silence?

Closing Prayer

Thank You Jesus for giving me the gift of the Holy Spirit, "The Great Silence." Help me not to wander away from His devouring fire and to always tend the silent fire of Pentecost so that I may always love You and through Your Spirit may rediscover the gift of silence.

Hidden Dispenser **Day 36**

The knowledge and implementation of the truth of man's restored dignity as an image of God, comes about by a sincere gift of himself to others. This is possible in Christ only through the work of the Holy Spirit.

"Man's intimate relationship with God in the Holy Spirit also enables him to understand himself, his own humanity, in a new way. Thus, that image and likeness of God which man is from his beginning is fully realized.... God comes close to man, and permeates more and more completely the whole human world. The Triune God ... giving himself in the Holy Spirit as gift to man, transforms the human world from within, from inside hearts and minds ... man discovers himself as belonging to Christ and discovers that in Christ he is raised to the status of a child of God, and so understands better his own dignity as man.... Thus it can truly be said that the glory of God is the living man, yet man's life is the vision of God: man, living a divine life, is the glory of God, and the Holy Spirit is the hidden dispenser of this life and this glory."

St. Pope John Paul II - *Dominum et Vivicantem*

In God's Presence Consider ...

Do I understand my humanity and how the Holy Spirit raises it and restores it to the status of being a child of God? Do I live my life for the glory of God?

Closing Prayer

Come, Holy Spirit, Hidden Dispenser of the Life of God. Help me to put into practice what it means to being created and restored as an image of God. Draw me close to God and help me to be permeated with His love and life. St. Pope John Paul II, pray for me.

Penetrating Earthly Existence **Day 37**

There is a need to live in the Spirit so as to be able to become Christlike. It is only the Holy Spirit living in the hearts of people that can reveal Christ. We can become the image of God in Christ only though the Spirit dwelling in us.

"In celebrating the two thousandth anniversary of Christian redemption we should never forget the following reality: The redemption is totally carried out by the Son as the Anointed One, who came and acted in the power of the Holy Spirit, offering himself finally in sacrifice on the wood of the cross. And this redemption is, at the same time, constantly carried out in human hearts and minds – in the history of the world – by the Holy Spirit, who is the other Counselor.

"The Spirit works in believers in the same way that he totally penetrated the earthly and eschatological existence of Christ. Believers are Christians insofar as they participate in the anointing of Jesus, that is, in the Holy Spirit. Believers are baptized and filled with the Spirit, who transforms them into Christ. Thus, the believer's life in Christ is possible only because, and to the extent that, it is life in the Spirit. 'Communion with Christ is the Holy Spirit' affirms St. Irenaeus.

THC - *The Holy Spirit, Lord and Giver of Life*

In God's Presence Consider …

Our redemption is constantly carried out in our hearts and minds by the Holy Spirit. Do I allow the Holy Spirit to penetrate me as He penetrated Christ? Do I see my participation in the anointing of Jesus as living a life in the Spirit?

Closing Prayer

Jesus, the Anointed One, come and act in the power of the Holy Spirit within me. Help me to deny myself daily, to pick up my cross, to follow You, and to live a life in the Spirit.

The Church is holy because she participates in the Trinitarian nature of the total otherness of God. The Holy Spirit is called holy because He is considered to be God's actual indwelling.

"The Holy Spirit is truly holy because nothing is holy to this degree and in this manner. It is not acquired holiness, but holiness in person. The Spirit is, in fact the communion between the Father and the Son, between Christ and humanity—the unity which constitutes the Church—and between the Church and the Father, so that through him both of us have access in One Spirit to the Father."

St. Gregory of Nazianzus - *Orations*, XXV, 16

In God's Presence Consider...

I have access to the Father and the Son through the Holy Spirit. Do I see the unity of the Church as a communion between the Father and the Son and the Son and humanity? Do I realize that my access to the Father is the work of the Holy Spirit within me?

Closing Prayer

Come, Holy Spirit, Spirit of Communion, and unite me to the Church that I may have access to You and become a part of Your holy people, Your holy priesthood, a people set aside for the wondrous works of God. St. Gregory of Nazianzus, pray for me.

The Holy Spirit is revealed as another divine person with Jesus and the Father. He is sent by the Father and the Son to be with us, to teach and to guide us into all truth.

"According to our human concept, a person is a being who is complete and distinct from other beings; a subsistent being, existing by itself; an intelligent being, free and capable of willing; and an affectionate being, capable of loving. All this is verified in the Holy Spirit in the most perfect manner: He, the breath of love of the Father and the Son, is a Person, and a divine Person. He is a complete being. He is God, and wholly God, not a part of God; although absolutely equal to the other two divine Persons, He is distinct from them; He is subsistent in Himself, knowing and loving. Because the Holy Spirit is a divine Person, we can have relations with Him just as we do with the Father and the Son."

Fr. Gabriel of St. Mary Magdalen, O.C.D. - *Divine Intimacy*

In God's Presence Consider …

Do I have a personal relationship with the Holy Spirit? Am I having difficulty with images of the Holy Spirit and in seeing Him as a Person? Do I ask for His help in clearing my confusion and developing a personal relationship with Him?

Closing Prayer

Come, Holy Spirit, into my soul like the sun, which finding no obstacle, no impediment, illuminates everything. Illuminate my whole being with Your love. Make my soul Your humble abode and prepare me to develop a personal relationship with You.

Intimate Source of Life **Day 40**

The word Trinity is not found in the New Testament. Although Jesus talks about God as Father and the Holy Spirit, who is Love, He does not use the word Trinity. This union of the Father and the Son in the Holy Spirit is a union of Love, thus the Trinity is a communion of Love and an intimate source of all life.

"In the Old Testament, from the Book of Genesis onwards, the Spirit of God was in some way made known, in the first place as a 'breath' of God which gives life, as a supernatural 'living breath.' In the Book of Isaiah, he is presented as a 'gift' for the person of the Messiah, as the one who comes down and rests upon him, in order to guide from within all the salvific activity of the 'Anointed One.' At the Jordan, Isaiah's proclamation is given a concrete form: Jesus of Nazareth is the one who comes in the Holy Spirit and who brings the Spirit as the gift proper to his own Person, in order to distribute that gift by means of this humanity.... In the Gospel of Luke, this revelation of the Holy Spirit is confirmed and added to, as the intimate source of the life and messianic activity of Jesus Christ.... What Jesus says of the Father and of himself—the Son—flows from that fullness of the Spirit which is in him, which fills his heart, pervades his own 'I,' inspires and enlivens his action from the depths.... His humanity belongs to the person of the Son of God, substantially one with the Holy Spirit in divinity."

St. Pope John Paul II - *Dominum et Vivicantem*

In God's Presence Consider ...

Have I ever thought about the reason Jesus, the Son of God, came to earth and took on our humanity was so that He could distribute the Gift of the Holy Spirit to us through His humanity? What do I do with this precious Gift? What does this Gift say about my humanity?

Closing Prayer

Come, Holy Spirit, You who are the Intimate Source of Life, fill me with Your fullness that I too will be enlivened by Your actions within my heart. Unite my humanity with Your divinity that I too may be one with the Father and the Son. St. Pope John Paul II, pray for me.

Holy Spirit Revealed in Symbols

The purpose of the Holy Spirit being sent was to make known and unfold what was hidden. This is what is behind the Spirit's inspiration of Sacred Scripture. It is to the Church that He has been given to safeguard and instruct the Word of God and to convey truth. All of this is for the salvation and sanctity of man.

"The Spirit came especially to 'glorify' Christ; and vouchsafes to be a shining light within the Church and the individual Christian, reflecting the Savior of the world in all His perfections, all His offices, all His works. He came for the purpose of unfolding what was yet hidden whilst Christ was on earth; and speaks on the house-tops what was delivered in closets, disclosing Him in the glories of His transfiguration, who once had no comeliness in His outward form, and was but a man of sorrows and acquainted with grief.... He inspired the Holy Evangelists to record the life of Christ, and directed them which of His words and works to select, which to omit.... He continued His sacred comment in the formation of the Church, superintending and overruling its human instruments, and bringing out our Savior's words and works.... Lastly, He completes His gracious work by conveying this system of Truth ... to the heart of each individual Christian in whom He dwells. Thus, He vouchsafes to edify the whole man in faith and holiness."

St. John Henry Newman - *Sermon 19*

In God's Presence Consider ...

How do I allow the "shining light" of the Holy Spirit to reflect outward to the world through Jesus living in me? Do I allow the Holy Spirit to continue to form me through the Church? How reverently do I treat the Holy Scriptures?

Closing Prayer

Jesus, You are the Word made flesh. Send Your Holy Spirit to dwell in me that thus inspired and formed by the Magisterium of the Church, I may convey Your Truth to the whole world in faith and holiness. St. John Henry Newman, pray for me.

Creator of Every Creature **Day 42**

St. Ambrose, in referring to Scripture, affirms western tradition's strong awareness of the creating role of the Spirit.

"... (The Scriptures) have not only taught that without the Spirit no creature could endure, but even that the Spirit is the creator of every creature. Who could deny that the creation of the earth was the work of the Holy Spirit? Who could deny that, if the creation of the earth was the work of the Holy Spirit, then its renewal is also the work of the Spirit? Do we believe that without the work of the Holy Spirit the substance of the earth would exist when without his action not even the vaults of heaven exists?"

St. Ambrose - *On the Holy Spirit, II*

In God's Presence Consider ...

Do you find it impossible to deny that the creation of earth is the work of the Holy Spirit? Could renewal of the earth, the Church, and me personally be done without the Holy Spirit? How important is the Holy Spirit to me?

Closing Prayer

Come, Holy Spirit, come. Renew in me Your Sanctifying work. You who give life to all creation, come and re-enkindle the fire of Your Love and renew the face of the earth. St. Ambrose, pray for me.

Like Glasses That Magnify **Day 43**

The closer we grow to God, the Holy Spirit acts as a magnifying glass helping us to see those areas of sin in our lives that we never noticed or considered faults in the past.

"The Holy Spirit is light and strength. He teaches us to distinguish between truth and falsehood, and between good and evil. Like glasses that magnify objects, the Holy Spirit shows us good and evil on a large scale. With the Holy Spirit we see everything in its true proportions; we see the greatness of the least faults. As a watch maker with his glasses distinguishes the most minute wheels of a watch, so we, with the light of the Holy Spirit, distinguish all the details of our poor life. Then the smallest imperfections appear very great, the least sins inspire us with horror. That is the reason why the most Holy Virgin never sinned. The Holy Spirit made her understand the hideousness of sin; she shuddered with terror at the least fault."

St. John Vianney - *Catechism on the Holy Spirit,* Chapter 3

In God's Presence Consider ...

Have I made excuses for or avoided to look at my small imperfections when the Holy Spirit begins to reveal them to me? Am I able to recognize and see the hideousness of my sin? Am I accustomed to wearing the glasses of the Holy Spirit?

Closing Prayer

O Holy Spirit, You who are Light and Truth, come help me to distinguish between truth and error, good and evil. Help me to see the horror and hideousness of my sins. St. John Vianney, pray for me.

The Torch of Illumination **Day 44**

The Holy Spirit makes Jesus present in our hearts and helps us to recall the things Jesus taught.

"Jesus tells us that His holy Disciples will be more courageous and more understanding when they would be, as the Scripture says, 'Endowed with power from on high' (Luke 24:49), and that when their minds would be illuminated by the torch of the Spirit they would be able to see into all things, even though no longer able to question Him bodily present among them. The Savior does not say that they would no longer as before need the light of His guidance, but that when they received His Spirit, when He was dwelling in their hearts, they would not be wanting in any good thing, and their minds would be filled with most perfect knowledge."

St. Cyril of Alexandria - *Commentary on Luke*

In God's Presence Consider …

Does Jesus dwell in my heart? Do I allow my mind to be illuminated by the Holy Spirit? Do I see Jesus giving me guidance through the Holy Spirit working in me? Do I accept the personal work of the Holy Spirit within me?

Closing Prayer

Jesus, come into my heart and dwell. Illumine me with the torch of Your Spirit that I may be healed of my spiritual blindness and be filled with Your perfect knowledge and guidance. St. Cyril of Alexandria, pray for me.

Fr. Apostoli tells us that for the ancient peoples, breath, like wind, had a mysterious quality that they associated with life. Quoting Gen. 2:7 we read: "The Lord God formed man out of the clay of the ground and blew into his nostrils the breath of life, and so man became a living being"

"For the Hebrews, a person's breath was the source of his life.... Human breath was seen as the breath of God in us. His breath was thought to give life to us as well as to all creation; furthermore, it kept all things in existence.

"In our spiritual life, it is the Holy Spirit as the Breath of God Who breathes into us the spark of divine life. His presence in the soul is the origin of our supernatural life. His continued guidance is the means of sustaining the divine life of Sanctifying Grace in us and allowing us to continue to grow.... The Holy Spirit is then the breath of God blowing in us."

Fr. Andrew Apostoli, C.F.R. - *The Gift of God: The Holy Spirit*

In God's Presence Consider ...

Do I see a direct connect to every breath I take and God breathing life into me? Do I see the Holy Spirit as the breath of God blowing in me?

Closing Prayer

Breathe on me, O Breath of God, and spark the divine life within me. You are the origin of my supernatural life. I ask that You would continue to guide and sustain me in that life.

The Breath and Kiss of God

Day 46

The Holy Spirit is the very love of the Father and Son; the very Breath, the origin of our being and life.

"Because the Holy Spirit is the effusion of divine love, He is called 'Spirit' according to the Latin sense of the word which means air, respiration, the vital breath. In us, respiration is a sign of life; in God, the Holy Spirit is the expression, the effusion of the life and love of the Father and the Son, but a substantial personal effusion, which is a Person. It is in this sense that the third Person of the Blessed Trinity is called the 'Spirit of the Father and the Son,' and also 'the Spirit of love in God,' that is, the 'breath' of love of the Father and the Son, the 'breath' of divine love. It was in this sense that the Fathers of the Church called the Holy Spirit 'the kiss of the Father and the Son, a sweet, but secret kiss,' according to the tender expressions of St. Bernard."

Fr. Gabriel of St. Mary Magdalen, O.C.D. - *Divine Intimacy*

In God's Presence Consider ...

Just as the wind within nature surrounds us and makes its presence felt, so too the Holy Spirit makes Himself felt in our spiritual lives. Have I ever experienced the Holy Spirit as God's breath in my life? How might this be important for me in growing in my relationship with God?

Closing Prayer

Come, Holy Spirit, Spirit of Love. Come, that You may enkindle in my heart the flame of charity and be the breath of God that fills my soul.

St. Augustine tells us that once we have begun the journey of our spiritual life, the road becomes long and monotonous. The Church Fathers loved comparing the Holy Spirit to a precious ointment whose fragrance constantly renews the vessel that contains it. We are those vessels!

"Our life time here on earth is a period of continuous effort to live faithful Catholic Christian lives. At times, it can appear like a seemingly endless waiting for the Lord's return. This takes its toll on many. Some grow weary and barely manage to trudge along; others lose their way for a while; still others abandon the struggle altogether. It is at this point of weariness or discouragement that the Spirit of Life sustains and renews us throughout our long journey. Like a runner in a marathon race, we need a new breath of fresh air, our 'second wind' in order to have the energy to endure to the end. The Holy Spirit breathes that spiritual 'second wind' into our lives just when we need it.

"And how does Jesus refresh us? Precisely by sending us His Holy Spirit who constantly revives and renews us along the journey of life … when we begin to lose our fervor and are in danger of falling into a state or an attitude of mediocrity, lukewarmness, and indifference—the Holy Spirit breathes back into us renewed life.

Fr. Andrew Apostoli, C.F.R. - *The Gift of God: The Holy Spirit*

In God's Presence Consider …

Have I been at a point of weariness and discouragement where the Holy Spirit has sustained and renewed me? Do I ever seek the 'second wind' of the Holy Spirit to breathe back into me renewed life?

Closing Prayer

Come Second Wind of God, come and pour Yourself out on my dryness. Give strength to my weary legs and drooping heart. Grant me the wings of an eagle to soar to God in praise. Help me to finish the journey of faith renewed in Your life and love.

A Mighty Wind **Day 48**

From the very beginning, the Holy Spirit has shared with the saving work of the Father and the Son. One of the ways His work among us has been symbolized is by wind.

"In the beginning God created the heavens and the earth. The earth was without form and void, and darkness was upon the face of the deep; and the Spirit of God was moving over the face of the waters." Gen. 1:1–2

"Then Moses stretched out his hand over the sea, and the Lord drove the sea back by a strong east wind all night, and made the sea dry land, and the waters were divided." Gen. 14:21

"The wind blows where it wills, and you hear the sound of it, but you do not know where it comes from or where it goes; so it is with everyone who is born of the Spirit." Jn. 3:8

"When the day of Pentecost had come, they were all together in one place. And suddenly a sound came from heaven like the rush of a mighty wind, and it filled all the house where they were sitting." Acts 2:1–2

In God's Presence Consider …

Have I ever experienced the Holy Spirit as wind? How does the image of wind help me to understand the movement and work of the Holy Spirit in my life?

Closing Prayer

Come, Holy Spirit, Ruah, the Breath of God. Come as a mighty wind and move me along the path God intends me to walk this day.

Free as the Wind **Day 49**

There are four things: wind, breath, water, and fire, which were closely connected with life in the sacred Scriptures. In some way these symbols are also used in helping us understand the Holy Spirit as the Spirit of Life.

"Wind and breath are closely linked to the Spirit of Life by the biblical Hebrew word ruah. The ancient Jewish people used this same word to mean 'wind' or 'breath', or 'spirit.' This was because in biblical times, these three realities were thought to be connected. The basic root of the word ruah means 'air in motion,' and this is the WIND. But it can also mean air inhaled and exhaled in respiration, and this is BREATH. Finally, the ancient Hebrews observed that when breathing stops, life also departs from inside the person. This led them to assume that there is also an inner source of life in each person, a kind of 'inner breath,' and this is the human spirit or soul.

"For ancient peoples, 'wind' had a certain mystery about it. They could not explain wind in terms of its origin or its movements. Three qualities of the wind can help us in better understanding the Holy Spirit: it is unpredictable; it is known by its effects; and it can be very forceful.

"The Holy Spirit's ways will often be mysterious and unpredictable.... We must respect the freedom of the Spirit in directing our lives. Just as the wind can only be known by its effects, so too, the Holy Spirit can only be genuinely known by the effects of His fruits in our spiritual lives."

Fr. Andrew Apostoli, C.F.R. - *The Gift of God: The Holy Spirit*

In God's Presence Consider ...

If the work of the Holy Spirit can be examined by using the symbols of wind and breath, how do I detect the presence and work of the Holy Spirit in my life? How have I experienced the qualities of wind associated with the Holy Spirit: unpredictable, its effects, forceful, gentle?

Closing Prayer

O God, Almighty Father and Jesus, Your Beloved Son, breath on me Your Spirit, that I may be moved along Your paths and filled with Your life.

Soul of Our Souls **Day 50**

The process of sanctifying a soul can be compared to the lyre. God's gifts are the strings and when He plays them, they are in perfect harmony and make a beautiful symphony of love.

"The seven gifts are a divine means for making our souls fit to receive the motion of the Spirit. The celestial influence of this intimate Guest is called inspiration; its action is the breath of wind, delicately soft and irresistibly strong, that impels our life toward heaven, the warm and powerful wind of love that cleanses, eases, rectifies, consoles, refreshes—but also moves, carrying along all that is before it.

"Imagine a fine lyre whose perfectly harmonized strings vibrate at the blowing of the wind, each giving its own sound and all together composing a beautiful symphony. This is the soul of a just man when the Holy Spirit possesses it fully and has harmonized all the faculties by means of his gifts. Each one of them, like the strings of a living lyre, gives its own sound when the wind of the Spirit blows.... What else would the Holy Spirit, the personal love of God, produce, but a song if it is proper to love to sing?

Servant of God (SOG) Archbishop Louis M. Martinez - *The Sanctifier*

In God's Presence Consider ...

Do I reflect on the motions of the Holy Spirit as a delicately soft and irresistibly strong wind? Do I see the cleansing, consoling, refreshing, and rectifying work of the Holy Spirit within me? Am I allowing the Spirit to harmonize all my faculties through the reception and use of His gifts and producing a love song to God?

Closing Prayer

O Soul of my Soul, fine tune the strings of my heart that I may be perfectly harmonized as a fine lyre. Make my strings perfectly vibrate at the blowing of Your breath.

In comparing the Holy Spirit to the Wind, Fr. Apostoli makes the point that the force of the Spirit in our lives will vary. We must be tuned in to the workings of the Holy Spirit in order to feel His gentle nudge or His strong inspiration otherwise we might miss or run away from Him.

"As for the force of the wind, that varies quite a bit. Sometimes it is a gentle breeze which can be very refreshing on a hot summer day. Sometimes the wind can be fierce and powerful as in a gale or hurricane. Sometimes the wind can speed us up when it is to our backs, or slow us down if we are moving against it.

"Like the wind, the force of the Spirit varies in our lives. Most often, the Spirit's lead is gentle, almost imperceptible. He inspires us in a low-key way, and nudges us along, slowly but surely. (After all, there are many more gentle breezes in life than there are hurricanes!) But there are also times when the Spirit is unmistakably directing us in a certain way. We get the message 'loud and clear'; there is no mistaking what He wants of us. These are the times when the Spirit's promptings are forceful and undeniable. We may even want to avoid them or run from them. Do we not often resist, for example, His inspirations to greater generosity in service and sacrifice? How many people try to run from the thought of serving God in the Priesthood or Religious life?

"Like Jeremiah, we invent all kinds of excuses to God's call (Jer. 1:6).... There are times when there is absolutely no 'safe place' to run to and hide from the Spirit!"

Fr. Andrew Apostoli, C.F.R. - *The Gift of God: The Holy Spirit*

In God's Presence Consider ...

Have I ever experienced the Holy Spirit as a breeze or as a hurricane? Are there times that I avoid or run from the Spirit's promptings? Do I resist His inspiration and make excuses?

Closing Prayer

Come Mighty Breath of God. Come, as a gentle breeze or a mighty gale. Come and inspire me, help me to gratefully accept Your promptings to greater generosity, service, and sacrifice.

Fire — Day 52

Fire transforms that which it is consuming from one form to another.

"… fire symbolizes the transforming energy of the Holy Spirit's actions. The prayer of the prophet Elijah who 'arose like fire' and whose 'word burned like a torch,' brought down fire from heaven on the sacrifice on Mount Carmel (1Kings 18:38–39). This event was a 'figure' of the fire of the Holy Spirit, who transforms what he touches. John the Baptist … proclaims Christ as the one who 'will baptize you with the Holy Spirit and with fire.' (Lk. 1:17, 3:16) 'I came to cast fire upon the earth; and would that it were already kindled!' (Lk. 12:49) In the form of tongues 'as of fire' the Holy Spirit rests on the disciples on the morning of Pentecost and fills them with himself (Acts 2:3–4). The spiritual tradition has retained this symbolism of fire as one of the most expressive images of the Holy Spirit's actions. 'Do not quench the Spirit.' (1 Thes. 5:19)"

CCC #696

In God's Presence Consider …

Am I on fire with the Holy Spirit? Do I allow or seek His transforming energy to work in my life? How do I quench the Holy Spirit's fire within me?

Closing Prayer

Come, Holy Spirit, let Your fire fall. Come, Holy Spirit, set my heart on fire.

In the Old Testament, fire was often a mysterious sign of God's presence. In the New Testament, fire is linked to the coming and presence of the Holy Spirit.

"We can learn something about the Hoy Spirit's working in us from the very nature of fire. Fire gives us light and warmth; the Holy Spirit gives us these in a spiritual sense. By His light, the Holy Spirit assists our minds to better know the Lord and the truths He has revealed to us. By His warmth, the Holy Spirit moves our wills. This enables us to follow with eagerness and determination a course of action which will work to God's greater glory, to our salvation and sanctification, and to the building up of the Church, the Mystical Body of Christ.

"Fire also has the capability of purifying, as when gold or steel are placed in intense fire and all foreign elements are burned away. The Holy Spirit's fire cleanses us of our sins and sinful attachments, freeing our hearts so that we may belong entirely to the Lord....

"The 'tongues as of fire' which appeared over the heads of the disciples on Pentecost signified not only their reception of the Holy Spirit, but also prefigured the zeal that would characterize their preaching of the Gospel message. In fact, they immediately began to make 'bold proclamation as the Spirit prompted them' (Acts 2:4). The disciples had been fearful up to this time. Now they were bold...."

Fr. Andrew Apostoli, C.F.R. - *The Gift of God: The Holy Spirit*

In God's Presence Consider ...

Do I experience the Holy Spirit as a fire of light or warmth? Do I follow Jesus with a sense of eagerness and determination? Do I possess a zeal and boldness to proclaim the Good News of Jesus?

Closing Prayer

Come, Holy Spirit, fill the hearts of Your faithful, and enkindle in them the fire of Your Divine Love.

Throughout the Old Testament, the Spirit of God came down upon God's people, helped accomplish a task, and departed. Pentecost marks the New Covenant, for the Holy Spirit is given to reside interiorly, as in a Temple, within believers.

"'When the day of Pentecost had come, they were all together in one place. And suddenly a sound came from heaven like the rush of a mighty wind, and it filled all the house where they were sitting. And there appeared to them tongues as of fire, distributed and resting on each one of them. And they were all filled with the Holy Spirit and began to speak in other tongues, as the Spirit gave them utterance.' Act 2:1–4

"The sound from heaven, like that of a mighty wind, was an external sign of the mysterious and powerful action of the Holy Spirit; and at the same time the tongues of fire which rested upon each of the Apostles symbolized what was to be accomplished in their souls.... Here the symbolism is as clear as it can be. As fire purifies, enlightens, and gives warmth, so the Holy Ghost in this moment most deeply purified, enlightened and inflamed the souls of the Apostles. This was truly the profound purging of the spirit.

"The Holy Ghost came into them to increase the treasures of His grace, of the virtues and the gifts, giving them light and strength in order that they might be capable of witnessing to Christ even to the ends of the earth, and at the peril of their lives. The tongues of fire are a sign that the Holy Ghost enkindled in their souls that living flame of Love of which St. John of the Cross speaks."

Rev. Garrigou-Lagrange, O.P. - *The Three Ways of the Spiritual Life*

In God's Presence Consider ...

How do I experience the powerful actions of the Holy Spirit in my life? How has the Holy Spirit increased His grace within me? How might I prepare my soul for a renewal, a deepening of He who dwells within me?

Closing Prayer

O Holy Spirit, come as a mighty wind with your tongues of fire to purge me of all fear and those things which are hindering You from dwelling in Your fullness within me.

Full of Unwonted Joy **Day 55**

St. Philip Neri was known for his great joy. His body and soul bore the marks of his extraordinary encounter with the Holy Spirit.

"Here is how one of his [St. Philip Neri] biographers, Father Bacci, describes it: 'While he was with the greatest earnestness asking of the Holy Ghost His gifts, there appeared to him a globe of fire, which entered into his mouth and lodged in his breast; and thereupon he was suddenly surprised with such a fire of love, that, unable to bear it, he threw himself on the ground, and, like one trying to cool himself, bared his breast to temper in some measure the flame which he felt. When he had remained so for some time, and was a little recovered, he rose up full of unwonted joy, and immediately all his body began to shake with a violent tremor; and putting his hand to his bosom, he felt by the side of his heart, a swelling about as big as a man's fist, but neither then nor afterwards was it attended with the slightest pain or wound.'

"… sometime after his death, an autopsy found that two ribs had been broken and curved outward to accommodate his enlarged heart, which 'had been dilated upon the sudden impulse of love."

The Catholic Encyclopedia

In God's Presence Consider...

Do I earnestly and continuously ask the Holy Spirit for His gifts? Do I seek to have a heart dilated with love? What holds me back from seeking the Holy Spirit working in my heart?

Closing Prayer

Come, Holy Spirit, come. Pour out Your brilliance upon me. Dissipate the darkness of my sins which covers me and help me to seek You with my whole heart and to be filled with the love of God. St. Philip Neri, pray for me.

Melt Down **Day 56**

God's love can be likened to a source of heat which has the power to melt and transform what It touches. Like the Sequence for Pentecost says, "Melt the frozen, warm the chill...."

"We must say that melting is characteristic of love. My soul melted when he spoke (Sg. 5:6). Before a thing melts, it is hard and bound together in itself. If it melts, it is diffused and extends itself to another thing. Fear also becomes hard at times when it is not great, and likewise love; because when love conquers, then man extends himself to another thing which was before him. And concerning this kind of melting, it can be applied to Christ, according as he is our Head. For to be melted in this wise is the work of the Holy Spirit who is in the midst of us, that is in our affections—for he is Love, and our affections tend to love...."

St. Thomas Aquinas, O.P. -
Summa Theologica, Of the Effects of Love, Art. 5

In God's Presence Consider ...

Do I think of God's Love as a consuming fire? Am I consumed in this fire? Is my heart melting by the presence and work of the Holy Spirit within me?

Closing Prayer

Come, Holy Spirit, Fire of God's Love. Melt my hardness, warm my cold, that I may be drawn into Your eternal embrace. St. Thomas Aquinas, pray for me.

Hebrews 12:29 tells us that "God is a consuming fire." The CCC tells us in #696 that fire transforms, and thus fire symbolizes the Holy Spirit. We say that the Holy Spirit is the "Fire of God's Love." St. Padre Pio, in a letter to Fr. Benedetto, his spiritual director, in 1914 writes of his experience of God's fire.

"As soon as I begin to pray, my heart is invaded by a fire of loving love. This flame has nothing whatsoever to do with flames of this world below. It is a delicate, sweet flame that consumes but causes no pain at all. It is so sweet and delightful that, although the soul experiences great pleasure in it and is content, it still does not lose the intense desire for it. Oh God! This is so marvelous that I may never understand it until I am in my heavenly home.

"That desire for more, far from impinging on the complete contentment the soul experiences, refines the soul even more. The enjoyment the soul feels, rather than being diminished by the desire, becomes even more intense."

St. Pio of Pietrelcina, O.F.M. Cap. -
Padre Pio's Spiritual Direction for Every Day

In God's Presence Consider ...

Do I experience my heart being invaded by the Holy Spirit and burning like a fire with love for God in prayer? Do I experience prayer as something sweet and delightful giving me great pleasure and at the same time feel a more intense desire for God?

Closing Prayer

St. Pio, pray that the Fire of God's love would invade my heart and thus consumed, I may find great pleasure and a strong desire for more of the Holy Spirit in prayer.

God created man with his five senses. We take information from outside of us and through our senses bring it into us to process a response. Thus God uses symbols and things our senses can relate to in order to communicate His truths to us.

"The symbolism of water signifies the Holy Spirit's action in Baptism, since after the invocation of the Holy Spirit it becomes the efficacious sacramental sign of new birth: just as the gestation of our first birth took place in water, so the water of Baptism truly signifies that our birth into the divine life is given to us in the Holy Spirit. As 'by one Spirit we were all baptized,' so we are also 'made to drink of one Spirit' (1 Cor. 12:13). Thus the Spirit is also personally the living water welling up from Christ crucified (Jn. 19:34, 1 Jn. 5:8) as its source and welling up in us to eternal life (Jn. 4:10–14)."

CCC #694

In God's Presence Consider …

Efficacious means that the sign not only points to a spiritual reality, but confers the grace that is signified, and makes what it points to happen. Am I living my life in a way that reflects the new life and the living water of the Holy Spirit that I first received in my baptism?

Closing Prayer

Come, Holy Spirit, Source of Divine Life and renew within me the graces of my baptism, helping me to renounce Satan and all his empty promises and live for God alone.

Fr. Apostoli compares water as a life symbol with the Holy Spirit. Two of water's most basic uses are for drinking and for bathing. The Holy Spirit gives us supernatural life as the Living Water of our souls and this is precisely the Spirit's role—to be the constant source of Eternal Life within our souls!"

"… Old Testament passages where water symbolizes life and salvation. For example, the floodwaters in the story of Noah are used as a sign of the destruction of sin and the preservation of those who are just. In the story of the Israelite's crossing the Red Sea, the parting of the waters is a symbol of the waters of Baptism.

"In the New Testament, the symbol of water frequently refers to the Spirit as Life-Giver. This is especially true in the Gospel of John…. In Our Lord's conversation with the Samaritan woman at the well (Jn. 4:4–42) … the Holy Spirit as 'Living Water.' He will be poured forth into our souls to give us spiritual life, much as water poured on plants sustains them, and when needed, even revives them. St. John refers to water as a symbol of the life-giving Spirit. 'Everyone who drinks this water (at the well) will be thirsty again. But whoever drinks the water I give him will never be thirsty; no, the water I give shall become a fountain within him, leaping up to provide eternal life.' (Jn. 4:13–14) … the 'Living Water' He wants to give us, the Holy Spirit, Who would satisfy the thirst of our soul and becomes like a fountain within us, springing up to provide eternal life.

Fr. Andrew Apostoli, C.F.R. - *The Gift of God: The Holy Spirit*

In God's Presence Consider …

The Holy Spirit has been poured into my soul giving me spiritual life. Am I allowing this Living Water to sustain me? To revive me? Do I draw near the well to receive the Living Water anew? Is the Spirit dwelling in me as a fountain springing up to eternal life?

Closing Prayer

O God, who have brought us to rebirth by the word of life, pour out upon us your Holy Spirit, that, walking in oneness of faith, we may attain in our flesh the incorruptible glory of the resurrection.

Collect from the 3rd reading of the Vigil Mass for Pentecost

The Nicene and Constantinople Councils of 325 and 381 A.D. proclaim the Holy Spirit as the "Lord and Giver of Life."

"According to the Gospel of John, the Holy Spirit is given to us with the new life, as Jesus foretells and promises on the great day of the Feast of Tabernacles: 'If any one thirst, let him come to me and drink. He who believes in me, as the scripture has said, 'Out of his heart shall flow rivers of living water.' (Jn. 7:37–40) And the Evangelist explains: 'This he said about the Spirit, which those who believed in him were to receive.' It is the same simile of water which Jesus uses in his conversation with the Samaritan woman, when he speaks of 'a spring of water welling up to eternal life,' (Jn. 4:14) and in his conversation with Nicodemus when he speaks of the need for a new birth of water and the Holy Spirit in order to enter the kingdom of God (Jn. 3:5)

"The Church ... has proclaimed since the earliest centuries her faith in the Holy Spirit, as the giver of life, the one in whom the inscrutable Triune God communicates himself to human beings, constituting in them the source of eternal life.... This faith, uninterruptedly professed by the Church, needs to be constantly reawakened and deepened in the consciousness of the People of God.... In our own age, we are called anew by the ever ancient and ever new faith of the Church to draw near to the Holy Spirit as the giver of life."

St. Pope John Paul II - *Dominum et Vivicantem*

In God's Presence Consider ...

Do I trust God to give me living water and new life through the Holy Spirit? Do I think of the "living water" as the Holy Spirit, the Lord and Giver of Life?

Closing Prayer

O Lord, I thirst for You; I long to enter Your kingdom. Send Your Holy Spirit into my heart that I may receive the source of eternal life and be born anew. St. Pope John Paul II, pray for me.

A Vital Water Supply **Day 61**

The Holy Spirit, as the Living Water, becomes a spring or a fountain within the soul of everyone who believes in Jesus and seeks to make Him the Lord of their life.

"… The Spirit will flow as living water from the Heart of Christ into the heart of the individual, and there the Spirit will become like a Fountain. Just as a spring of water in a desert land can produce a life of rich vegetation, so too, the Spirit in us will bring our soul to life and will allow us to bring forth the fruits of Christian holiness.

"Like a tree planted near running water, that yields its fruit in due season, and whose leaves never fade. Whatever he does prospers.' (Ps 1:3) Thus, a good person—one deeply rooted in the Holy Spirit—is like 'a tree planted near running water." Even in a desert, the roots of a tree planted near flowing water often reach to the bed of the stream itself to get its needed water. In such a case, the tree will always have a vital water supply. This accounts for the effects produced. Its leaves never fade but retain their vital texture all year round. Furthermore, such a tree 'yields its fruit in due season.' Being alive and thriving, despite the hot sun, the tree will produce its own fruit once or twice during the year at the appropriate seasons.

"All this beautiful imagery describes the soul of someone rooted in the 'Living Water,' the Holy Spirit.

Fr. Andrew Apostoli, C.F.R. - *The Gift of God: The Holy Spirit*

In God's Presence Consider …

A good person is one who is deeply rooted in the Holy Spirit. How rooted am I in the Holy Spirit? Is my spiritual life alive and thriving? Am I producing the fruits of the Holy Spirit?

Closing Prayer

O Sacred Heart of my Redeemer, O Immaculate Heart of Mary, and Pure Heart of St. Joseph, pour into my heart the living water of the Holy Spirit. May He become a spring, a fountain of water, that I may be alive and thriving in my relationship with You and others.

St. Ambrose compares the life-giving quality of water to the Holy Spirit, which he says, never fails. He speaks of the Holy Spirit as a large river, by which the mystical Jerusalem is watered.

" … yet lest they should judge anything injuriously from this comparison taken from creatures, let them learn that not only is the Holy Spirit called Water, but also a River, as we read: From his belly shall flow rivers of living water. But this He said of the Spirit, Whom they were beginning to receive, who were about to believe in Him. (Jn. 7:38–39)

"So, then, the Holy Spirit is the River, and the abundant River, which according to the Hebrews flowed from Jesus in the lands, as we have received it prophesied by the mouth of Isaiah. (Is. 66:12) This is the great River which flows always and never fails. And not only a river, but also one of copious stream and overflowing greatness, as also David said: The stream of the river makes glad the city of God.

"For neither is that city, the heavenly Jerusalem, watered by the channel of any earthly river, but that Holy Spirit, proceeding from the Fount of Life, by a short draught of Whom we are satiated, seems to flow more abundantly among those celestial Thrones, Dominions and Powers, Angels and Archangels, rushing in the full course of the seven virtues of the Spirit. For if a river rising above its banks overflows, how much more does the Spirit, when He touches them, make glad that heavenly nature of the creatures with the larger fertility of His sanctification."

St. Ambrose - *Book 1 On the Holy Spirit*

In God's Presence Consider …

Do I ever ponder the Holy Spirit being the Living Water Jesus talked about? Am I satiated with this Living Water? Because the Holy Spirit desires to sanctify me in His Living Water, do I rejoice, give thanks, and allow myself to become fertile ground?

Closing Prayer

St. Ambrose, pray that the Holy Spirit, the River of Life, wash over me with His overflowing greatness and remove all that stands in the way of my receiving the living water of God's love. Make me a city of gladness.

Simple and Indivisible **Day 63**

St. Cyril says that the Holy Spirit gives of Himself through various gifts and actions for the common good, taking into consideration the differences of people, yet His nature remains the same.

"But why did Christ call the grace of the Spirit water? Because all things are dependent on water; plants and animals have their origin in water. Water comes down from heaven as rain, and although it is always the same in itself, it produces many different effects, one in the palm tree, another in the vine, and so on throughout the whole of creation. It does not come down, now as one thing, now as another, but while remaining essentially the same, it adapts itself to the needs of every creature that receives it.

"In the same way the Holy Spirit, whose nature is always the same, simple and indivisible, apportions grace to each man as he wills.... The Spirit makes one man a teacher of divine truth, inspires another to prophesy, gives another the power of casting out devils, enables another to interpret holy Scripture. The Spirit strengthens one man's self-control, shows another how to help the poor, teaches another to fast and lead a life of asceticism, makes another oblivious to the needs of the body, trains another for martyrdom. His action is different in different people, but the Spirit himself is always the same. In each person, Scripture says, the Spirit reveals his presence in a particular way for the common good."

St. Cyril of Jerusalem - *Instructions to Catechumens*

In God's Presence Consider ...

Do I depend on the graces of the Holy Spirit as much in my spiritual life as I depend on water in my physical life? Do I envy someone else's gifts or how the Spirit reveals His presence in them? Do I ever give much thought to living my life for the common good?

Closing Prayer

Pray for me, St. Cyril, that I may receive the Waters of the Holy Spirit in my life revealing and sharing the Spirit's presence for the common good.

Hidden in God **Day 64**

The Holy Spirit is a part of the central mystery of our Faith, and as mystery, the truth about the Holy Spirit is inaccessible to our reason alone and needs God's help and enlightenment. We can grow in our understanding of mystery while never exhausting the mystery.

"The mystery of the Most Holy Trinity is the central mystery of Christian faith and life. It is the mystery of God in himself. It is therefore the source of all the other mysteries of faith, the light that enlightens them. It is the most fundamental and essential teaching in the hierarchy of the truths of faith. The whole history of salvation is identical with the history of the way and the means by which the one true God, Father, Son, and Holy Spirit, reveals himself to men and reconciles and unites with himself those who turn away from sin.

"The Trinity is a mystery of faith in the strict sense, (and) his inmost Being as Holy Trinity is a mystery that is inaccessible to reason alone or even to Israel's faith before the Incarnation of God's Son and the sending of the Holy Spirit."

CCC #234, 237

In God's Presence Consider …

Have I tried to understand the Holy Spirit with merely my reason? God sent the Holy Spirit into my life at Baptism. How might this gift and grace aid me in coming to understand who the Holy Spirit is and what He does in my life?

Closing Prayer

Come, Holy Spirit, Divine Creator, the true source of light and fountain of wisdom. Pour forth your brilliance upon my intellect, dissipate the darkness which covers me, that of sin and of ignorance. Grant me a penetrating mind to understand, a retentive memory, method and ease in learning, the lucidity to comprehend, and abundant grace in expressing myself. Guide my exploration of who you are, direct its progress, and bring it to successful completion. This I ask through Jesus Christ our Lord, living and reigning with you and the Father, God forever and ever.

(Accredited to St. Thomas Aquinas)

The Father's Gift in His Son **Day 65**

The Holy Spirit is given as a gift and a guide to those who believe and are baptized.

"There is one Creator of all things, for in God there is one Father from whom all things have their being. And there is one only-begotten Son, our Lord Jesus Christ, through whom all things exist. And there is one Spirit, the gift who is in all. So all follow their due order, according to the proper operation of each: one power, which brings all things into being, one Son, through whom all things come to be, and one gift of perfect hope. Nothing is wanting to this flawless union: in Father, Son, and Holy Spirit, there is infinity of endless being, perfect reflection of the divine image, and mutual enjoyment of the gift.

"Since our weak minds cannot comprehend the Father or the Son, we have been given the Holy Spirit as our intermediary and advocate, to shed light on that hard doctrine of our faith, the incarnation of God."

St. Hilary - *Treatise on the Trinity*

In God's Presence Consider …

The proper operation of the Holy Spirit is that He is the gift who is in all. How have I experienced this gift of the Holy Spirit in my life? How has the Holy Spirit shed light on hard doctrines and things of our faith for me?

Closing Prayer

O Holy Spirit, the Gift of all gifts, help my weakened mind to comprehend the great mysteries of our Faith, especially the Father and the Son. St. Hilary, pray for me.

Personal Expression **Day 66**

It is through the Holy Spirit that the love of the Blessed Trinity comes to man as gift.

"Through grace, man is called and made capable of sharing in the inscrutable life of God. In his intimate life, God is love, the essential love shared by the three divine Persons: personal love is the Holy Spirit as the Spirit of the Father and the Son.... It can be said that in the Holy Spirit the intimate life of the Triune God becomes totally gift, and exchange of mutual love between the divine Persons, and that through the Holy Spirit God exists in the mode of gift. It is the Holy Spirit who is the personal expression of this self-giving, of this being-love. He is Person—Love. He is Person—Gift."

St. Pope John Paul II - *Dominum et Vivicantem*

In God's Presence Consider ...

The Scripture tells us that God pours out His love into our hearts through the Holy Spirit. Do I personally experience and accept this love as gift, or do I merely have head knowledge that God is love?

Closing Prayer

O God, Your love is a consuming fire. Let the Fire of Your Holy Spirit consume me, that I may receive Your love as Your gift to me. St. Pope John Paul II, pray for me.

Christian revelation never speaks of an impersonal God, of a force that threatens or inspires terror. It reveals a marvelous and exciting divine reality, who becomes personally involved. The God Jesus reveals is a personal God and is a communion of three persons.

"We believe in one God but his intimate life is so rich that it is formed by three persons distinct among themselves.... Every divine person, by the very fact that he is distinct from the others, by appropriation has his own activity in the history of salvation, has a relationship with creation, and, above all, has a relationship with humanity.

"The differences in the actions of the three persons might be described in this way: everything comes from the Father, everything is accomplished and actualized by the Son, and everything reaches humanity and becomes present to and experienced by humanity through the Holy Spirit.

"Hence the whole Christian life is a communion with each of the divine persons, without in any way separating them. Everyone who glorifies the Father does so through the Son in the Holy Spirit; everyone who follows Christ does so because the Father draws him and the Spirit moves him."

THC - *The Holy Spirit, Lord and Giver of Life*

In God's Presence Consider ...

If the Father's plan has been accomplished and actualized by the Son, do I see the role of the Holy Spirit as the one who makes the Father's plan and the Son's work present to me? If the Father draws me and I follow Christ, do I give the Spirit credit for moving me towards God?

Closing Prayer

Father, draw me to You, that in following Christ Your Son and moved by Your Spirit, I may glorify You with my whole life and may live for all eternity in communion with You. Help me never to be separated from You.

As the Love of the Father and the Son — Day 68

The Father and the Son love each other totally and completely. This total and complete giving of themselves in love to each other is the Holy Spirit, who they in turn pour into our hearts as the "Gift that contains all gifts." CCC #1082

"The Father and His Word, mutually beholding Their infinite goodness and beauty, love each other from all eternity, and the expression of this unitive love is a third Person, the Holy Spirit.... The Holy Spirit proceeds from the Father and the Son by way of love. This love is a Person, the third Person of the Most Holy Trinity, to whom the Father and the Son, by the sublime fruitfulness of their love, communicated their very own nature and essence, without losing any of it Themselves.

"... having ascended into heaven, Jesus, in union with the Father, sends us the Holy Spirit. The Father and the Holy Spirit loved us to the point of giving us the Word in the Incarnation; the Father and the Word so loved us as to give us the Holy Spirit. Thus, the three Persons of the Trinity give Themselves to man, stooping to bring him into Their own intimacy. Such is the excessive charity with which God has loved us; and the divine gift to our souls reaches its culminating point in the gift of the Holy Spirit, who is the Gift par excellence. The Spirit is given to be able to complete the work of our sanctification. By His descent upon the Apostles under the form of tongues of fire, the Holy Spirit shows us how He, the Spirit of love, is given to us in order to transform us by His charity, and having transformed us, to lead us back to God."

Fr. Gabriel of St. Mary Magdalen, O.C.D. - *Divine Intimacy*

In God's Presence Consider ...

God's divine gift of His love culminates in His giving us His Spirit. Do I seek the manifestations, charisms, and experiences of the Holy Spirit in my life or do I seek the Gift that contains all gifts? Do I accept the Holy Spirit as the ultimate Gift the Father and the Son gives to me?

Closing Prayer

Father, thank You for giving me Jesus and the Holy Spirit. Help me to focus more on the Giver of the gifts and not merely on the gifts that the Holy Spirit brings.

The Breath Who Confirms **Day 69**

The Church believes that God creates everything, giving existence and life through Christ in the Spirit. It is the Holy Spirit, the divine person, through whom God the Father immediately animates life. The Spirit is a life-giving force, the energy at work in the actions of creation. He is the perfecter and giver of life.

"You could have learned of the communion of the Spirit with the Father and with the Son from the initial act of creation.... The Father, since he creates by his very will, would not have needed the Son; but he wants to create through the Son. The Son would not even have needed cooperation, since he acts in the same way as the Father, but even the Son wanted to perfect the work through the Spirit.... You understand, therefore, that there are three; the Lord who orders, the Word who creates, the Breath who confirms. Who else could have been the confirmation if not the one who perfects?"

St. Basil - *On the Holy Spirit,* XVI, 38

In God's Presence Consider ...

The Holy Spirit is the One who perfects the work of the Father and the Son. Do I see the perfecting work of God being done in me through the Holy Spirit? Am I open to the renewal of life that the Spirit desires to do within me?

Closing Prayer

Breathe on me, O Breath of God, and perfect in me that which the Father and the Son has started. St. Basil, pray for me.

Completing the Perfections of God **Day 70**

The Holy Spirit is the most mysterious, most misunderstood, and most vaguely known Person of the Trinity. He is One with the other two Persons while His work seems to be inflaming love within man and enlightening their minds. He continues the work Jesus completed while on earth.

"He is the equal of the Father and the Son, of the same nature, power, and substance, eternally existent with Them, participating in the same divine life, forming with Them the ever-blessed Three-in-One. He represents to our human point of view that wonderful mystery, the personified love that proceeds from Father and from Son forever, and by this act completes the perfections of God … it was the Holy Spirit who is the love of the Father and the Son…. He loves forever the same, but it is we who, by our sins, have the power to shut off that love from effecting anything good in our souls.

"He (Jesus) had to die and rise and ascend, and then from the right hand of the Father, His own work would continue in a ceaseless intercession for all the children of men. On earth, however, His place would be taken by the Holy Spirit, who would teach the Apostles all things and bring back to their minds whatever He had taught them. In this way was guaranteed the infallibility and growth in doctrine that is the work of the Spirit…. The work, then, of the Holy Spirit is twofold: to inflame the love and to enlighten the mind."

Fr. Bede Jarrett, O.P. - *Classic Catholic Meditations*

In God's Presence Consider …

Do I cooperate with the Holy Spirit's work of inflaming God's love within me and enlightening my mind, or do I shut off His love preventing anything good in my soul? Do I use my human point of view to judge who the Holy Spirit is, what He does, and what I allow Him to do within me and for me?

Closing Prayer

O Lord, help me to never shut off Your love from working in me. Fan the flame of Your love within me and enlighten my mind, that, filled with Your Light and Truth, I may have Your vision to view my life.

Holy Spirit Known through Actions

A Share in the Holy Spirit **Day 71**

Origen lived between the years 185–254. He is speaking to a very young Church about the mystery of the oneness of the Three Persons of the Blessed Trinity and their shared work. Regeneration (conversion) unto salvation that is true is to obtain salvation with what he calls, "the co-operation of the entire Trinity." To be in a relationship with one of the Persons is to be in a relation with the other two Persons also.

"As now by participation in the Son of God one is adopted as a son, and by participating in that wisdom which is in God is rendered wise, so also by participation in the Holy Spirit is a man rendered holy and spiritual. For it is one and the same thing to have a share in the Holy Spirit, which is (the Spirit) of the Father and the Son, since the nature of the Trinity is one and incorporeal. And what we have said regarding the participation of the soul is to be understood of angels and heavenly powers in a similar way as of souls, because every rational creature needs a participation in the Trinity."

Origen - *De Principiis, Book IV Chapter I*

In God's Presence Consider …

Do I participate in the life of the Holy Spirit seeking to become holy and spiritual? Do I find myself fostering a relationship with one Person of the Trinity and not wanting or ignoring the other Two?

Closing Prayer

St. Joseph Most Faithful, offer my heart to God so that He may dwell in it as a throne of love and mercy. Present the movements of my soul and all the affections of my heart to God so that through your intercession I will always be faithful to the grace and inspirations of the Holy Spirit.

Prayer of Blessed Bartolo Longo

Inundated in Happiness **Day 72**

The interior life of God is a union of love with the Three Persons who are One. When we are united with One, we are also united to all Three Persons of the Trinity. When united to the Holy Spirit, our soul is inundated with the same happiness that nourishes the saints. This is the essence of the Beatific Vision to which we are all called.

"On one occasion, God's presence pervaded my whole being, and my mind was mysteriously enlightened in respect to His Essence. He allowed me to understand His interior life. In spirit, I saw the Three Divine Persons, but Their Essence was One. He is One, and One only, but in Three Persons; none of Them is either greater or smaller; there is no difference in either beauty or sanctity, for They are One. They are absolutely One. His love transported me into this knowledge and united me with Himself. When I was united to One, I was equally united with the Second and to the Third in such a way that when we are united with One, by that very fact, we are equally united to the two Persons in the same way as with the One. Their will is One, One God, though in Three Persons.

"When One of the Three Persons communicates with a soul, by the power of that one will, it finds itself united with the Three Persons and is inundated in the happiness flowing from the Most Holy Trinity, the same happiness that nourishes the saints. This same happiness that streams from the Most Holy Trinity makes all creation happy; from it springs that life which vivifies and bestows all life which takes its beginning from Him."

St. Maria Faustina Kowalska - *Diary of Divine Mercy*

In God's Presence Consider …

Do I lack an understanding and knowledge of who the Holy Spirit is and what it means to be united to the One is really a uniting with all Three Persons? Do I reflect the happiness of God in my spiritual life?

Closing Prayer

Come O Holy Spirit, fill me with understanding and acceptance of the happiness that nourishes me and streams from the Most Holy Trinity. Help me to push past my fears and vivify my life with my union with You. St. Faustina, pray for me.

The Secret Presence of God — Day 73

God's love for us is mirrored in the gift of the Holy Spirit.

"The condescension of the Blessed Spirit is as incomprehensible as that of the Son. He has ever been the secret Presence of God within the Creation: a source of life amid the chaos, bringing out into form and order what was at first shapeless and void, and the voice of Truth in the hearts of all rational beings, turning them into harmony with the intimations of God's Law, which were externally made to them. Hence He is especially called the 'life-giving' Spirit; being (as it were) the Soul of universal nature, the Strength of man and beast, the Guide of faith, the Witness against sin, the inward Light of patriarchs and prophets, the Grace abiding in the Christian soul, and the Lord and Ruler of the Church. Therefore let us ever praise the Father Almighty, who is the first Source of all perfection, in and together with His Co-equal Son and Spirit, through whose gracious ministrations we have been given to see 'what manner of love' it is wherewith the Father has loved us."

St. John Henry Newman - *Sermon 19*

In God's Presence Consider …

Do I ever look for the secret Presence of God within creation? God is a God of order, harmony, and life. Do I see the Holy Spirit as the Source of all perfection and the very presence of God in my life?

Closing Prayer

Father, I praise and thank You for Your Spirit, who You have given to me as the source of all life, goodness, beauty, and truth. Let Your Love through Him, always help me to be in harmony with Your laws and guide me in all matters of faith. St. John Henry Newman, pray for me.

The Holy Spirit is God, therefore when God fully gives Himself to man, this wholly self-giving God is giving us the Holy Spirit without which there is no gift and no life.

"The ultimate thirst of men cries out for the Holy Spirit. He, and he alone, is, at a profound level, the fresh water without which there is no life. In the image of a spring, of the water that irrigates and transforms a desert that man meets like a secret promise the mystery of the Spirit becomes visible in an ineffable fashion that no rational meditation can encompass. In man's thirst, and in his being refreshed by the water, is portrayed that infinite, far more radical thirst that can be quenched by no other water....The Holy Spirit is eternally, of his very nature, God's gift, God as wholly self-giving, God as sharing himself as gift. In that sense, the inner reason and basis for creation and salvation history do after all lie in this quality of being of the Holy Spirit, as donum and datum.... He is the content of Christian prayer. He is the only gift worthy of God: as God, God gives nothing other than God; he gives himself and thereby everything. This is why proper Christian prayer, again, does not beg for just anything; rather, it begs for the gift of God that is God himself, begs for him."

Pope Benedict XVI - *The Fellowship of Faith*

In God's Presence Consider ...

Do I ever experience a thirst in my soul during times of prayer? Water is needed for life. If the Holy Spirit is the living water, do I drink fully of the Holy Spirit in my spiritual life? Do I accept the gift of God, His whole self-giving, the only gift worthy of God, Himself as the Holy Spirit? Do I beg God for the Holy Spirit?

Closing Prayer

Holy Spirit, Living Water sent from God Himself, I beg that You would come and quench my thirst and transform the desert of my heart.

The Christian family, like the Holy Trinity, is a communion of persons. The love the Father has for the Son and the Son has for the Father, bring forth Life. This love and life is the Holy Spirit who is one and coequal with the Father and the Son.

"How has God revealed himself? God is a communion of Persons: Father, Son, and Holy Spirit. Each Person of the Godhead is fully God: holy, wise, just, true, love—so how do we tell them apart? We are able to differentiate the Father, Son, and Holy Spirit by their relations. From all eternity, the Father fathers the Son in self-donating love. The Son, in imitation of the Father, pours himself back to the Father in self-donating love. And the bond between them is more than a spirit of love; it constitutes the very Person of the Holy Spirit. God's inner life of total self-donation creates an intimate communion of love and life. God is not just loving; he is the very essence of love (1Jn. 4:8). He is the source of all life.... God did not create man and woman because he was lonely. Rather, as an expression of his life-giving love, the Triune God created us for the joy of creating us and making us life-giving lovers like himself. Man and woman were made to reflect God's inner life and love."

Kimberly Hahn -
Life Giving Love: Embracing God's Beautiful Design for Marriage

In God's Presence Consider ...

How has God revealed Himself to me? How do I experience the Person of the Holy Spirit? How have I become a life-giving lover through the work of the Holy Spirit?

Closing Prayer

Blessed Triune God, the God of Love who loves and pours out that love upon me, help me to imitate Your self-donating love so that I too may reflect and share Your inner life and love to others.

God is three Persons who share the one Nature: God. Pope Leo cautions us not to separate the one Nature in looking at each of the Persons, but to honor and adore the Trinity through each of the Persons signifying both the Trinity of Persons and the Unity of Nature who we equally owe supreme glory and worship.

"… Not that all perfections and eternal operations are not common to the Divine Persons; for the operations of the Trinity are indivisible, even as the essence of the Trinity is indivisible; because as the three Divine Persons are inseparable, so do they act inseparably. But by a certain comparison … these operations are attributed … to One Person rather than to the others…. The Holy Ghost is the ultimate cause of all things, since, as the will and all other things finally rest in their end, so He, who is the Divine Goodness and the Mutual Love of the Father and Son, completes and perfects, by His strong yet gentle power, the secret work of man's eternal salvation.

"Among the external operations of God, the highest of all is the mystery of the Incarnation of the Word, in which the splendor of the divine perfections shines forth so brightly that nothing more sublime can even be imagined, nothing else could have been more salutary to the human race. Now this work, although belonging to the whole Trinity, is still appropriated especially to the Holy Ghost, so that the Gospels thus speak of the Blessed Virgin: 'She was found with child of the Holy Ghost.' and 'that which is conceived in her is of the Holy Ghost.' (M1:18, 20) And this is rightly attributed to Him who is the love of the Father and the Son."

Pope Leo XIII - *Divinum Illud Munus*

In God's Presence Consider …

Have you ever thought of the Holy Spirit as the ultimate cause of all things? Do you acknowledge and give the Holy Spirit thanks for completing and perfecting your salvation?

Closing Prayer

Come O Divine Goodness and Mutual Love of the Father and Son; come with Your strong yet gentle power and complete and perfect in me the great gift of eternal salvation.

The "We" in the Origin — Day 77

Our comprehending the Holy Spirit depends on our participation in His life, His operations: remembrance, listening. He can bring about our understanding of Him as we participate in the whole body of knowledge which is given us through the Church.

"How does the Holy Spirit operate? First of all, by bestowing remembrance, a remembrance in which the particular is joined to the whole, which in turn endows the particular, which hitherto had not been understood, with its genuine meaning.

"A further characteristic of the Spirit is listening: he does not speak in his own name; he listens, and teaches how to listen. In other words, he does not add anything but rather acts as a guide into the heart of the Word, which becomes light in the act of listening. The Spirit does not employ violence; his method is simply to allow what stands before me as an other to itself and to enter into me. This already entails an additional element: the Spirit effects a space of listening and remembering, a 'we' which in the Johannine writings defines the Church as the locus of knowledge. Understanding can take place only with this 'we' constituted by participation in the origin. Indeed, all comprehension depends on participation."

Pope Benedict XVI - *The Nature and Mission*

In God's Presence Consider ...

How does the Holy Spirit operate in me? Does the Holy Spirit guide me into the heart of Jesus? Do I make efforts to remove myself from busyness and noise to listen to the Holy Spirit? Do I participate in the life of the Holy Spirit thus comprehending Him more?

Closing Prayer

Come and operate in me Holy Spirit. Call to mind those things to me that Jesus taught. Help me to listen and guide my heart into the heart of Jesus.

Murmuring in Souls **Day 78**

Jesus and the Father send the Holy Spirit in order to bear witness to Them and that we also may come to know and bear witness to Them.

"… The Father sends the Son; when the Son is in glory he prays to the Father to send the Spirit…. The Spirit, then, comes from the Father, through the Son. But in turn the Spirit brings us to the knowledge of the Son, which is life in him, so that, brought into the nuptial chamber of the Bridegroom, we come at last to the loving knowledge of the Father.

"The Spirit, Jesus says, will bring us into truth, making known to the Church and murmuring in the souls of the faithful all that he has learnt in the heart of the Trinity: what he will proclaim is what he has received, Jesus himself … Father, Son and Holy Spirit are all deeply involved in the story of our salvation; they turn towards us to bring life to our souls. In this world the Blessed Trinity becomes light and holiness."

Bernard Piault - *What is the Trinity?*

In God's Presence Consider …

It is the Holy Spirit who brings us into the nuptial chamber of the Bridegroom, Jesus. Do I allow the Holy Spirit to bring me into this oneness with Jesus? Do I listen to the murmuring of the Spirit in my soul? Do I allow all Three Persons of the Trinity to work salvation in my soul?

Closing Prayer

Come, Holy Spirit, the true source of light and fountain of wisdom. Bring me into the loving knowledge and intimate relationship with the Blessed Trinity. Help me to hear Your murmurings in my soul.

The Blessed Trinity is One and at the same time Three. God has one nature yet is three Persons sharing in God's work. The Father creates, The Son redeems, the Holy Spirit Sanctifies.

"The One whom the Father has sent into our hearts, the Spirit of his Son, is truly God … the Spirit is inseparable from them, in both the inner life of the Trinity and his gift of love for the world … the Church's faith also professes the distinction of persons. When the Father sends his Word, he always sends his Breath. In their joint mission, the Son and the Holy Spirit are distinct but inseparable. To be sure, it is Christ who is seen, the visible image of the invisible God, but it is the Spirit who reveals him.

"The whole divine economy is the common work of the three divine persons. For as the Trinity has only one and the same nature, so too does it have only one and the same operation: 'The Father, the Son, and the Holy Spirit are not three principles of creation but one principle.' However each divine person performs the common work according to his unique personal property…. Everyone who glorifies the Father does so through the Son in the Holy Spirit; everyone who follows Christ does so because the Father draws him and the Spirit moves him."

Cf. CCC #689–690; #258–259

In God's Presence Consider …

Do I have a personal intimate love relationship with Jesus? Have I ever considered that it is the Holy Spirit who has revealed Jesus to me and who has moved me to that relationship? Have I ever considered that my adoption by the Father is the work of the Holy Spirit?

Closing Prayer

Come, Holy Spirit, You who are inseparable from the Father and the Son; come and make me one with the Blessed Triune God.

It is the Holy Spirit who helps us discover the values that lie beyond facts and the freedom that lies beyond law. Pope Benedict encourages us to reflect on our responsibilities and choices regarding the Holy Spirit that go beyond a purely rational thinking to one of discovering the truth and values of the Holy Spirit as love.

"What is the real Christian message of Pentecost? What is this 'Holy Spirit' of which it speaks?....World history is a struggle between two kinds of love: self-love to the point of hatred of God, and love of God to the point of self-renunciation. This second love brings the redemption of the world and the self. In my opinion it would already be a giant step forward if during the days of Pentecost we were to turn to a reflection on our responsibility; if these days were to become the occasion for moving beyond purely rational thinking, beyond the kind of knowledge that is used in planning and can be stored up, to a discovery of 'spirit,' of the responsibility truth brings, and of the values of conscience and love....The Holy Spirit is truly 'spirit' in the fullest possible sense of the word. In all probability we must make our stumbling way to him anew from the midst of a world profoundly changed."

Pope Benedict XVI - *The Fellowship of Faith*

In God's Presence Consider ...

Who are You Holy Spirit? What is it that You do? What is my responsibility in regards to You? How can Pentecost become more real for me?

Closing Prayer

Come, Holy Spirit, help me to discover You. Sharpen my values and consciousness in love. Help me, in my stumbling attempts at understanding You, and not to fear the changes You desire to bring about in my life; so that I might truly live the gift of redemption.

It is through the special communion between Christ and the Holy Spirit that has its original source in the Father that the Holy Spirit ushers in the new era of the Church.

"In the light of what Jesus says in the farewell discourse in the Upper Room the Holy Spirit is revealed in a new and fuller way. He is not only the gift to the person (the person of the Messiah), but is a Person-gift. Jesus foretells his coming as that of 'another Counselor' who, being the Spirit of truth, will lead the Apostles and the Church 'into all truth'.... Coming from the Father the Holy Spirit is sent by the Father (Jn. 14:26; 15:26). The Holy Spirit is first sent as a gift for the Son who was made man, in order to fulfill the messianic prophecies. After the 'departure' of Christ the Son, the Johannine text says that the Holy Spirit 'will come' directly (it is his new mission), to complete the work of the Son. Thus it will be he who brings to fulfillment the new era of the history of salvation."

St. Pope John Paul II - *Dominum et Vivicantem*

In God's Presence Consider ...

Have I ever seen the work of the Holy Spirit as His sharing and completing the work of Jesus? Do I ever consider that God the Father desires to send me the Holy Spirit to work out my salvation?

Closing Prayer

St. Pope John Paul II, pray that the Holy Spirit, the Spirit of truth and the Person-gift of God may come and lead me into all truth. May He come and complete the work of salvation in me that Jesus has started.

Jesus is fully human and divine. His humanity is limited just like us. During His Passion, His spirit will suffer beyond His human capacity, but there is no possibility for His spiritual strength to stretch his bodily strength indefinitely. God the Father sends the help He needs in Simon of Cyrene.

"… the Holy Spirit, who is totally devoted to the work of the Incarnation of the Son and his task on earth, to whom the Father and the Son had entrusted the hour of the birth and so the task of overshadowing and who keeps to the hour fixed by the Father for the Son's death, … takes care that the Son does not die from exhaustion before his time but receives the necessary assistance to help him reach the Father's hour, which is also the Son's. He inspires Simon, not yet a believer, not to refuse giving help, and through this act the Holy Spirit can take possession also of his soul."

Adrienne von Speyr - *The Passion from Within*

In God's Presence Consider …

Do I ask God for the Holy Spirit's help when my humanity is stretched to its breaking point? Do I believe the Holy Spirit can help me carry my crosses? Who are the Simons of Cyrene that the Holy Spirit has brought into my life to help carry my crosses?

Closing Prayer

Father, help me to follow the inspiration of the Holy Spirit that He may take full possession of my soul and help me not refuse giving help to someone in need.

Forged and Transformed **Day 83**

Pope Francis, in his Apostolic Exhortation reminds us that God wants all of us to be saints and not to settle for a bland and mediocre existence. This call to holiness is a call to a relationship with the Holy Spirit forging us to reflect Jesus Christ to the world. Our response is to allow the Spirit to transform us.

"The Father's plan is Christ, and ourselves in him. In the end, it is Christ who loves in us, for 'holiness is nothing other than charity lived to the full,' (Benedict XVI, General Audience April 13, 2011). As a result, 'the measure of our holiness stems from the stature that Christ achieves in us, to the extent that, by the power of the Holy Spirit, we model our whole life on his,' (Ibid). Every saint is a message which the Holy Spirit takes from the riches of Jesus Christ and gives to his people.

"You too need to see the entirety of your life as a mission. Try to do so by listening to God in prayer and recognizing the signs that he gives you. Always ask the Spirit what Jesus expects from you at every moment of your life and in every decision you must make, so as to discern its place in the mission you have received. Allow the Spirit to forge in you the personal mystery that can reflect Jesus Christ in today's world … let yourself be transformed. Let yourself be renewed by the Spirit … lest you fail in your precious mission."

Pope Francis - *Gaudete et Exsultate* #21–23

In God's Presence Consider …

Do I ever think of myself as part of God's plan? Do I consider myself being transformed into a saint that becomes a message of God's riches to others? Do I allow the Spirit to forge in me the mystery of Jesus Christ that is meant to bear witness to the world?

Closing Prayer

Come O Creator Spirit; visit me and fill me with Your grace, making my heart holy. Forge and transform me that I may carry out my mission and reflect Christ to the world.

Jesus' work of salvation continues to be carried out in His Body the Church where He invites all into His life and in particular His sacramental life where He secures for them the life of divine grace which brings them into the life of heaven. This work and mission are shared with the Holy Spirit.

"He (Jesus) did not will to entirely complete and finish this office Himself on earth, but as He had received it from the Father, so He transmitted it for its completion to the Holy Ghost…. He made it clear that the Holy Ghost is equally sent by-and therefore proceeds from-Himself and the Father; that He would complete, in His office of Intercessor, Consoler, and Teacher, the work which Christ Himself had begun in His mortal life. For, in the redemption of the world, the completion of the work was by Divine Providence reserved to the manifold power of that Spirit, who, in the creation, adorned the heavens and filled the whole world."

Pope Leo XIII - *Divinum Illud Munus*

In God's Presence Consider …

How does the Holy Spirit bring to completion the saving work of Jesus? Have you ever thought about the Holy Spirit actually completing the work Jesus came to earth to do? How have you experienced the life-giving love of the Holy Spirit?

Closing Prayer

Come, Holy Spirit, Life-giving Love, complete the work that You and Jesus have begun in me and the world.

The Holy Spirit not only inspired the authors of Sacred Scripture, but can inspire me through the reading of the Sacred Scriptures. The coming to life of the Word of God is the work of the Holy Spirit.

"There can be no experience of God in the Scriptures if it is not inspired by the Spirit.... Sacred Scripture, in that it is the Word of God directed to human beings, offers the possibility of encountering God in a vital and open dialogue. It is impossible that God's self-revelation in his Word come without the Spirit who renders visible the invisible and palpable the impalpable. Present in the Spirit is the unique dynamism that reaches the Son from the Father and from the Son in the Spirit reaches every human being. This means that the experience of God through his Word is given by the action of the Holy Spirit, who orients human beings toward the search for truth.

"The Spirit is the power of incarnation, of presence, of truth, and of acceptance: without him the Word remains ineffective, inoperative, exteriorized, and inconsistent.... At the same time, the Spirit prepares the human heart for listening, makes the heart capable and desirous of welcoming the Word. In this, the act of faith is a gift of the Spirit.... The Holy Spirit is the one who illuminates the revelation of God executed by Jesus."

THC - *The Holy Spirit, Lord and Giver of Life*

In God's Presence Consider ...

Do I always pray to the Holy Spirit seeking His inspiration and for the gift of faith before I read Scripture? Do I allow the Holy Spirit to work within me by His preparing me to listen and be illuminated by the word God?

Closing Prayer

O God, You who taught the hearts of the faithful by the light of the Holy Spirit, by this same Spirit, help the Holy Scriptures become alive within me that I may grow in the perfection of the gift of faith. Help my heart to listen and welcome Your Word in me.

Truly a Person **Day 86**

Fr. Hampsch first addresses the heretical opinion held by many that the Holy Spirit is merely a symbol of God's presence or power, and not a living entity. He then sites six facts found in Scripture that show the Holy Spirit is truly a Person who is also truly God. This is his 6th point.

"The recorded activities of the Holy Spirit bespeak personhood, for instance: He speaks (Acts 13:2); He intercedes (Rom. 8:26); He testifies (Jn. 15:26); He guides (Jn. 16:13); He commands (Acts 16:6–7); He appoints (Acts 20:28); He leads (Rom. 8:14); He reproves and convicts of sin (Jn. 16:8); and He shapes the individual's and community's life (Rom. 8:1–17).

"Thus, by Scripture we know that the Holy Spirit acts as a Person, with an intellect, emotions, and will, and can be 'grieved.' The Spirit generally acts in and through the Church, directly or indirectly, but always by his own choice, as affirmed by Jesus' descriptive analogy in reference to the Spirit: 'The wind blows wherever it pleases' (Jn. 3:8)."

Fr. John H. Hampsch, CMF - *Receiving the Gift of the Holy Spirit*

In God's Presence Consider …

Have you ever thought of the Holy Spirit as a person possessing an intellect, emotions, and will who can be grieved? How could my life be grieving the Holy Spirit? Do I relate to the Holy Spirit as a Person or as a symbol/power of God acting?

Closing Prayer

Come, Holy Spirit, come and be my guest. Come and help me to see You as a Person in relationship with the Father, Son, and His Body the Church.

One is a disciple of Jesus who allows the Holy Spirit to dwell in their hearts and to transform them to be other-worldly; orientated to Heaven and conformed to be another Christ.

"It can easily be shown from examples both in the Old Testament and the New that the Spirit changes those in whom he comes to dwell; he so transforms them that they begin to live a completely new kind of life....

"Does this not show that the Spirit changes those in whom he comes to dwell and alters the whole pattern of their lives? With the Spirit within them it is quite natural for people who had been absorbed by the things of this world to become entirely other-worldly in outlook, and for cowards to become men of great courage. There can be no doubt that this is what happened to the disciples. The strength they received from the Spirit enabled them to hold firmly to the love of Christ, facing the violence of their persecutors unafraid. Very true, then, was our Savior's saying that it was to their advantage for him to return to heaven: his return was the time appointed for the descent of the Holy Spirit."

St. Cyril of Alexandria - *Commentary on the Gospel of John*

In God's Presence Consider ...

What is it that disturbs me or makes me feel uncomfortable with the Holy Spirit dwelling in me and allowing Him to transform my life to be a true disciple of Jesus? Am I fearful of change? Have I grown comfortable with where I am in my spiritual life? How do I hold firmly onto the love of Christ?

Closing Prayer

Grant, we pray, almighty God, that your Church may always remain that holy people, formed as one by the unity of the Father, Son and Holy Spirit, which manifests to the world the Sacrament of your holiness and unity and leads it to the perfection of your charity.

Collect from the 1st reading of the Vigil Mass for Pentecost

Fearful before Pentecost, the Apostles, men without education, are now enlightened, receive the fullness of contemplation, and are filled with courage, even to the point of martyrdom.

"The transformation which the Apostles had undergone is shown also in their sanctifying influence, in the transport of intense fervor which they communicated to the first Christians.... As the Acts show, (Acts 2:42–47) the life of the infant Church was a life of marvelous sanctity; 'the multitude of the believers had but one heart and one soul'; they had all things in common, they sold their goods and brought the price of them to the Apostles that they might distribute to each according to his needs. They met together every day to pray, to hear the preaching of the Apostles, and to celebrate the Eucharist. They were often seen assembled together in prayer, and men wondered to see the charity that reigned among them.

"They are strong in the face of peril, but they are tender in the love of their brethren; the almighty Spirit who guides them well knows the secret of reconciling the most opposite tensions.... He gives them a heart of flesh made tender by charity and He makes them hard as iron or steel in the face of peril. He strengthens and He softens, but in a manner all His own. For these are the same hearts of the disciples, which seem as diamonds on their invincible firmness, and which yet become human hearts and hearts of flesh by brotherly love. This is the effect of the heavenly fire that rests upon them this day. It has softened the hearts of the faithful, it has, so to speak, melted them into one."

Rev. Garrigou-Lagrange, O.P. - *The Three Ways of the Spiritual Life*

In God's Presence Consider...

Have I experienced the transforming power of the Holy Spirit in my life? How has the Holy Spirit softened my heart to be reconciled with those with different views, opinions, or who have hurt me?

Closing Prayer

O Holy Spirit, the Great Transformer, come with Your heavenly fire. Rest upon me; soften my heart with Your tender charity toward my neighbor, yet make me hard as steel in the face of peril.

Evangelism is first of all about a person; Person of Jesus Christ. Jesus, the Word of God, is present to us through the Holy Spirit.

"Evangelism is not first and foremost a matter of strategies, plans and projects but rather of being filled with the Holy Spirit and allowing that divine life within us to burst forth in both word and action.... Jesus Himself was filled with the Holy Spirit at His baptism in the Jordan River.... Jesus was sinless; He did not need to repent for anything.... He would be counted among sinners and would bear the penalty for sin.... John the Baptist himself speaks of Jesus. 'He will baptize you with the Holy Spirit and fire' (Lk. 3:16) .... Jesus would baptize people in the Spirit because He Himself had been baptized in the Spirit.... The essence of baptism in the Holy Spirit is to have the love of God the Father poured into one's heart by the Holy Spirit (see Romans 5:5).

"... After His baptism, Jesus was 'full of the Holy Spirit' (Lk. 4:1). Curiously, the first thing the Holy Spirit did was to lead Him into the desert to be tempted by the devil. Why would the Spirit lead Jesus to be tempted? To be led by the Holy Spirit means to resist those evil spirits that seek to deflect us from our God-given mission. In the Holy Spirit, we have a God-given authority to defeat the enemy and break his influence.... His (Jesus) whole mission was a work of dismantling the kingdom of darkness and liberating those who had been captive to it.... Jesus chose to live as a man, dependent on the Holy Spirit"

Randy Clark & Mary Healy - *The Spiritual Gifts Handbook*

In God's Presence Consider ...

To be baptized in the Holy Spirit is to have the love of the Father poured into us. Do I accept this great outpouring? Jesus, as man, was dependent on the Holy Spirit. Am I dependent on Him? Do I make myself available to be refilled and re-enkindled with the Holy Spirit?

Closing Prayer

Help me O Holy Spirit to direct my life to God as my last end; so that having loved Him and served Him in this life, I may have the happiness of possessing Him eternally in the next.

Prayer of St. Alphonsus Ligouri

Jesus chose twelve weak, rude, ignorant, timid, and fearful men to be His Apostles. Even after three years of following as His disciples, who watched Him, listened to Him, and asked Him questions, they still remained dull of comprehension, slow to grasp His teachings, and when Jesus needed them the most, they ran and hid, leaving Him alone. With the sending of the Holy Spirit, everything changed.

"When, the Holy Ghost descended upon them at Pentecost, they were at once changed. In an instant, the Holy Ghost made them understand all that Jesus had been teaching them for three years but which they had failed to grasp. All their fears vanished, and they went into the midst of their enemies preaching Jesus Christ.

"They then divided the whole world among themselves, preaching the Gospel, casting down the false idols, and planting the doctrine of Christ in their place. They did not fear the Roman emperors, nor the proud philosophers of Greece and Rome, whom they confounded.

"What happened to the Apostles is still happening to all those who do not know and love the Holy Ghost. They are blind and cannot see. Their ideas are vague and erroneous. They must begin at once to love and pray to the Holy Ghost."

Fr. Paul O' Sullivan, O.P. - *The Holy Ghost Our Greatest Friend*

In God's Presence Consider …

Jesus had told His disciples to wait until they were "clothed with power" before they started their ministry. In a twinkling of an eye, they were transformed and made new. Do I believe that I can be clothed with God's power? Do I seek the Holy Spirit to change me? Do I believe that the Pentecost experience continues to be offered to me today?

Closing Prayer

Come, Holy Spirit and fall afresh on me. Let Your tongues of fire rest upon me, clothing me with Your power that I may set the world on fire with love for Jesus.

Showing His Influence **Day 91**

The Holy Spirit penetrates our deepest being and bears witness to the reality that we are adopted children of God the Father.

"Paul reflects on the Spirit showing his influence not only on the Christian's action but over his very being. In fact, he says that 'the Spirit of God dwells in us' (cf. Rom. 8:9; 2 Cor. 3:16) and that 'God has sent the Spirit of his Son into our hearts' (Gal. 4:6).

"For Paul, therefore, the Spirit penetrates our most intimate personal depths. In this connection, these words have a relevant meaning: 'For the law of the spirit of life in Christ Jesus has freed you from the law of sin and death.... For you did not receive a spirit of slavery to fall back into fear, but you received a spirit of adoption, through which we cry, Abba, Father!' (Rom. 8:2, 15), given that we are children, we can call God Father."

Pope Benedict XVI - *Zenit News*

In God's Presence Consider ...

Am I led by a spirit of fear when it comes to the things of God and especially to the things of the Holy Spirit? I might have thought about the Spirit influencing my actions, but have I ever thought about the Spirit's influence over my very being?

Closing Prayer

Abba, Father, as Your child, I thank You for pouring Your Spirit into my heart. May He penetrate my inmost being setting me free from the slavery to my sins, and helping me truly live as Your child.

Pentecost is the turning point for the Apostles in bearing witness to Jesus. The Sacrament of Confirmation is to be our Pentecost experience.

"But the Apostles were not only enlightened on the day of Pentecost; they were also strengthened and confirmed. Jesus had promised them: 'You shall receive the power of the Holy Ghost coming upon you.' (Acts 1:8) Fearful before Pentecost, they are now full of courage, even to the point of martyrdom. Peter and John, arrested and hauled before the Sanhedrin, declare that 'there is no salvation in any other' than in Jesus Christ. Arrested again, and beaten with rods, 'they went forth from the presence of the council rejoicing that they were accounted worthy to suffer reproach for the name of Jesus. And every day they ceased not, in the temple and from house to teach and preach Christ Jesus' (Acts 5:41). They all bore testimony to Christ in their blood. Who had given them the strength to do this? The Holy Spirit by enkindling the living fire of charity in their hearts."

Rev. Garrigou-Lagrange, O.P. - *The Three Ways of the Spiritual Life*

In God's Presence Consider …

Do I see my Sacrament of Confirmation as a Pentecost? Do I experience courage in defending the faith? Do I share Jesus and my Catholic Faith ceaselessly?

Closing Prayer

Come, Holy Spirit, let Your fire fall. Renew within me the grace of my confirmation that I may truly be a soldier and ambassador of Christ.

Left to the Care of... **Day 93**

Jesus gave the Holy Spirit to the Church with the promise that He would be with her until the end of time, that the gates of hell would not prevail against the Church, and that the Holy Spirit would guide and teach her in all truth.

"According to the Creed, the Christian believes firstly in God the Father, in Christ incarnate, in the Holy Spirit, and "one, holy, catholic, and apostolic Church." This is a great mystery and, though Jesus carried it out completely, he did not tell us everything. He left it to the care of the Holy Spirit to guide the Church to all truth (Jn. 16:12-13). It is the Spirit who transmits and explains the Word of the Lord to us. It is he who teaches us how to live as faithful followers of Christ. It is through him that we put into practice the new law of love, the new ark that is the means of our salvation."

Fr. El Khoury - *A Light from the East*

In God's Presence Consider ...

Have you ever thought of the Holy Spirit completing the ministry Jesus started, through guiding the Church? How do I work with the Holy Spirit to be able to put into practice the law of love?

Closing Prayer

O Holy Spirit, Guide of the Church, guide me into all truth. Explain to me the Word of the Lord, and teach me to be a faithful follower of Jesus.

The Old Testament understanding and experience of the Holy Spirit prepares the way for the New Testament's revealing of the Holy Spirit as a person. The same outpouring of the Holy Spirit at Pentecost is the same outpouring on the People of God today.

"The Spirit of Yahweh was active (Gen. 1:2) This spirit he breathed into man, the breath of life (Gen. 2:7) that makes him like God (Gen. 1:26), yet, when he wished, he could take it away (Gen. 6:3).

"To the Spirit of God is attributed the mysterious phenomena which are beyond human control: power over the outcome of wars; of carrying men off through the air; inspired the prophets.

"The Spirit of God is said to also dwell in man. By the time of the great prophets the action of the Spirit is no longer seen as intermittent and passing, it has become permanent; the Spirit of the Lord dwells in man to make him act righteously. On the other hand, without the Spirit of the Lord the spirit of man, goes raving mad.

"The role of the Spirit of the Lord is vividly presented. What is this Spirit in itself? Not a distinct person in God but a force, a creative sanctifying power which comes forth from him to carry out in the world the work he wishes to accomplish there, particularly when his actions assume a religious character."

St. Pope John Paul II - *Dominum et Vivicantem*

In God's Presence Consider …

Do I find that because the Holy Spirit is beyond human control, I fear His dwelling in and working in me? Do I think of the Holy Spirit as a person God sends to me to work what He wishes and to dwell in me?

Closing Prayer

Come, Holy Spirit and make of me a permanent dwelling place for You. St. Pope John Paul II, pray for me.

The Holy Spirit, who is the "Master of the Interior Life" (CCC #1995) works within the human heart to bring about our conversion and to turn us back to God.

"If we wish a more profound understanding of this mysterious action of the divine Paraclete in the sacred soul of Jesus, it will suffice to think of what He accomplishes in a soul who has reached the transformation of love. St. John of the Cross teaches that, in this very exalted state, the Holy Spirit invades the soul, henceforth totally docile to His motions; He directs it and moves it in all its acts, impelling it unceasingly toward God by a perfect adherence to His divine will. The Holy Spirit accomplished immeasurably more in the soul of Christ which was supremely capable of docility and correspondence to His inspiration. The divine Spirit encountered the sublime creature, the soul of Jesus; He invaded it, directed it, guided it in the accomplishment of its mission and brought it to God with unparalleled transports, because it was completely under His sway."

Fr. Gabriel of St. Mary Magdalen, O.C.D. - *Divine Intimacy*

In God's Presence Consider...

Am I docile to the invasion and motions of the Holy Spirit in my soul? To what degree do I allow myself to be completely under the Holy Spirit's sway?

Closing Prayer

O Holy Spirit, You who worked with such plenitude in the most holy soul of Jesus, deign to operate also in my poor soul and take it entirely under Your direction, so that every act, interior as well as exterior, may be according to Your inspiration, Your choice, Your good pleasure.

Wake Up and Believe **Day 96**

Often people are so caught up with the experiences of God's wonders that they fail to see the God who acts powerfully in their midst; they focus more on the gifts and the experience than the Giver of the gifts who is the Gift.

"The Spirit is the Spirit of Jesus who makes Jesus present in power in our midst. This Spirit calls us to expectant faith that reaches to Jesus as our healer. Our faith should not be preoccupied with wonders but with the Lord who is acting in our midst.

"The Spirit speaks to the Churches. He calls them to a new fullness of life. He affirms the good of using the gifts of God to develop competent leaders and professional specialists in so many areas, to organize to better serve the poor, to research and study the meaning of the Scriptures and those traditions developed under the inspiration of the Spirit. But this Spirit has this against the Churches: they so easily forsake their greatest source of power, the life-giving power that flows from the Lordship of Jesus....

"The Spirit says wake up and believe. Get up and work while there is light. Be compassionate as I your God am compassionate; heal my people, my chosen people whom I love and desire to gather under my wing. Heal them!"

Fr. Michael Scanlan, T.O.R. - *Inner Healing*

In God's Presence Consider ...

Have I ever thought of the Holy Spirit as the Gift Giver who makes the gift of Jesus present to me? Am I so preoccupied with life and other distractions that I miss the wonder of the Lord acting in my life?

Closing Prayer

Jesus send Your Holy Spirit to awaken in me an expectant faith and the grace to see that all power to heal and to be healed flows from You. You are calling me to continue Your work by giving me Your gifts. Help me to focus not on the wonders You perform, but upon seeing You acting in my midst. Gather me under Your wing that through the Holy Spirit I may be healed and be a source of healing for Your People.

The Holy Spirit does not remain idle in a soul that is open to His divine work. The Spirit influences our whole being as He sets about His work of transformation and places within us His divine gifts. Through His inspirations, the gifts influence the way we live, love, and respond to God.

"The soul's delightful Guest does not remain idle in his intimate sanctuary. Being fire and light, as the Church calls him, he hardly takes possession of the soul before his beneficent influence extends itself to the whole being and begins with divine activity its work of transformation.

"The Holy Spirit lives in the center of the soul, in that profound region of the will where he himself has diffused charity. From that center he pours himself out, so to speak, over the whole man with a divine unction, like the sacred perfume of which the Scriptures speak....

"Like the victor who, on taking possession of a kingdom places in each city men to execute his orders and act as his regents, governing the place he has conquered, so the Holy Spirit, the loving conqueror of souls, places some divine gifts in each of the human faculties, that through his holy inspiration the whole man may receive his vivifying influence."

SOG Archbishop Louis M. Martinez - *The Sanctifier*

In God's Presence Consider ...

Have I experienced the divine work of transformation within my life by the Holy Spirit? Have I allowed the Holy Spirit to conquer my heart and then to govern it? Am I receptive to the inspirations and vivifying influence of the Holy Spirit?

Closing Prayer

O Holy Spirit, fire and light of Christ; come and take possession of my soul. Work Your divine activity in me that I may be transformed and anointed with Your divine unction.

In the Gospel of John, we read that even though we have never seen God, if we love one another, God lives in us and His love is perfected in us. It is through God giving us His Holy Spirit that we know that we abide in Him and He in us.

"This does not refer to an exterior dwelling of the Spirit but to a presence which touches the essence of the person and transforms him, transfiguring him and consecrating him. The indwelling of the Spirit in the soul derives from the original and primary reality of the dwelling of the Spirit in the body of Christ, which is the Church. Just as in the baptism of Christ, the Spirit 'sanctified' and 'consecrated'* Christ's body of flesh, so at Pentecost did he sanctify and consecrate Christ's mystical body, the Church.... Here is seen the action of the Holy Spirit, who exercises a continuing discernment in the need of purification, which connotes the road of the conversion of the Church."

THC - *The Holy Spirit, Lord and Giver of Life*

In God's Presence Consider ...

Do I allow the Holy Spirit to touch the essence of my being? Do I believe that I can renew my Confirmation and ask the Holy Spirit to be stirred into action where I have allowed Him to lie dormant? Am I open for the Holy Spirit's continuous discernment and transforming work of conversion?

Closing Prayer

Come, Holy Spirit and renew Your life within me that I received in my baptism and confirmation. Purify me and continue to help me discern the need of conversion and renewal within me. Stir into Fire the Love You are who dwells in me as You dwell in Christ.

*Please consult the Catechism #536–37, #1225 for a better understanding of what the Commission is addressing here.

Perceptible and Perpetual Guidance **Day 99**

The Holy Spirit has been sent in order to continually sanctify the Church and to help those who believe have access to the Father and to share in His divine life, thus perpetuating Pentecost in the Church.

"With the coming of the Spirit they (the Apostles and Mary) felt capable of fulfilling the mission entrusted to them. They felt full of strength. It is precisely this that the Holy Spirit worked in them, and this is continually at work in the Church, through their successors. For the grace of the Holy Spirit which the Apostles gave to their collaborators through the imposition of hands continues to be transmitted in Episcopal Ordination … and, through the Sacrament of Confirmation, ensure that all who are reborn of water and the Holy Spirit are strengthened by this gift. And thus, in a certain way, the grace of Pentecost is perpetuated in the Church."

St. Pope John Paul II - *Dominum et Vivicantem*

In God's Presence Consider …

Do I believe that the same Holy Spirit given at Pentecost is the same Spirit given to me at Baptism and Confirmation? Do I allow the Holy Spirit the freedom to live and move within me, manifesting His graces as He chooses or do I tie His graces up and force the Holy Spirit into dormancy from my fears and wanting to have control of my life?

Closing Prayer

Come, Holy Spirit and strengthen the graces of my Baptism and Confirmation that I may become thus renewed and may experience a new Pentecost in my life. St. Pope John Paul II, pray for me.

The "Constitution on the Church", (Lumen Gentium), coming out of Vatican II, stresses the universal call we all have to grow and be holy. The Holy Spirit's direction is paramount in our growing in holiness. His working sanctity in us is often very gentle and sweet, not forcing our response but respecting our free will.

"… the work that has to be accomplished in man is divine. It is the reproduction of Jesus, the masterpiece of God, and for such an exalted undertaking the direction of the Holy Spirit is necessary. Sanctity is impossible without this direction….

"The spirit's teaching is unction. He teaches us by pouring himself into us gently and penetratingly. He teaches us as mothers teach their children, with kisses of love, with indefinable outpouring of tenderness. We learn from him as we perceive the fragrance of a perfume, as we savor the sweetness of a fruit or enjoy the caress of a breeze that enfolds us…. United intimately to divine things through the work of the Holy Spirit, the soul tastes the fruit of love by a direct divine experience … the Holy Spirit takes our faculties and moves and guides them—so firmly that they do not stray, and at the same time so gently that our activities continue to be vital, spontaneous, and free."

SOG Archbishop Louis M. Martinez - *The Sanctifier*

In God's Presence Consider …

How have I experienced the gentleness, tenderness, and sweet caress of the Holy Spirit in my life? Am I allowing the Holy Spirit to reproduce Jesus within me? Do I seek to have holiness and becoming a saint as a priority in my life?

Closing Prayer

Come, Holy Spirit, come. Wash the stains of guilt away, bend the stubborn heart and will; melt the frozen, warm the chill, guide the steps that go astray.

Sequence of the Mass of Pentecost

To Bear Much Fruit **Day 101**

The joint mission of Jesus and the Holy Spirit is to bring Christ's faithful to share in communion with the Father. This mission is brought to completion in the Church. Note that everything the Spirit does is directed to Jesus.

"The Spirit prepares men and goes out to them with his grace in order to draw them to Christ. The Spirit manifests the risen Lord to them, recalls his word to them and opens their minds to the understanding of His Death and Resurrection. He makes present the mystery of Christ, supremely in the Eucharist, in order to reconcile them, to bring them into communion with God, that they may bear much fruit.

"Through the Church's sacraments, Christ communicates, pours out his Holy and sanctifying Spirit to the members of his Body to nourish, heal, to give them life, send them to bear witness, and associate them to his self-offering to the Father and to his intercession for the whole world."

CCC #737, 739

In God's Presence Consider …

Is the Eucharist something I do or does the Eucharist bring about within me reconciliation and communion with God? Do I allow the Holy Spirit to make Jesus present to me in the Eucharist? Do I go out to bear witness to Jesus or do I keep my Catholic faith personal and private?

Closing Prayer

Come, Holy Spirit, and give me a penetrating mind to understand the mystery of Christ made present to me in the sacraments and draw me into a deeper communion with the Father, the Son, and You.

Invoke with Confidence **Day 102**

The Holy Spirit works the restoration of man to the divine likeness that was lost through sin. This is why we can have confidence in invoking Him.

"… He helps us to overcome actual difficulties. For example, we very often find ourselves struggling against a fault which we seem unable to overcome, or trying unsuccessfully to acquire a certain virtue, or endeavoring to solve some problem; but at a certain point, without our knowing how, things change: our former doubt is resolved and we are able to accomplish with ease what at first seemed impossible. This, too, is the result of the action of the Holy Spirit in our soul; it explains why His initiatives are so precious for us, and why we should desire Him and invoke Him with so much confidence."

Fr. Gabriel of St. Mary Magdalen, O.C.D. - *Divine Intimacy*

In God's Presence Consider …

Do I remember a time in my life where I asked God for help in overcoming a difficulty and later realize that things have changed and resolved themselves? Do I ever give the Holy Spirit credit for helping me? Do I thank Him?

Closing Prayer

You are the God of impossibilities. Increase and perfect the virtues of faith, hope, and charity in me that I may invoke the Holy Spirit with confidence in overcoming the difficulties and struggles I will encounter this day.

The work the Holy Spirit did in the infant Church is the same work He desires to do in all ages for He never ceases to give life.

"Such were the fruits of the transformation of the Apostles and the disciples by the Holy Spirit.... But was the Holy Spirit sent to produce these marvelous fruits only in the infant Church? Evidently not. He continues the same work throughout the course of ages. His action in the Church is apparent in the invincible strength that He gives her; a strength which may be seen in the three centuries of persecution which she underwent, and in the victory that she won over so many heresies.

"Every Christian community, then, must conform to the example of the infant Church. What must we learn from her?

"To be one heart and one soul, and to banish all divisions amongst us. To work for the extension of the kingdom of God in the world, despite the difficulties with which we are confronted. To believe firmly and practically in the indefectibility of the Church, which is always holy, and never ceases to give birth to saints. Like the early Christians we must bear with patience and love the sufferings which God sends us. Let us with all our hearts believe in the Holy Spirit who never ceases to give life to the Church, and in the Communion of Saints."

Rev. Garrigou-Lagrange, O.P. - *The Three Ways of the Spiritual Life*

In God's Presence Consider ...

Do I pooh-pooh the work of the Holy Spirit today by believing He was only sent for the infant Church? Do I pray daily for the Holy Spirit to continue the work He has begun in the Church and in me? Do I seek His marvelous fruits in my life and for the life of the Church?

Closing Prayer

Come, Holy Spirit, with Your marvelous fruits that I may be of one heart and soul with Your Church. Banish all divisions from among us. Help us as a Church to believe in You and bear witness to Your presence and work in our midst.

Receives of Mine

Day 104

The unity of the Trinity can be seen in how the Son and Holy Spirit say and do only those things that God the Father has said and done.

"But the Holy Ghost does not speak His own things, but those of Christ, and that not from himself but from the Lord; even as the Lord also announced to us the things that He received from the Father. For, says He, 'the word which ye hear is not Mine, but the Father's who sent Me.' And says He of the Holy Ghost, 'He shall not speak of Himself, but whatsoever things He shall hear from Me.' And He says of Himself to the Father, 'I have,' says He, 'glorified Thee upon the earth; I have finished the work which, Thou gavest Me; I have manifested Thy name to men.' And of the Holy Ghost, 'He shall glorify Me, for He receives of Mine.'"

St. Ignatius of Antioch -
The Epistle of Ignatius to the Ephesians Chapter IX

In God's Presence Consider …

Are God's words a part of my life? Does my life give God glory? Do I share with others the fruits of the words God speaks to me?

Closing Prayer

Come, Holy Spirit, You who inspired the Holy Scriptures, inspire me, move me, speak to me anew the words You have received from the Father and the Son. Help me to glorify You O Blessed Trinity with my life. St. Ignatius of Antioch, pray for me.

Vatican II exhorts the faithful to remember that we are to promote union among Christians. The best way to do this is to try to live holier lives according to the Gospel.

"He gave his followers a new commandment to love one another, and promised the Spirit, their Advocate, who, as Lord and life-giver, should remain with them forever....After being lifted up on the cross and glorified, the Lord Jesus poured forth the Spirit whom he had promised, and through whom he has called and gathered together the people of the New Covenant, which is the Church, into a unity of faith, hope and charity...It is the Holy Spirit dwelling in those who believe and pervading and ruling over the entire Church, who brings about that wonderful communion of the faithful and joins them together so intimately in Christ that he is the principle of the Church's unity.

"There can be no ecumenism worthy of the name without interior conversion. For it is from newness of attitudes of mind, from self-denial and unstinted love, that desires of unity take their rise and develop in a mature way. We should therefore pray to the Holy Spirit for the grace to be genuinely self-denying, humble, gently in the service of others and to have an attitude of brotherly generosity toward them."

Vatican II - *Unitatis Redintegratio,* #2, 7a

In God's Presence Consider ...

The Catechism tells us in #1434 that the Holy Spirit brings sin to light and moves the human heart to conversion and repentance. Do I spend time each day examining my life and how I sin in my lack of self-denial, my actions or words against unity, and my prejudices and sins of omission in the service of others and Christian unity?

Closing Prayer

O Holy Spirit, You who are the Spirit of Unity, grant me the grace to be genuinely self-denying, humble, gentle in the service of others, and to have an attitude of brotherly generosity toward others.

Life in the Holy Spirit fulfills the vocation of man. It is the Holy Spirit who gives us the new life that Jesus won for us on the Cross and through His grace the Holy Spirit restores what sin had damaged in us.

"… Christians are called to lead henceforth a life worthy of the gospel of Christ (Phil. 1:27). They are made capable of doing so by the grace of Christ and the gifts of his Spirit, which they receive through the sacraments and through prayer.

"Christians have become the temple of the Holy Spirit. This Spirit of the Son teaches them to pray to the Father and, having become their life, prompts them to act so as to bear the fruit of the Spirit by charity in action. Healing the wounds of sin, the Holy Spirit renews us interiorly through a spiritual transformation. He enlightens and strengthens us to live as children of light through all that is good and right and true (Eph. 5:8–9)."

CCC #1692, 1695

In God's Presence Consider …

Am I living a life worthy of the gospel of Jesus? Am I using the gifts of the Holy Spirit given to me in the sacraments and prayer? Do I take my call to be a saint seriously? Is the Holy Spirit my life?

Closing Prayer

Come, Holy Spirit, into my heart, that You will enlighten and strengthen me to live as a child of the light and that my life will reflect Your presence living in me.

With the committing of original sin, man's rank and dignity was deeply wounded and marred. Because of concupiscence, our condition was unfixable by mere human efforts. God, infinite in mercy, sends His Son and His Spirit to restore mankind to the dignity and rank He intended.

"No one can express the greatness of this work of divine grace in the souls of men. Wherefore, both in Holy Scripture and in the writings of the Fathers, men are styled regenerated, new creatures, partakers of the Divine Nature, children of God, god-like, and similar epithets. Now these great blessings are justly attributed of sons. Whereby we cry 'Abba, Father' (Gal. 4:6). He fills our hearts with the sweetness of paternal love. 'The Spirit Himself giveth testimony to our spirit that we are the sons of God' (Rom. 8:15–16)."

Pope Leo XIII - *Divinum Illud Munus*

In God's Presence Consider …

What is the great work of the Holy Spirit Pope Leo is writing about? How has the Holy Spirit given testimony to me about this great gift? Do I reflect on the importance of my baptism and my baptismal promises?

Closing Prayer

Come, Holy Spirit; help me to be faithful to my baptismal promises and Your working in my life. Restore the life I have forfeited through my decisions to sin and help me to live as a son or daughter of God.

Not Without Cost **Day 108**

In the Gospel of John 17, Christ's departure through His death on the Cross is an indispensable condition for the sending and coming of the Holy Spirit.

"The Holy Spirit comes at the price of Christ's departure. While this departure caused the Apostles to be sorrowful, and this sorrow was to reach its culmination in the Passion and Death on Good Friday.... For Christ will add to this redemptive departure the glory of his Resurrection and Ascension to the Father. Thus the sorrow with its underlying joy is, for the Apostles in the context of their Master's departure, an advantageous departure, for thanks to it another Counselor will come (Jn. 16:7). At the price of the Cross which brings about the Redemption, in the power of the whole Paschal Mystery of Jesus Christ, the Holy Spirit comes in order to remain from the day of Pentecost onwards with the Apostles, to remain with the Church and in the Church, and through her in the world."

St. Pope John Paul II - *Dominum et Vivicantem*

In God's Presence Consider ...

Jesus' Paschal Mystery brings about sorrow and joy, death and redemption. Do I embrace sorrow and suffering as a means of sharing in the work of the Paschal Mystery? Do I see the sending of the Holy Spirit as continually present and manifested in the Church today? In my life?

Closing Prayer

Come, Holy Spirit, into my heart that I may grow in my understanding in living the mystery of my salvation and in the power of Redemption; that I may be renewed in the Love the Father and Son have for me in You.

Communion among Ourselves **Day 109**

The principle work of the Spirit, who is the Spirit of communion, consists in rendering the Church ever more a sign of God's Trinitarian love. St. Pope John Paul II spoke in his encyclical letter "Ut Unum Sint" that "to believe in Christ means to desire unity; and to desire unity means to desire the Church; to desire the Church means to desire the communion of grace which corresponds to the Father's plan for all eternity."

"Because the Spirit is communion with the Father and with the Son, they have wished for us to have communion among ourselves and with them in the Holy Spirit, who is God and the gift of God.... It is in him that the people of God are joined in unity.... The Church is the very work of the Holy Spirit and outside of him there is no remission of sins."

St. Augustine - *Sermons, LXXI*

In God's Presence Consider ...

God desires unity. Do I live my life in unity with the Church and in communion with her members, or am I a source of disunity, skepticism, and discord through my grumbling and lack of obedience to her and those she has placed over me in authority?

Closing Prayer

Father, send forth Your Spirit that we may be one as You are one. Unite Your Church and bring us into Your communion of love. St. Augustine, pray for me.

The Second Vatican Council (1962–65), was called by St. Pope John XXIII, who sought to bring renewal to the Church and greater dialogue with the world. This was a work he believed was the work of the Holy Spirit. St. Pope Paul VI stated in his general audience June 6, 1973, "The Christology and particularly the ecclesiology of the Council must be succeeded by a new study of and devotion to the Holy Spirit, precisely as the indispensable complement to the teaching of the Council."

"In our own age, then, we are called anew by the ever ancient and ever new faith of the Church, to draw near to the Holy Spirit as the giver of life.... The Holy Spirit is the one who points out the ways leading to the union of Christians, indeed as the supreme source of this unity, which comes from God himself.

"... the Holy Spirit, who proceeds from the Father and the Son; with the Father and the Son he is adored and glorified: a divine Person, he is at the center of the Christian faith and is the source and dynamic power of the Church's renewal."

St. Pope John Paul II - *Dominum et Vivicantem*

In God's Presence Consider ...

Do I believe the Holy Spirit to be the source and dynamic power of renewal and unity in the Church? In my life? What kind of relationship do I have with the Holy Spirit?

Closing Prayer

Come, Holy Spirit, Source of Unity, come. You who proceed from the Father and the Son and with the Father and Son are adored and glorified. Come and move me to a deeper penetration into the mystery of the Trinity and to fellowship with You. St. Pope John Paul II, pray for me.

St. Pope John Paul II speaks of the holiness of Jesus constituting the principle and lasting source of holiness in human and world history.

"The union of divinity and humanity in the one Person of the Word-Son, that is the 'hypostatic union' (hypostasis: 'person') is the Holy Spirit's greatest accomplishment in the history of creation and in salvation history. Even though the entire Trinity is its cause, still it is attributed by the Gospel and by the Fathers to the Holy Spirit, because it is the highest work wrought by divine Love … in order to communicate to humanity the fullness of holiness in Christ: all these effects are attributed to the Holy Spirit (St. Thomas, Summa Theol., III, q. 32, a.1).

"The Pope goes on to show how this type of holiness is a result of the unique consecration effected in Christ by the Spirit.... We can say, therefore, that in the Incarnation the Holy Spirit lays the foundations for a new anthropology which sheds light on the greatness of human nature as reflected in Christ. In him, in fact, human nature reaches its highest point of union with God.... It was not possible for man to rise up higher than this high point, nor is it possible for human thought to conceive of a closer union with the divinity."

Fr. O'Carroll, CSSp, - *John Paul II*

In God's Presence Consider …

Jesus communicates the fullness of holiness that the Spirit brings about, to show us the Holy Spirit's highest work of divine love. Do I meditate on the mystery of the Incarnation? Do I allow the Holy Spirit to take me places that are impossible for me to reach on my own in my spiritual walk? Have I consecrated my life to Jesus? To the Holy Spirit?

Closing Prayer

May the wondrous flame that appeared above the disciples, powerfully cleanse your hearts from every evil and pervade them with its purifying light.

Solemn Blessing of Vigil Mass for Pentecost

Superhuman Loveliness **Day 112**

Humanity was created in the image and likeness of God. Because of sin, our dignity was disfigured, wounded, corrupted, and deprived of the glory of God. It is through Jesus and the work of the Holy Spirit that man is restored to the Father's "likeness." St. Cyril tells us that we are so united with the Holy Spirit that we are composed of body, soul, and the Holy Spirit.

"The Holy Spirit impresses on us the divine image and gives us superhuman loveliness. We are temples of the Holy Spirit, who truly lives in us. On this account we are called gods. Because of our union with the Holy Spirit, we share the divine, incomprehensible nature of God. We have not merely the enlightenment of the Holy Spirit, but He Himself dwells within us. Man is composed of body and soul and the Holy Spirit."

St. Cyril of Alexandria

In God's Presence Consider …

Even though man is disfigured by sin, man remains in the image of God. Have I ever thought of the glory of my dignity being the Holy Spirit? What kind of attention do I need to give to being the temple of the Holy Spirit that I am? Have I ever thought of being a composite of body, soul, and the Holy Spirit?

Closing Prayer

St. Cyril, pray with me, that I may be a temple worthy of the Holy Spirit's indwelling. Through your prayers, help me to be open to bear the divine image that He impresses upon me.

No Jealousy or Quarrelsomeness **Day 113**

The work of unity with the Body of Christ and the Pope is a testimony to the presence and work of the Holy Spirit.

"The Apostles of the Son of God had once disputed concerning the primacy; but now that the Holy Spirit has made them of one heart and one soul they are no longer jealous or quarrelsome. It seems to them that through Peter they all speak, that with him they all reside, and if his shadow heals the sick the whole Church has its part in this gift and praises our Lord for it. In the same way we ought to regard one another as members of the same mystical body, of which Christ is the head, and, far from allowing ourselves to give way to jealousy or envy, we ought to rejoice with a holy joy in the good qualities of our neighbor; for we profit by them as the hand derives advantage from what the eye sees, or the ear hears."

Rev. Garrigou-Lagrange, O.P. - *The Three Ways of the Spiritual Life*

In God's Presence Consider …

Do I tend to be jealous or quarrelsome with other members of the Church? Do I speak negatively about the Pope? Do I find joy in the qualities and good works of the members of the Body of Christ or do I tend to find faults and pass judgments on others?

Closing Prayer

Bind us together Holy Spirit, that as one body we may bear witness to the love of Jesus and find great joy in the good of our neighbor.

St. Paul speaks of the new covenant God has made with man that is written on the human heart through the Holy Spirit who gives life. St. Faustina's relationship with Jesus shows how intimate this new life in the Spirit can be.

"Why are You sad today, Jesus? Tell me, who is the cause of Your sadness? And Jesus answered me, 'Chosen souls who do not have My spirit, who live according to the letter (cf. 2 Cor. 3:6) and have placed the letter above My spirit, above the spirit of love....'

"I knew, more directly, then ever before, the Three Divine Persons.... But their being, their equality, and their majesty are one. My soul is in communion with these Three.... Whoever is united to One of the Three Persons is thereby united to the Whole Blessed Trinity, for this Oneness is indivisible."

St. Maria Faustina Kowalska - *Diary: Divine Mercy in My Soul*

In God's Presence Consider ...

Do I have the Holy Spirit in me and am I living a life with and in Him? Do I place the letter of the law above the Holy Spirit? Is my spiritual life reflective of all Three Persons or toward the Father and Son, leaving out the Holy Spirit?

Closing Prayer

O Jesus, keep me in holy fear, so that I may not waste graces. Help me to be faithful to the inspirations of the Holy Spirit. Grant that my heart may burst for love of You, rather than I should neglect even one act of love for You.

Prayer of St. Faustina - *Diary #1557*

Through the death and resurrection of Jesus and the cleansing waters of Baptism, we become adopted sons and daughters of the Father. St. Basil describes the inheritance that becomes ours through this adoption done by the Holy Spirit.

"The Holy Spirit makes us spiritual. There is the readmission to Paradise, the return to the status of Children, the courage to call God, Father. We become participators in the grace of Christ, are called children of the light, and share eternal glory."

St. Basil the Great - *Treatise on the Holy Spirit* #36

In God's Presence Consider …

Do I spend time periodically reflecting on the great gift of my Baptism and what it means to be an adopted child of God? Do I live as a child of the light? Do I long for the time to share in eternal glory?

Closing Prayer

Make me spiritual Holy Spirit. Help me to grow in my appreciation of being a child of God. Give me the courage to approach God and to call Him, Father. St. Basil the Great, pray for me.

The Highest Expression of Love **Day 116**

Love unites thus the union of the Holy Spirit with creatures is the highest expression of love.

"Unification is love, creative love. The activity of God outside himself does not proceed otherwise.... The creature totally filled with this love, with divinity, is the Immaculata, without the slightest stain of sin, the one who never deviated from God's will in anything. She is joined in an ineffable manner with the Holy Spirit, because she is his Bride.

"Of what kind is that union? It is above all inner union; it is the union of her being with the being of the Holy Spirit. The Holy Spirit dwells in her, lives in her, and that from the first moment of her existence, always and eternally. What does this life of the Holy Spirit in her consist of? He himself is love in her, the love of the Father and of the Son, the love with which God loves himself, the love of the whole Most Holy Trinity, fruitful love, conception. In created semblances the union of love is the closest union. The Scriptures assert that they will be two in one flesh (Gen. 2:24), and Jesus emphasizes: 'Therefore now they are not two, but one flesh.' (Mk. 10:8) In a way incomparably more rigorous, more interior, more essential, the Holy Spirit lives in the soul of the Immaculata, in her being and makes her fruitful and that from the first moment of her existence for her whole life, that is forever.... Thus, this is the highest expression of love."

St. Maximilian Kolbe - *The Writings of St. Kolbe, Volume II*

In God's Presence Consider ...

Do I look at myself as being the bride of the Holy Spirit? How might this union make me more fruitful and help Christ to be born anew within me? Could my relationship with the Blessed Mother help me to live with the Uncreated Love in a more tangible way? And how does it?

Closing Prayer

Come O Holy Spirit, the Uncreated Love of the Most Blessed Trinity, come and dwell within me; live in me, that from this moment on, always and eternally, You will fill me with Your Love, with the Divine Presence, and with our Blessed Mother Mary, Your Spouse, to never deviate from God's will in anything. St. Maximilian Kolbe, pray for me.

Conjoined and Ordered to the Son **Day 117**

What we as Catholics believe about Mary is based on what we believe about Christ. What we believe about Mary tells us more about what God has done in and for Mary. What we believe about Mary illumines and is to lead us to faith in her Son.

"… the Son of God assumed a human nature in order to accomplish our salvation in it.

"The mission of the Holy Spirit is always conjoined and ordered to that of the Son. The Holy Spirit, 'the Lord, the giver of Life,' is sent to sanctify the womb of the Virgin Mary and divinely fecundate it, causing her to conceive the eternal Son of the Father in a humanity drawn from her own.

"The Father's only Son, conceived as man in the womb of the Virgin Mary, is 'Christ,' that is to say, anointed by the Holy Spirit, from the beginning of his human existence…."

Cf. CCC #461 485, 486, 490, 493

Lumen Gentium #56 says that in order for Mary to become the mother of our Savior, she was enriched by God with special graces, gifts appropriate to such a role. In order for Mary to be able to give the free assent of her faith and say "Yes," it was necessary she would be free of every personal sin from the moment of her conception and through her whole life.

In God's Presence Consider …

Do I believe that the Spirit is sent to sanctify and make my life fruitful? Do I believe that God enriches me with His Holy Spirit who gives me the gifts appropriate to my vocation and role? Do I allow the Spirit to fashion and form me as a new creature?

Closing Prayer

Blessed Mother Mary, pray for me that I will give my free assent to the workings of your "Beloved Spouse" who seeks to fashion and form me into a new creature, in the image of your Son.

Holy Spirit: Spouse of the Virgin Mary

The fruit of Mary's pondering the things of God led to her deep longing for the coming of the Messiah; a longing expressing itself in a docility and entrusting of her heart to God's promises. Guided by the promptings of the Spirit, her Yes makes her Theotokos, God bearer, thus becoming a model for our trusting in God.

"Mary, who conceived the incarnate Word by the power of the Holy Spirit and then in the whole of her life allowed herself to be guided by his interior activity, will be contemplated and imitated … as the woman who was docile to the voice of the Spirit, a woman of silence and attentiveness, a woman of hope who, like Abraham, accepted God's will 'hoping against hope' (Rom. 4:18). Mary gave full expression to the longing of the poor of Yahweh and is a radiant model for those who entrust themselves with all their hearts to the promises of God."

St. Pope John Paul II - *Apostolic Letter Tertio Millennio Adveniente*

In God's Presence Consider …

Do I allow the Holy Spirit to guide me by His interior activity as Mary did? Am I collaborating with the Holy Spirit allowing Him to overshadow me and help me to become another Theotokos (God-bearer)?

Closing Prayer

I pray, I pray, O Holy Virgin, that I should have Jesus by that same Spirit by which you engendered Jesus. May my soul receive Jesus, by the work of that Spirit through whom your flesh conceived Jesus himself…. May I love Jesus in that same Spirit in whom you worship him as Lord and contemplate him as Son.

The prayer of St. Ildephonsus of Toledo

"So that the provisions of the Gospel and the activity of the Holy Spirit develop in us, Christ must be born in us." St. Gregory of Nyssa

"Mary has an indispensable place in the economy of salvation … without the extraordinary action of the Spirit she might have remained an anonymous woman of Palestine. Furthermore, her free and loving collaboration with the Spirit makes her a model of every relationship with the sanctifying Holy Spirit.

"For Jesus to be born in every soul and continue the mystery of Theotokos (God-bearer), the Creator must put himself into the very hearts of his creatures and the divine Spirit must overshadow them … Christ must be born in us."

THC - *The Holy Spirit, the Lord and Giver of Life*

In God's Presence Consider …

Do I use Mary as the model of my loving collaboration with the Holy Spirit? Do I ponder and see myself in the mystery of being another Theotokos? Is Jesus born anew in me?

Closing Prayer

Come, Holy Spirit, come by means of the powerful intercession of the Immaculate Heart of Mary your well beloved spouse.

Fatima Prayer

Following the example of Mary's maternity, the Church, as mother, loves, cares for, nourishes, instructs, protects, and engenders her members to God and God to her members. The extent of our personal and collective love for the Church is the extent of the Holy Spirit dwelling within us.

"The wonder of the maternity of Mary is reflected in the Church, who, by the unique grace of the Holy Spirit, engenders God in humanity and humanity in God. The universality of the maternal mediation of Mary is also realized and completed through the Church. The maternity of the Church adds charm and happiness to all the joys of the faith.... The rule of faith becomes living and familiar, a loved and harmonious voice.

"Our love for the Church is the sign that we are preserving within us the divine gift of charity, the living and personal pledge of Infinite Love for us, who is the Holy Spirit. Loving the Church, we are loving unity and our love, multiplying itself by all the love that is in the Church, grows to infinity, loses itself in the unity of love, and prepares its consummation. Saint Augustine says, 'We, therefore, receive the Holy Spirit if we love the Church, if we are joined together by charity, if we make the Catholic name and faith our joy. Believe it, brethren, to the extent that one loves the Church, to that extent he has the Holy Spirit within him.'"

Fr. Humbert Clerissac, O.P. - *The Mystery of the Church*

In God's Presence Consider ...

How have I experienced the maternity of the Church? Do I ever think of the connection between my love of the Church and the Holy Spirit within me as the divine gift of Charity given through the Holy Spirit? We receive the Holy Spirit if we love the Church. How much do I love and care for the Church?

Closing Prayer

O God, who bestow heavenly gifts upon your Church, safeguard, we pray, the grace you have given, that the gift of the Holy Spirit poured out upon her may retain all its force and that this spiritual food may gain her abundance of eternal redemption.

Prayer after Communion for the Mass of Pentecost

Docile Resting Place **Day 121**

Mary's transformation by the Spirit was so profound from the beginning as to touch her very essence. This is the real reason why Mary was all holy from the first moment of her existence.

"The Father predestined her but the sanctifying virtue of the Spirit visited her, purified her, made her holy and, so to say, immaculate."

St. John Damascene - *Homily on the Dormition I, 3*

"Mary from the beginning was united with the Spirit, author of life; everything that she experienced she shared with the Spirit so that her participation in the Spirit became a participation in being.

Theophanes of Nicea, - *Discourse on the Mother of God, 30*

In God's Presence Consider …

Do I believe that the Holy Spirit's transformation of Mary touched her very essence making her immaculate? Do I share my whole life with the Holy Spirit allowing Him to participate in my being?

Closing Prayer

Mary, Mother of God, pray that my union with your Beloved Spouse will make me a docile resting place for Him. St. John Damascene, pray for me.

Name Changer **Day 122**

The eternal Immaculate Conception (the Holy Spirit) can produce an immaculate manner of divine life in our soul which sets it apart for God and makes it a dwelling place for Love.

"This eternal Immaculate Conception, which is the Holy Spirit, produces in an immaculate manner divine life itself in the womb and in the depths of Mary's soul, making her … the human Immaculate Conception. And the virginal womb of Mary's body is kept sacred for him; there he conceives in time—because everything that is material occurs in time—the human life of the Man-God.

"… If among human beings the wife takes the name of her husband because she belongs to him, is one with him, becomes equal to him, and, is with him the source of new life, with how much greater reason should the name of the Holy Spirit, who is the divine Immaculate Conception be used as the name of her in whom he lives as uncreated Love, the principle of life in the whole supernatural order of grace?"

St. Maximillian Kolbe - *The Immaculate Conception and the Holy Spirit*

In God's Presence Consider …

Do I allow the Holy Spirit to keep my heart and soul a sacred place for God to dwell? Am I a source of new life because of my union with the Holy Spirit?

Closing Prayer

Come, Holy Spirit, God's Divine Life and spouse of the ever Virgin Mary, make me in an immaculate manner a sacred place, a dwelling place for God, where He can love me with a spousal love. St. Maximillian Kolbe, pray for me.

It is not that Mary was so gifted and worthy that God could work miraculously through her, but because of her profound humility and docility to the workings of grace, that she became the resting place of the Spirit, the Mother of God, the Mother of the Church, and our spiritual mother.

"She (Mary, Mother of God) had personal experience (humility) through the Holy Spirit who illuminated and instructed her … she learned from the Holy Spirit the great knowledge that God did not want to manifest his power in any way other than elevating that which is low and lowering that which is high."

Martin Luther - *Werke, Kritische Gesamtausgabe 7, 546*

"… let all Christian peoples add their prayers also, invoking the powerful and ever-acceptable intercession of the Blessed Virgin. You know well the intimate and wonderful relations existing between her and the Holy Ghost, so that she is justly called His Spouse.… May she continue to strengthen our prayers with her suffrages that, in the midst of all the stress and trouble of the nations, those divine prodigies may be happily revived by the Holy Ghost."

Pope Leo XIII - *Divinum Illud Munus*

In God's Presence Consider …

What role does humility play in my life? Am I open and docile to the Holy Spirit's desire to illumine and instruct me? Do I invoke the powerful intercession of the Blessed Mother when I seek to know more about who the Holy Spirit is and the role He plays in my life?

Closing Prayer

Holy Virgin Mary, there is no one similar to you born in the world among women, daughter and maidservant of the All High King, the heavenly Father, mother of the holiest Lord Jesus Christ, bride of the Holy Spirit; pray for us with St. Michael the Archangel and with all the powers of heaven, and with all the saints, to your most holy beloved Son, our Lord.

St. Francis of Assisi - Officium Passionis

The Second Vatican Council referred to Mary's union with the Holy Spirit as a "sanctuary" of the Holy Spirit. Other Saints, have referred to Mary as the "spouse" of the Holy Spirit. It is her total self-gift to God that brings about her being the Mother of God.

"The Holy Spirit, who comes down upon Mary during the Annunciation, is the one who, in the Trinity's relationship, expresses in his Person the marital love of God, the 'eternal' love … for the Son of God who was conceived in the womb of the Virgin 'not by natural generation, nor by human choice, nor by man's decision, but of God' (Jn. 1:13) But it especially expresses the supreme union in love, brought about between God and a human being by the power of the Holy Spirit…. In the divine marriage with humanity; Mary answers the angel's announcement with the love of a spouse who is able to respond and to adjust to the divine choice in a perfect way. For this reason, especially since St. Francis of Assisi's time, the Church calls her the spouse of the Holy Spirit. Only this perfect marital love, deeply rooted in her total self-gift to God, could have brought it about that Mary became the 'Mother of God' in a conscious and worthy fashion through the mystery of the Incarnation.

"In Mary's act and gesture, she stands out in humanity's spiritual history as the new Spouse, the new Eve, the Mother of the living, the type and model of the New Covenant as a nuptial union of the Holy Spirit…."

St. Pope John Paul II - *A Dictionary of His Life and Teachings*

In God's Presence Consider …

Do I look upon the Holy Spirit as expressing the marital love of God? Have I ever thought about asking the Holy Spirit's spouse, Mary, to help me grow in my love for Him? Does my spiritual life reflect a nuptial union with the Holy Spirit?

Closing Prayer

Dear Blessed Mother, Daughter of the Father, Spouse of the Holy Spirit, Mother of the Son, please act on my behalf to introduce me anew to your beloved Spouse, the Holy Spirit. Thus united, may I grow in my nuptial union with Him, in my total self-gift to God. St. Pope John Paul II, pray for me.

A Celestial Delight **Day 125**

Everything that Mary became with her free consent and collaboration, she owes to the Father's choice and invitation, her son, Jesus, and the action of the Holy Spirit. Because of her participation and cooperation with the Holy Spirit she bears the fruits of the Spirit dwelling in her.

"To live spiritually is to have our affections and our actions in order. St. Augustine defined virtue by saying that it is order in love. Order in love produces order in our actions, in our thoughts, and in our faculties.... Whenever part of our soul is perfected, it receives an effusion of heavenly consolations. Therefore, if we desire to obtain the fruits of the Spirit, we need to work, to try to purify our souls little by little, to advance little by little on the road to perfection.... The plants that produce the fruits of the Holy Spirit are the virtues and especially the gifts of the Holy Spirit.... Accordingly, there are three things that we must do to possess those celestial delights. We must pray; we must purify our soul; eliminating all that hinders us from perceiving the sweetness and mildness of the heavenly fruits; then, by also working ceaselessly and struggling against our interior and exterior enemies, we can be assured that the precious fruits will fill our souls with sweetness."

SOG Archbishop Louis M. Martinez - *The Sanctifier*

In God's Presence Consider ...

Do I share with the Holy Spirit everything that I experience? Do I define my identity based on what I do or who I am? What fruits grows in the garden of my heart? What do I do to possess the celestial delights?

Closing Prayer

Come, Holy Spirit; Come by means of the powerful intercession of the Immaculate Heart of Mary, Your well-beloved spouse.

A Fatima Prayer

St. Maximilian Kolbe, one of our greatest Marianist, spent years reflecting on the Immaculate Conception and asking: "Who are you Immaculate Conception?" Two hours before his arrest by the Gestapo, he penned the answer to his reflections.

"At the apparitions in Lourdes, Mary didn't say to St. Bernadette 'I was immaculately conceived' but rather 'I am the Immaculate Conception.' This seems to be a problem … through a special grace from God, she was conceived in the womb of her mother, St. Anne, without any stain of original sin by the foreseen merits of her Son. So why does she speak so strangely? Why does she make the grace she received at her conception her very name? Doesn't this almost seem as if she were making herself divine? Clearly, Mary is not God. Kolbe wrestled with this apparent 'divinity problem' for decades, and it led to the following solution.

"The Immaculate Conception is divine. But the one I'm talking about isn't Mary. It's the Holy Spirit. Kolbe believed there are two Immaculate Conceptions. Before the created Immaculate Conception (Mary), there is the uncreated Immaculate Conception, the One (Holy Spirit) who for all eternity springs from God the Father and God the Son as an uncreated conception. So, the Father begets: the Son is begotten; the Spirit is the conception that springs from their love.

"Now, the Holy Spirit is a conception in the sense of being the Life and Love that springs from the love of the Father and the Son. The Holy Spirit is an immaculate conception because, being God, he is obviously without sin. And finally, the Holy Spirit is an eternal uncreated conception because, again, he is God."

Fr. Michael Gaitley, MIC - *33 Days to Morning Glory*

In God's Presence Consider …

Do I ponder my relationship with God in the light of a conception of life and love?

Closing Prayer

Come, Holy Spirit, Uncreated Conception of Love and Life; beget in me the Love and Life of the Father and the Son.

The Holy Spirit and the Blessed Virgin Mary are indispensable in the work of sanctifying our souls, transforming them into the image of Jesus. The cooperation of these two artisans is necessary for personal sanctification.

"The first sanctifier by essence because he (the Holy Spirit) is God, who is infinite sanctity, because he is the personal Love … the sanctity of God … it belongs to him to communicate to souls the mystery of that sanctity. The Virgin Mary, for her part, is the cooperator, the indispensable instrument in and by God's design. From Mary's maternal relation to the human body of Christ is derived her relation to his Mystical Body….

"The Holy Spirit and Mary, are the indispensable artificers of Jesus, the indispensable sanctifiers of souls…. The cooperation of these two artisans of Jesus is so necessary that without it souls are not sanctified…. For the Holy Spirit pours charity into our hearts, makes a habitation of our souls and directs our spiritual lives my means of his gifts. The Virgin Mary has the efficacious influence of Mediatrix in the most profound and delicate operations of grace in our souls. Finally, the action of the Holy Spirit and the cooperation of the most holy Virgin Mary are constant; without them, not one single character of Jesus would be traced on our souls, no virtue grow, no gift be developed, no grace increase, no bond of union with God be strengthened in the rich flowering of the spiritual life."

SOG Archbishop Louis M. Martinez - *The Sanctifier*

In God's Presence Consider …

Do I see one of the roles of the Holy Spirit to communicate to my soul the mystery of God's love and sanctity? Do I ever ponder that the Blessed Virgin Mary and the Holy Spirit are crucial to my sanctity and growing in my relationship with God?

Closing Prayer

Grant, we pray, O Lord, that, as promised by your Son, the Holy Spirit may reveal to us more abundantly the hidden mystery of this sacrifice and graciously lead us into all truth.

Prayer over the Offerings for the Mass of Pentecost

Mary's union with the Holy Spirit is deeper than what we understand by a spousal relationship. A union to which we are all invited to participate in.

"What type of union is this (between the Holy Spirit and Mary)? It is above all an interior union, a union of her essence with the essence of the Holy Spirit. The Holy Spirit dwells in her. This was true from the first instant of her existence. It was always true; it will always be true.

"In what does this life of the Spirit in Mary consist? He himself is uncreated Love in her; the Love of the Father and of the Son, the Love by which God loves himself, the very love of the Most Holy Trinity. He is a fruitful Love, a 'Conception.' Among creatures made in God's image, the union brought about by married love is the most intimate of all (see Mt. 19:6). In a much more precise, more interior, more essential manner, the Holy Spirit lives in the soul of the Immaculata, in the very depths of her very being. He makes her fruitful, from the very first instant of her existence, all during her life, and for all eternity."

St. Maximilian Kolbe - *The Immaculate Conception and the Holy Spirit*

In God's Presence Consider …

Have I ever thought of uniting the essence of my being, with the essence of God? Do I fear the intimate union of the Holy Spirit dwelling in me? What is my relationship with Mary? How could Mary help me grow in my spiritual fruitfulness?

Closing Prayer

St. Kolbe intercede for me to Our Lady and the Holy Spirit, the Uncreated Love, that He may live in me; that I may be united with God; and may be fruitful like His Spouse our Blessed Mother. Through your prayers, remove me from all my fears and hesitancies so that I will allow Mary to love me into an intimate union with God as she has.

Forgotten Yet Necessary **Day 129**

The Holy Spirit is necessary to bring about Christian perfection and reproducing Jesus in our souls. This transformation of souls into the image of Jesus, this reproducing Jesus in our souls, is a work that both the Holy Spirit and the Virgin Mary can only bring about.

"... because he is more forgotten—the Holy Spirit must be given his proper place, the place that rightfully belongs to him in Christian life and Christian perfection. Devotion to the Holy Spirit must become ... something not superficial and intermittent, but constant and profound, filling the depths of souls and impregnating lives with sweet unction of infinite love.

"Christian life is the reproduction of Jesus in souls; and perfection, the most faithful and perfect reproduction, consists in the transformation of souls into Jesus ... this mystical reproduction is brought about in souls ... with the conciseness and precision of an article of faith: 'who was conceived by the Holy Spirit ... of the Virgin Mary.' That is the way Jesus is always conceived.... Two artisans must concur in the work that is at once God's masterpiece and humanity's supreme product: the Holy Spirit and the most holy Virgin Mary. Two sanctifiers are necessary to souls, the Holy Spirit and the Virgin Mary, for they are the only ones who can reproduce Christ."

SOG Archbishop Louis M. Martinez - *The Sanctifier*

In God's Presence Consider ...

Do I ever reflect on how my Christian Life is to be about the reproducing and transforming of my soul into the image of Jesus? Are the two sanctifiers: the Holy Spirit and the Virgin Mary an integral part of my spiritual life? How can I work with them in this process of reproducing Christ within me?

Closing Prayer

Almighty and ever-living God, your Spirit made us your children, confident to call you Father. Increase your Spirit of love within us and bring us to our promised inheritance.

Liturgy of the Hours - Easter Monday Week 2

Man's fullness or emptiness is proportionate on their relationship with the Holy Spirit. The Russian, St. Seraphim, speaks of the aim of the Christian life as a relationship with a person, not our Christian practices and devotions.

"Know thou, that every man is either empty or full. For if he has not the Holy Spirit, he has no knowledge of the Creator; he has not received Jesus Christ the Life; he knows not the Father who is in heaven; if he does not live after the dictates of reason, after the heavenly law, he is not a sober-minded person, nor does he act uprightly: such a one is empty. If, on the other hand, he receives God, who says, 'I dwell with them, and walk with them, and I will be their God," such a one is not empty but full."

St. Irenaeus - *Ante-Nicene Fathers Vol. 1*

"Prayer, fastings, vigils, and all other Christian practices.... do not constitute the aim of our Christian life: they are by the indispensable means of attaining that aim. For the true aim of Christian life is the acquisition of the Holy Spirit of God."

St. Seraphim of Sarov - *The Holy Spirit, Lord and Giver of Life*

In God's Presence Consider ...

Is my faith reasonable and inspired by the Holy Spirit? Am I empty or full as St. Irenaeus defines? How true am I to the aim of Christian life? Have my spiritual practices become a means to my end or the end?

Closing Prayer

Come, Holy Spirit, and fill me with Your presence that I may know the Father and the Son, and together with You live an upright, fruitful and full life as the Father has intended. Sts. Irenaeus and Seraphim of Saroy, pray for me.

Holy Spirit as Master of Interior Life

Vatican II, in Gaudium et Spes, (The Church in the Modern World) stresses the respect for the human person and that everyone should look upon their neighbor as another self, bearing in mind above all their life and the means necessary for living it in a dignified way.

"Conformed to the image of the Son who is the firstborn of many brothers, the Christian man 'receives the first fruits of the Spirit' (Rom. 8:23) by which he is able to fulfill the new law of love. By this Spirit, who is the 'pledge of our inheritance' (Eph. 1:14), the whole man is inwardly renewed, right up to the 'redemption of the body' (Rom. 8:23). 'If the Spirit of him who raised Jesus from the dead dwells in you, he who raised Christ Jesus from the dead will give life to your mortal bodies also through his Spirit who dwells in you' (Rom. 8:11). The Christian is certainly bound both by need and by duty to struggle with evil through many afflictions and to suffer death; but, as one who has been made a partner in the paschal mystery, and as one who has been configured to the death of Christ, he will go forward, strengthened by hope, to the resurrection.

"It is the Father's will that we should recognize Christ our brother in the persons of all men and love them with an effective love, in word and in deed, thus bearing witness to the truth; and it is his will that we should share with others the mystery of his heavenly love. In this way men all over the world will awaken to a lively hope (the gift of the Holy Spirit) that they will one day be admitted to the haven of surpassing peace and happiness in their homeland radiant with the glory of the Lord."

Vatican II - *Gaudium et Spes* #22d, 93

In God's Presence Consider ...

It is only by the work of the Holy Spirit in us that we can fulfill the new law of love. Do I see myself as a partner in the Paschal Mystery and a dwelling place for the Holy Spirit?

Closing Prayer

Father, conform me to the image of Your Son, that I may recognize Him and through Your Spirit dwelling in me, will love all others with an effective love and lively hope.

Reproducing the Heavenly Image **Day 132**

St. Ambrose speaks of the Holy Spirit as being the One responsible for our participation in the divine nature by making us into the image and likeness of God.

"The Holy Spirit reproduces in us the outline of the heavenly image. Who dares to say that the Spirit is separated from God the Father and from Christ? Through him we merit being in the image and likeness of God, for it is through him that there takes place what the apostle Peter calls our participation in the divine nature (2 Pet. 1:4)."

St. Ambrose - *On the Holy Spirit, I*

In God's Presence Consider …

I am made into the outline of the heavenly image of God by the power of the Holy Spirit. Do I see myself with such a sacred dignity? Does my life reflect this sacred dignity? Do I see my participation in the divine nature as the work of the Holy Spirit?

Closing Prayer

O Triune God, I am nothing without You. I have nothing without You. I neither seek nor desire to have anything that is apart from You. St. Ambrose, pray for me that the Holy Spirit restores me to the image and likeness of God that I have forfeited through my sin and help me live my sacred dignity as His child.

Sweet Intimacy — Day 133

To possess the Gift of God, the Holy Spirit, is like possessing a treasure whose value is unknown and cannot be enjoyed fully. Our imperfect spiritual life is similar. Our soul does not know what it possesses nor can it enjoy fully its value. We need the Holy Spirit to bring about this knowledge and possessing.

"This is precisely the work of the Holy Spirit in souls: to bring to holy maturity, to happy plentitude, that germ of life, which he himself deposited in them.

"The spiritual life is the mutual possession of God and the soul, because it is essentially their mutual love. When the Holy Spirit possesses a soul completely and the soul attains the full possession of the Gift of God, this is union, perfection, and sanctity.... Then the soul ... can freely know God ... love him with a true and profound love ... belongs wholly to God, and God to the soul ... belongs to him completely and enjoys God with confidence, with liberty, and with the sweet intimacy that we use with our own."

SOG Archbishop Louis M. Martinez - *The Sanctifier*

In God's Presence Consider ...

Has the Gift of God been deposited within my soul? Have I attained full possession of the Gift of God? Do I belong wholly to God and God wholly to me? What prevents this sweet intimacy?

Closing Prayer

O God, who open wide the gates of the heavenly Kingdom to those reborn of water and the Holy Spirit, pour out on your servants an increase of the grace you have bestowed, that, having been purged of all sins, they may lack nothing that in your kindness you have promised.

Collect from Tuesday of the 3rd week of Easter

Disposed for Union **Day 134**

Fr. Garrigou-Lagrange, OP, talks about the importance of our constant developing of interior spiritual life through prayer and the theological virtues of faith, hope, and charity. This helps us to see and enter into the Holy Spirit's work of love and union within the Trinity helping us to contemplate Their inner life and bringing about our union with Them.

"The interior life is for all, the one thing necessary. It ought to be constantly developing our souls more so than what we call our intellectual life, more so than our scientific, artistic, or literary life.

"But, above all, our interior union must be a life of faith, hope, charity, and union with God by unceasing prayer … to see the ineffable breathing of the Holy Spirit, the issue of the common Love of the Father and the Son, which unites them in the most complete outpouring of themselves.... In this way we shall enter into the mysteries of faith and relish them more and more. In other words, our whole interior life tends towards the supernatural contemplation of the mysteries of the inner life of God and of the Incarnation and Redemption; it tends, above all, towards a more intimate union with God, a preliminary to that union with Him, ever actual and perpetual, which will be the consummation of eternal life."

Fr. Garrigou-Lagrange, O.P. - *The Three Ways of the Spiritual Life*

In God's Presence Consider …

Is my interior life treated as the most important and necessary thing in my heart? Do I experience the "ineffable breathing" of the Holy Spirit in my prayer life? Is my spiritual life merely an intellectual exercise, or is it leading me to deeper levels of union with God?

Closing Prayer

Come, Holy Spirit, help me to cooperate with Your working in my interior life. Prepare me to see God in the Beatific Vision and to be united with the Triune God here, now on earth and for all eternity.

Origen is talking about salvation being the shared work of the Trinity when he states his opinion that the Holy Spirit works only in those people that are disposed to walking the way of Jesus, perform good works, and who seek to abide in God.

"I am of opinion, then, that the working of the Father and of the Son takes place as well in saints as in sinners, in rational beings and in dumb animals; nay, even in those things which are without life, and in all things universally which exist; but that the operation of the Holy Spirit does not take place at all in those things which are without life, or in those which, although living, are yet dumb; nay, is not found even in those who are endued indeed with reason, but are engaged in evil courses, and not at all converted to a better life. In those persons alone do I think that the operation of the Holy Spirit takes place, who are already turning to a better life, and walking along the way which leads to Jesus Christ, i.e., who are engaged in the performance of good actions, and who abide in God."

Origen - *De Principiis, Book I Chapter III*

In God's Presence Consider …

According to Origen, in order for the Holy Spirit to work in a person's heart, there needs to be openness, a disposition to Jesus and goodness. Do I have a disposition to following Jesus wherever He leads? Am I converted to a better life?

Closing Prayer

St. Joseph, Vicar of the Holy Spirit, introduce the Holy Spirit to my will in order to ignite it with God's holy love. Present my will to the Most Holy Trinity so that my desires may always be at God's disposal.

Prayer of Blessed Bartolo Longo

The Holy Spirit empowers and illumines the Church in her mission to bring Christ to the nations.

"The Church is, as we know, enlightened and guided by the Holy Spirit, Who is still ready, if we implore Him and listen to Him, to fulfill without fail the promise of Christ…. (Jn. 14:26).

"The interior life still remains the great source of the Church's spirituality, her own proper way of receiving the illuminations of the Spirit of Christ, the fundamental and irreplaceable manifestation of her religious and social activity, an impregnable defense as well as an inexhaustible source of energy in her difficult contact with the world…. It is especially important that the baptized person should have a highly conscious esteem of his elevation, or, rather, of his rebirth to the most happy reality of being an adopted Son of God, to the dignity of being a Brother of Christ, to the good fortune, we mean to the grace and joy of the indwelling of the Holy Spirit, to the vocation to a new life…. He must truly look upon it, as did the Christians of old, as an illumination, which, by drawing down upon him the life-giving ray of Divine Truth, opens heaven to him, sheds light upon earthly life, and enables him to walk as a child of the light towards the vision of God, the spring of eternal happiness."

St. Pope Paul VI - *Ecclesiam Suam*

In God's Presence Consider …

Note that the Holy Spirit is still ready to enlighten and guide, and to fulfill the promises of Christ, if we do our part. Do I implore and listen to Him? Am I open to receive the Spirit's illuminations in my prayer life? Do I seek the life-giving ray of Divine Truth that baptism opened to me through the Holy Spirit?

Closing Prayer

Holy Spirit, I implore Your enlightenment and guidance and ask that You would help me to reflect upon my baptism and on the good fortune of the grace and joy Your indwelling brings about. Draw down upon me Your life-giving ray of Divine Truth and enable me to walk as a child of the light. St. Pope Paul VI, pray for me.

St. Cyril makes the point of the importance of being filled with the Holy Spirit in order to live our life in Christ and to combat temptations.

"After Christ had completed his mission on earth, it still remained necessary for us to become sharers in the divine nature of the Word. We had to give up our own life and be so transformed that we would begin to live an entirely new kind of life that would be pleasing to God. This was something we could do only by sharing in the Holy Spirit.

"... It was necessary for him (Jesus) to be united through his Spirit to those who worshiped him, and to dwell in our hearts through faith. Only by his own presence within us in this way could he give us confidence to cry out, Abba, Father, make it easy for us to grow in holiness, and through our possession of the all-powerful Spirit, fortify us invincibly against the wiles of the devil and the assaults of men."

St. Cyril of Alexandria - *Commentary on John*

In God's Presence Consider ...

How do I share in the divine nature of God? Why are self-denial, mortification, and dying to self so important in my spiritual life? Do I seek the Holy Spirit's presence in fortifying me against the enemies of my spiritual life?

Closing Prayer

O God, who in fire and lightning gave the ancient Law to Moses on Mount Sinai and on this day manifested the new covenant in the fire of the Spirit, grant, we pray, that we may always be aflame with that same Spirit whom you wondrously poured out on your Apostles, and that the new Israel, gathered from every people may receive with rejoicing the eternal commandment of your love.

Collect from the 2nd reading of the Vigil Mass for Pentecost

Sr. Ruth Burrow, O.C.D., defines the essence of prayer as being in the presence of God and allowing Him to love us on His terms. This deep intimacy of communion with the Blessed Trinity is impossible for man to achieve on his own. We need Jesus, who is the way, and the Holy Spirit, who helps us through our inabilities and weaknesses into the love of God.

"I saw that my total helplessness was expressing a fundamental truth: we cannot save ourselves, cannot attain God, cannot cope with God, still less show off in His presence.... God has given us Jesus ... Jesus is really our own Savior.... God has done it all for us in giving us Jesus. Our part is to use him to the uttermost ... living only in Jesus without any self-claim, is what it means to be in the Holy Spirit.

"Nothing runs so counter to nature as the experience of our spiritual poverty and a practical love for it such as this can only be the work of the Holy Spirit, the Spirit of Jesus.... It is the Spirit who continually upholds our natural weakness with divine strength; who is always praying deep within us even when our hearts seem mute, uttering our own most authentic desires, desires that we hardly know we have. The Holy Spirit, who proceeds from the Father and yet is sent to us by Jesus himself, is nothing less than the love between the Father and Son, their "communion".... Our prayer is one with that communion of love between Jesus and His Father, which is the Holy Spirit."

Sr. Ruth Burrows, O.C.D. - *Essence of Prayer*

In God's Presence Consider ...

Love has come to us, is with us, for us, and has us in His heart. How have I experienced my total helplessness before God? Has this helplessness opened up vistas of grace for me? Have I felt the Spirit uphold me with His divine strength?

Closing Prayer

Almighty Triune God, thank You for faith in the midst of my weakness and mute heart. Thank You for sending me Jesus and the Holy Spirit that I may enter into and experience Your love.

Consecrated to God **Day 139**

The summit of the spiritual life is communion with God. This transformation and union in the life of God is the work of the Holy Spirit.

"... under the influence of the Holy Spirit, souls are purified, illuminated, and enkindled until they are transformed into Jesus, who is the ultimate ideal of God's love and of the aspirations of the soul, the glorious summit of the mystical ascent where we find peace and happiness: where we find God.

"What is devotion to the Holy Spirit but a loving and constant cooperation with his divine influence, with his sanctifying work.... To be devoted to the Holy Spirit is to possess him and to let ourselves be loved and moved according to his good pleasure ... let him infuse into us a new life, the marvelous participation in the life of God.

"When a temple is consecrated to God it is a place set apart for him alone.... We were consecrated to be temples of the Holy Spirit on the day of our baptism."

SOG Archbishop Louis M. Martinez - *The Sanctifier*

In God's Presence Consider ...

Am I under the influence of the world or the Holy Spirit? Do I have a loving and constant cooperation with the Holy Spirit's influence and sanctifying work? Have I consecrated myself to the Holy Spirit as a temple is consecrated to God?

Closing Prayer

May your Spirit, O Lord, we pray, imbue us powerfully with spiritual gifts, that he may give us a mind pleasing to you and graciously conform us to your will.

Collect from Thursday of the 7th week of Easter.

St. Basil says the Holy Spirit is both simple and personal in His relationships. St. Pope John Paul says man's life in God exists through the Holy Spirit and this life develops and flourishes by the Holy Spirit.

"The Holy Spirit, while simple in essence and manifold in his virtues.... extends himself without undergoing any diminishing, is present in each subject capable of receiving him as if he were the only one, and gives grace which is sufficient for all."

St. Basil - *De Spiritu Sancto*

"Under the influence of the Holy Spirit this inner, spiritual man matures and grows strong.... In this Spirit, who is the eternal gift, the Triune God opens himself to man, to the human spirit. The hidden breath of the divine Spirit enables the human spirit to open in its turn before the saving and sanctifying self-opening of God. Through the gift of grace, which comes from the Holy Spirit, man enters a new life, is brought into the supernatural reality of the divine life itself and becomes a dwelling–place of the Holy Spirit, a living temple of God. For through the Holy Spirit, the Father and the Son come and take up their abode with him. Man is raised up to the supernatural level of divine life. Man lives in God and by God: he lives 'according to the Spirit,' and 'sets his mind on the things of the Spirit.'"

St. Pope John Paul II - *Dominum et Vivicantem*

In God's Presence Consider ...

The Holy Spirit makes me capable of receiving the divine life. Do I live my life under the influence of the Holy Spirit? Do I make myself capable of receiving the Holy Spirit and becoming His dwelling place? Have I set my mind on the things of the Holy Spirit?

Closing Prayer

Come, Holy Spirit, help me to receive You with total confidence, for You are sufficient for my every need. Help me to allow You to work within me and make me a dwelling place, a temple for this communion of grace with the Trinity. St. Pope John Paul II, pray for me.

The Holy Spirit is sent as a means of hope and restoration, when everything seems so hopeless and despairing. Like in Ezekiel 37, the dry bones of our lives are represented in our brokenness, helplessness, and hopelessness. God has Ezekiel prophesy and breathe over the bones to bring about renewal of God's people.

"Sometimes we may even feel we have reached the point of despair. We may believe that we are at the end of our rope and we just do not seem to be able to hang on any longer. This can happen in experiences which St. John of the Cross called the 'dark night.' God may seem very far away, quite unconcerned. Like the frightening experience the apostles once had on the Sea of Galilee, we may well feel that the Lord is apparently fast asleep while we are battling the storms of life that appear to be overwhelming us. (Mk. 4:37–38)

"… Our human situation may seem to be without any possible solution. All seems lost! If our spiritual lives are genuine, we will inevitably experience such circumstances. All apparent reason to hope or to continue on the journey will seem gone! This is precisely when the Spirit of Life comes to renew us.

Fr. Andrew Apostoli, C.F.R. - *The Gift of God: The Holy Spirit*

In God's Presence Consider …

Have I experienced the "dark night" where God seems far away or unconcerned about me? Do I have situations in my life that seem impossible and where I feel at the end of my rope? Do I seek the Spirit of Life to give me hope and renewal?

Closing Prayer

Holy Spirit, Divine Consoler, come and dispel the darkness of the storms overwhelming my life, for all seems lost and I can hang on no longer. I believe that You are here in my storms and seek to renew me and fill me with hope. Come, Holy Spirit, come!

Superhuman Vision **Day 142**

St. Cyril tells us that the Holy Spirit helps us to see everything in a new way and enables us to interpret human history.

"It is like someone who was first in the darkness. After having suddenly seen the sun he has the eye of his body illuminated and sees clearly what he could not see before, Thus, those who have become worthy to receive the Holy Spirit have their souls illuminated and see in a superhuman way that which was not seen before. The body is on earth and the soul contemplates the heavens as if in a mirror.... Each human, so small, extends his glance over the universe, from the beginning to the end, over the time in between and over the successive kingdoms. He comes to know that which no one has taught him because he is side by side with the person who illuminates him."

St. Cyril of Jerusalem - *Catechesis, XV, 16*

In God's Presence Consider ...

What illuminates the eyes of my body? Can I see spiritual things clearly? Have I acquired superhuman sight? Am I side by side with the Person who seeks to illuminate me in the things of God?

Closing Prayer

Come, Holy Spirit, with Your gift of light, that I may have superhuman sight and thus illumined, contemplate the things of God. St. Cyril of Jerusalem, pray for me.

Exuberantly Intoxicated in the Spirit **Day 143**

When spiritually intoxicated, a person is out of his mind not because he is bereft of reason, as in the case with wine or drugs, but because he passes beyond reason into the light of God. He is so filled with joy, he has to bubble over.

"The Holy Spirit has come to abide in you; do not make him withdraw; do not exclude him from your heart in any way. He is a good guest; He found you empty and He filled you; He found you hungry and He satisfied you; He found you thirsty and He has intoxicated you. May He truly intoxicate you! The Apostle said, 'Do not be drunk with wine which leads to debauchery.' Then, as if to clarify what we should be intoxicated with, he adds, 'But be filled with the Spirit, addressing one another in psalms and hymns and spiritual songs, singing and making melody to the Lord with all your heart" (Eph. 5:18). Doesn't a person who rejoices in the Lord and sings to Him exuberantly seem like a person who is drunk? I like this kind of intoxication. The Spirit of God is both drink and light."

St. Augustine - *Sermon 225*

In God's Presence Consider …

How has the Holy Spirit taken care of my needs? Do I seek to be intoxicated in the Spirit? Does my worship and praise of God show the exuberance of the new wine of the Holy Spirit, or am I stuck in spiritual sobriety?

Closing Prayer

St Augustine, pray for me that I will be intoxicated with the new wine of the Holy Spirit. Thus filled, may I address others with psalms, hymns, and spiritual songs, making melody exuberantly to the Lord with all my heart.

Ezekiel is transported by the Holy Spirit to a valley of dry bones. God then places His Holy Spirit within them, thus giving them life.

"And he led me round among them; and behold, there were very many upon the valley; and behold, they were very dry. And he said to me, 'Son of man, can these bones live?' And I answered, 'O Lord God, you know.' Again he said to me: 'Prophesy to these bones, and say to them, O dry bones, hear the word of the Lord. Thus says the Lord God to these bones: Behold, I will cause breath (spirit) to enter you and you shall live. And I will lay sinews upon you, and will cause flesh to come upon you, and cover you with skin, and put breath (spirit) in you, and you shall live; and you shall know that I am the Lord.' So I prophesied as I was commanded; and as I prophesied, there was a noise, and behold, a rattling; and the bones came together, bone to its bone. And as I looked, there were sinews on them, and flesh had come upon them, and skin had covered them; but there was no spirit in them.

"Then he said to me, 'Prophesy to the spirit, prophesy, Son of man, and say to the spirit, thus says the Lord God: Come from the four winds, O spirit and breathe upon these slain, that they may live.' So I prophesied as he commanded me, and the spirit came into them, and they lived, and stood upon their feet, an exceedingly great host.... Behold I will open your graves, and raise you from your graves, O my people ... I will put my Spirit within you, and you shall live, and I will place you in your own land; then you shall know that I, the Lord, have spoken, and I have done it, says the Lord."

Ezekiel 37:1-14

In God's Presence Consider ...

How can I be led by the Holy Spirit? Do I allow God to breathe His Life into the dry bones of my life? Do I live a life in the Spirit that God breaths within me? Is obedience something important and is it a part of my life?

Closing Prayer

Come O Breath of God. Breathe new life within my dry bones that I may live in, with, and for God.

Fr. Michael Scanlan shares how, after the "bottom fell out of his stomach and something like panic set in" when he arrived to the seminary to take on his new assignment as rector, he sought the guidance of a holy person. After being directed to be baptized in the Holy Spirit, he shares his experience of deep union and satisfaction.

"I knew I was inadequate for this job. I knew that I lacked some basic equipment. I shared my misgivings with the holiest person I knew. She was Sister Caroline, the Superior of the Discalced Carmelite Sisters.... I told her how ill-equipped I was to be holy myself, not to speak of leading others to holiness. I told her about my inability to relate to people in love, about that gnawing, unfulfilled feeling that I had always had.

"'You need to be baptized in the Holy Spirit, Michael,' she said when I was finished. 'What is that?' I asked. 'I've never heard of it.'

"'... I want to be baptized in the Holy Spirit.' They laid hands on me.... The Spirit fell. It was primarily an experience of prayer, but prayer unlike any other I had experienced or studied. I was lost in God, one with the fullness of life. I wanted nothing more than to know God the way I knew him at that moment, intimately united to him. I let myself go in praise and prayer. God was all I had. He was all I wanted. He was all I needed'"

Fr. Michael Scanlan, T.O.R. - *Let the Fire Fall*

In God's Presence Consider ...

Do I ever feel ill-equipped to be a disciple of Jesus let alone a holy person? Do I seek to be lost in God, to be intimately united to Him? Do I seek the baptism of the Holy Spirit?

Closing Prayer

Lord, I want more of You. I want my gnawing unfulfilled feeling of desire for You, to be filled with deep intimate union with You. Please baptize me in Your Holy Spirit that You may become all I want and need.

It's Something God Does **Day 146**

There is a will-power Christianity: using our will to achieve our ideal of holiness, and there is empowered Christianity: allowing the Holy Spirit to use us to achieve God's ideal of holiness.

"This is the difference the Spirit makes. Power. Power to do easily what before was difficult or impossible. Power to call down God's healing on those who are hurting. Power to face danger with courage. Power to discern the will of the almighty God to follow him fearlessly.

"Power is the visible manifestations of the intimacy we have with God through the Holy Spirit.... We think and act with God's power after this event because we enter a new relationship of intimacy with each person of the Trinity.... In short, being baptized in the Spirit means being brought into God's household. We become part of the family. With the Father caring for us, our brother Jesus standing beside us, and the Spirit directing our thoughts and actions, is it any wonder that we can act with power?

"The graces and gifts that come with being baptized in the Spirit are not necessarily new gifts that come from the outside. They are also the release of graces we have always had, the fruition of a work the Lord began in us when we were baptized. That is when we receive the Holy Spirit and brought from death into life. Being baptized in the Holy Spirit is giving ourselves over to the Lord so that his presence and gifts can take over our lives. It is not something you do. It's something God does for you."

Fr. Michael Scanlan, T.O.R. - *Let the Fire Fall*

In God's Presence Consider ...

Am I a "will-power" Christian or an "empowered" Christian? Do I think and act with God's power as a member of His family or as an outsider trying to get in by what I do? Do I seek the Holy Spirit to stir into action the graces within me from my baptism?

Closing Prayer

Holy Spirit, help me to be empowered and to work with Your graces to turn away from all sin, seeking the Father's forgiveness, avoiding everything that leads me to wrongdoing, and seeking the Lordship of Jesus in my heart. Baptize me in Your Spirit, Lord.

St. Mary of Jesus Crucified shows us the important role that the Holy Spirit plays in helping the disciples of Jesus to come to find Him, to understand Him, and to remain with Him. The key is total abandonment of self to the Holy Spirit.

"This morning, I was feeling low in spirit because I did not feel the presence of God. It seemed to me that my heart was like iron, I could not think of God; I invoked the Holy Spirit saying: "It is you who made us know Jesus. The Apostles spent a long time with him without ever comprehending him; but the fire you sent down on them made them understand him. You will also make me understand him. Come, my consolation; come, my joy; come, my peace, my strength, my light. Come, give me the light to find the spring where I can quench my thirst. One ray of your light is enough to show me Jesus as he is. I ask you for no other learning, nor any other wisdom than the knowledge of how to find Jesus and the wisdom of remaining with him. O Most Holy Spirit, when you sent forth the ray of light, the disciples were transformed; they were no longer what they had been before; their strength had been renewed, offering sacrifices became easy; they then got to know Jesus better than they had ever known him when he was among them. Source of peace and light, come and enlighten me. I am hungry, come and feed me. I am poor, come and enrich me. Holy Spirit, I abandon myself to you."

St. Mary of Jesus Crucified - *Thoughts of Mary of Jesus Crucified*

In God's Presence Consider ...

Do I seek the fire of the Holy Spirit's understanding so that I may know Jesus in a personal and intimate way? Do I seek the Holy Spirit's power to melt my heart of iron and give me a heart of love? How much do I abandon myself to the Holy Spirit?

Closing Prayer

O Most Holy Spirit, I pray as St. Mary of Jesus Crucified prayed: Send forth the ray of Your light transforming and renewing me. Source of peace and light, come and enlighten me. I am hungry, come and feed me. I am poor, come and enrich me. Holy Spirit, I abandon myself to You. St. Mary of Jesus Crucified, pray for me.

Openness to Dynamic Union

The Holy Spirit calls each of us after the pattern of Mary and the Apostles in the Upper Room, to accept and embrace the baptism of His fire, as the power of personal and communal transformation needed to fulfill our mission as Church.

"A life baptized in the Spirit is marked both by an experience of dynamic union with God and by an experience of charisms given by the Spirit. These enable us to serve God in praise and worship, to serve one another in love by prophecy, healing and other gifts, and to empower our participation in the church's ministry and society. These charisms belong to the church today….

"While deeply personal, life in the Spirit is not individualistic, but a participation in the body of Christ…. The hallmark of such communities is self-sacrificing mutual love among brothers and sisters in Christ…. A renewed parish is a community worshiping in vibrant liturgy, bonded together by the Holy Spirit, serving one another, committed to ongoing conversion and growth, reaching out to the inactive, the unchurched and to the poor. Such parishes confront us with the gospel and evangelize our culture. In these communities, as in the Acts of the Apostles and the early church, the charisms of the Holy Spirit are identified and welcomed. Only in the Holy Spirit will we be able to respond to its pastoral needs and those of the world. God freely gives this grace, but it requires a personal response of ongoing conversion and openness to the transforming presence and power of Jesus and the Holy Spirit."

McDonnell and Montague - *Fanning the Flame*

In God's Presence Consider …

Am I alive in the Spirit where others notice the Spirit's fruits in my life? Am I a hallmark of Christian community by my self-sacrificing mutual love and in communion with my brothers and sisters? Am I seeking ongoing conversion to the Lordship of Jesus Christ?

Closing Prayer

Father, please stir up the Holy Spirit within me; rekindle His fire from my baptism; that transformed by the power and love of the Holy Spirit, I will seek ongoing conversion to Your Son Jesus.

An Invisible Visit to Our Soul — Day 149

Charity is at the same time both the condition for and the result of the indwelling of the Holy Spirit in our souls.

"… according to Jesus Himself, the three divine Persons dwell only in a soul who loves; it is the result, because 'the charity of God is poured forth in our hearts by the Holy Ghost, who is given to us' (Rom. 5:5). Divine love completely preceded us at baptism; without merit on our part and solely through the merits of Jesus, the Holy Spirit was given to us, and His charity was gratuitously diffused in us. Thereafter, each time we corresponded to the divine invitations, by making generous acts of charity, He renewed His invisible visit to our soul, giving us always new grace and charity. Thus our supernatural life has developed under the action of the Holy Spirit, it is caught up in the life-giving transforming current of His love. In this way we understand how the Feast of Pentecost can and should represent a new out-pouring of the Holy Spirit in our souls, a new visit in which He fills us with His gifts."

Fr. Gabriel of St. Mary Magdalen, O.C.D. - *Divine Intimacy*

In God's Presence Consider …

Do I accept and cooperate with the divine invitation to love and grow in intimacy with God? How do I allow myself to be caught up in the life-giving current of the Holy Spirit's love?

Closing Prayer

Come Fire of Divine Love, and renew in me Your transforming love, that I may be generous in my acts of love and service to others.

Artist of Souls **Day 150**

An artist can penetrate hard and shapeless materials transforming them into magnificent masterpieces. The instruments he uses can impart to these materials exquisite proportions and shapes. Because the Holy Spirit is Love, His transforming work as an artist is a work of love.

"The Holy Spirit loves him (Jesus) more than an artist loves his ideal. That love is his being, because the Holy Spirit is nothing but love, the personal Love of the Father and of the Word (The Word or Logos, that is, the second Person of the Trinity, who became incarnate.). With divine enthusiasm he comes to the soul—the soul, breath of the Most High, spiritual light that can merge with uncreated Light, exquisite essence that can be transformed into Jesus, reproducing the eternal ideal.... His action is not exterior nor intermittent, but intimate and constant. He enters into the depths of our souls, penetrates the innermost recesses, and takes up his permanent dwelling there to produce later on his magnificent work."

SOG Archbishop Louis M. Martinez - *The Sanctifier*

In God's Presence Consider ...

Do I have an enthusiasm for the Holy Spirit to come and dwell in my soul? Do I see myself as the medium the Holy Spirit wants to work with to reproduce in my soul the image of Jesus?

Closing Prayer

O Artist of Souls, come with Your constant and intimate breath of love. Enter into the depths of my soul with Your uncreated Light, transforming me into a magnificent work in whom the Father is well pleased and the Son enjoys.

As the spiritual life grows, the soul increases in sanctity and becomes marvelously sensible to the movement of the Spirit. SOG Archbishop Martinez tells us that our perfection can be measured by our docility to the Holy Spirit.

"The true Director of souls, the intimate Master, the soul of the spiritual life, is the Holy Spirit … without him there is not sanctity. The perfection of a soul is measured by its docility to the movement of the Spirit, by the promptness and fidelity with which its strings produce the divine notes of the song of love. A soul is perfectly holy when the Spirit of love has taken full possession of it, when the divine Artist finds no resistance or dissonance in the strings of that living lyre, but only celestial strains coming forth from it, limpid, ardent, and delightfully harmonized.

"The inspirations of the Holy Spirit are not, then something extraordinary and superfluous in the spiritual life; they are its vital, perfect impulse."

SOG Archbishop Louis M. Martinez - *The Sanctifier*

In God's Presence Consider …

How docile am I to the movements of the Holy Spirit? Would I recognize those movements? Have I allowed the Holy Spirit to take full possession of me and become my "perfect impulse"?

Closing Prayer

O Holy Spirit, You who are the intimate Master of my soul, help me to recognize and be docile to Your movements within me that I will put up no resistance to Your taking full possession of me. Help me to become a delightful harmonized song of love to our God.

Following the Impulse **Day 152**

Detachment frees us from the various bonds, cords, and ties to creatures we have that prevent us from being elevated and brought to God.

"… to cooperate with the action of the Holy Spirit, the first requirement is the painstaking effort to detach ourselves from everything, especially from ourselves. Detachment will free us from numerous bonds which, like cords, tie us to creatures, making our docility and submissiveness to the Holy Spirit an impossibility. Detachment breaks the thread which fastens us to earth, and our soul, thus freed, can follow every slightest impulse of the Holy Spirit, who will then take possession of it and direct it according to His good pleasure.

"We have said that the Paraclete is not content simply to invite us to what is good, but He wishes to take the initiative, impelling us more effectually toward God. However, He respects our liberty, and will not make Himself Master of our will unless we are disposed to give it to Him freely. The Holy Spirit would like to elevate us and bring us to God, but we do not accept His initiative and our lack of generosity retards the divine work. Perhaps we cooperate partially, giving Him something of what He asks, but we do not give Him 'all.' We must, therefore, cultivate the spirit of 'totality' which puts no limits to our giving. We must have a magnanimous heart and not retard the work of the Holy Spirit, who wills to bring us, not only to good actions but to generous, heroic, saintly ones."

Fr. Gabriel of St. Mary Magdalen, O.C.D. - *Divine Intimacy*

In God's Presence Consider …

Do I find it hard to detach from my ego and the people and things I enjoy, in order to grow in intimacy with God? What are obstacles I put up to keep the Holy Spirit at a distance and retard His divine work? What must I do to be generous, heroic, and saintly?

Closing Prayer

Come, Holy Spirit, O Holy Paraclete. Come and change my attitudes and habits that I may seek to detach myself from all things that fasten me to the earth. Give me a magnanimous heart that I will not retard the work You desire to do within me.

Fr. Garrigou-Lagrange compares the three ways of the spiritual life to the three levels of human development: childhood, adolescence, and adulthood. Each way is preceded by a process of conversion.

"This third conversion or purification is, evidently, the work of the Holy Spirit, who illuminates the soul by the gift of understanding.... This third purification comes about, as St. John of the Cross says, by 'an inflowing of God into the soul, which purges it from its ignorance's and imperfections, habitual, natural and spiritual, and which is called by contemplatives infused contemplation or mystical theology. Herein God secretly teaches the soul and instructs it in perfection of love, without its doing anything or understanding of what manner is this infused contemplation.' (Dark Night, Book II, Ch. 5)

"The fruits of this third conversion are the same as those of Pentecost, when the Apostles were enlightened and fortified, and being themselves transformed, transformed the first Christians by their preaching—as we learn from the Acts of the Apostles, where we are told of the first sermons of St. Peter and St. Stephen's discourse before his martyrdom.... But the most perfect fruit of this third conversion is a very great love of God, a very pure and very strong love, a love that hesitates before no contradiction or persecution, like the love of the Apostles who rejoiced to suffer for the sake of our Lord."

Rev. Garrigou-Lagrange, O.P. - *The Three Ways of the Spiritual Life*

In God's Presence Consider ...

Have I ever thought of conversion as a means of purification? Do I rejoice in my suffering for the sake of Jesus? Do I seek the enlightenment of the Spirit through His gift of understanding?

Closing Prayer

Holy Spirit, come into my heart; draw it to Thee by Thy power, O my God, and grant me charity with filial fear. Preserve me, O ineffable Love, from every evil thought; warm me, inflame me with Thy dear love, and every pain will seem light to me. My Father, my sweet Lord, help me in all my actions. Jesus, love, Jesus, love. Amen.

Prayer of St. Catherine of Siena

Divine Cycle **Day 154**

The Father sends the Son to redeem man and to re-establish a relationship between the Father and His people. To continue His work that He finished on earth, the Father and the Son send the Holy Spirit, Who draws mankind to Jesus and together They present mankind back to the Father. This cycle of love is then completed in the Father, for all things find their full perfection when they return to their origin.

"Now the divine cycle must be reproduced in each soul, for this is the glorious destiny of souls. The Gift of God will come to each one of them as it came to the Virgin Mary; and since, after Love itself, the Gift of divine love is Jesus, the Holy Spirit will bring to each soul the divine fecundity of the Father; in each the Word will take flesh mystically, and Jesus will sing the poem of his divine mysteries; and each, through him, will go to the Father.

"Only the souls of the saints, letting themselves be possessed by 'Christ's bestowal' (Eph. 4:7), will fully accomplish the designs of God. In them the work of the Holy Spirit will appear splendidly, finished, and perfected. The divine cycle will have been completed in all its majestic fullness."

SOG Archbishop Louis M. Martinez - *The Sanctifier*

In God's Presence Consider ...

I am to be the reproduction of the love of the Trinity and thus fully accomplish the designs of God. Does my spiritual life reflect this divine cycle of love? When the Holy Spirit abides in a soul and mutual possession occurs, there is a divine fecundity that occurs. Do I see my life as the fruit of Trinitarian Love? Am I willing to allow myself to be possessed as the saints are?

Closing Prayer

Come, Holy Spirit, and take possession of me that I may fully accomplish the designs of God and be completed in all majestic fullness.

It is through the waters of Baptism that the Holy Spirit first enters into the soul. His entry and the work He does is called a 'New Birth' or 'Regeneration.' All guilt and pollution of sin are burned away as by fire, the devil is driven out, all sin forgiven, and the whole man is consecrated to God. The Holy Spirit seals us for the day of Redemption.

"… as the potter molds the clay, so He impresses the Divine image on us members of the household of God. And His work may truly be called Regeneration; for though the original nature of the soul is not destroyed, yet its past transgressions are pardoned once and for ever…. Such is the real doctrine, which we hold as a matter of faith, and without actual experience to verify it to us.

"The heavenly gift of the Spirit fixes the eyes of our mind upon the Divine Author of our salvation. By nature we are blind and carnal; but the Holy Ghost by whom we are new-born, reveals to us the God of mercies, and bids us recognize and adore Him as our Father with a true heart. He impresses on us our Heavenly Father's image, which we lost when Adam fell, and disposes us to seek His presence by the very instinct of our new nature…. Being then the sons of God, and one with Him, our souls mount up and cry to Him continually … Abba, Father."

St. John Henry Newman - *Sermon 19*

In God's Presence Consider …

How am I holding up to the "potter's" wheel and the molding process? Where are my eyes fixed? On the world or on the Divine things? Am I disposed to seek God's presence and to be made new in the Father's image?

Closing Prayer

Abba Father, You are the potter. Impress upon me Your Divine Image, that I may be disposed to seek Your presence by every instinct of my new nature. St. John Henry Newman, pray for me.

Led by God **Day 156**

The Holy Spirit can help us in our lowliness and our nothingness before God, by leading us into greatness if we but give Him the chance.

"O my Children, how beautiful it is! The Father is our Creator, the Son is our Redeemer, and the Holy Spirit is our Guide.... Man by himself is nothing, but with the Holy Spirit he is very great. Man is all earthly and all animal, nothing but the Holy Spirit can elevate his mind, and raise it on high. Why were the saints so detached from the earth? Because they let themselves be led by the Holy Spirit. Those who are led by the Holy Spirit have true ideas; that is the reason why so many ignorant people are wiser than the learned. When we are led by a God of strength and light, we cannot go astray.... Those who have the Holy Spirit cannot endure themselves, so well do they know their poor misery. The proud are those who have not the Holy Spirit...."

St. John Vianney - *Catechism on the Holy Spirit, Ch. 3*

In God's Presence Consider ...

Do I see my nothingness before God? Am I detached from the earthly desires and have my eyes towards heaven? How might the Holy Spirit be an aid to me in my spiritual life?

Closing Prayer

Holy Spirit, help me to see my nothingness before God, to be detached from earthly desires, and to be led by You as my Guide. St. John Vianney, pray for me.

A life of prayer is to be in the habit of being in the presence of and in deep union, communion with God.

"According to Scripture, it is the heart that prays. If our heart is far from God, the words of prayer are in vain.... The heart is the dwelling-place where I am, where I live ... the heart is the place to which I withdraw. The heart is our hidden center, beyond the grasp of our reason and of others; only the Spirit of God can fathom the human heart and know it fully. The heart is the place of decision, deeper than our psychic drives. It is the place of truth, where we choose life or death. It is the place of encounter, because as image of God we live in relation; it is the place of covenant.

"Christian prayer is a covenant relationship between God and man in Christ. It is the action of God and of man, springing forth from both the Holy Spirit and ourselves, wholly directed to the Father, in union with the human will of the Son of God made man ... prayer is the living relationship of the children of God with their Father who is good beyond measure, with his Son Jesus Christ and with the Holy Spirit.... In the Holy Spirit, Christian prayer is a communion of love with the Father, not only through Christ but also in him...."

Cf. CCC #2562–2565, 2615

In God's Presence Consider ...

Do I know God personally? Is my heart a dwelling place; a place of encounter with God? Do I pray from my head or from my heart? Is my prayer a living relationship as a child of God with my Father? Is my prayer a communion of love with God?

Closing Prayer

Come, Holy Spirit, Master of the Interior Life. Breathe into my heart charity and infuse Your life and love within me. Wholly direct my life to the communion You long me to have with the Father and in the Son through You.

By Virtue of His Action **Day 158**

The highest degree of prayer according to St. Cyprian, is the Our Father, which he says, is an authentic spiritual prayer that prays "in Spirit and Truth."

"He who gave us the gift of life, with the same benevolence with which he bestowed his other gifts on us, also taught us how to pray. Turning to God with the prayer dictated by the Son, we can be more easily heard. Christ already foretold that a time was to come in which the true worshipers would worship the Father 'in Spirit and truth.' He made this come to pass earlier than he promised so that we, who by virtue of his sanctification have received the Spirit and the Truth, by virtue of his action also worship 'in Spirit and truth.' What could be more spiritual than the prayer given by Christ, he who also sent the Holy Spirit?"

St. Cyprian - *On the Lord's Prayer*

In God's Presence Consider …

How has God taught me through the Holy Spirit to pray? What do I do with the Spirit and Truth that Jesus and the Father have sent me? Is my prayer truly inspired by the Holy Spirit dwelling in me?

Closing Prayer

Come, Holy Spirit, and become the desire of my heart; You who have caused me to want You. Come my Breath and my Life. Come forth from within me and lead me to worship the Father in Spirit and in Truth. St. Cyprian, pray for me.

The Holy Spirit is the interior Master of prayer, the artisan of prayer, who inspires, recalls, teaches, and unites. We are to live and walk by the Holy Spirit thus being sensitive to the presence of God in our midst.

"… Every time we begin to pray to Jesus it is the Holy Spirit who draws us on the way of prayer by his prevenient grace. Since he teaches us to pray by recalling Christ, how could we not pray to the Spirit too? That is why the Church invites us to call upon the Holy Spirit every day, especially at the beginning and the end of every important action…. Only the Spirit by whom we live can make 'ours' the same mind that was in Christ Jesus…. The heart that offers itself to the Holy Spirit turns injury into compassion and purifies the memory in transforming the hurt into intercession. If we live by the Spirit, let us also walk by the Spirit (Gal. 5:25)

Cf. CCC #2670, 2672, 2673, 2842–43, 2848–49

In God's Presence Consider …

The Holy Spirit teaches us to pray by recalling Christ. Is the Holy Spirit a part of my daily prayers? Do I allow the Interior Master of Prayer to form me? Am I angry and hold on to offenses or injuries others have caused me or do I live in the strength of the Holy Spirit who helps me forgive and be healed?

Closing Prayer

Come, Holy Spirit, fill the hearts of your faithful and enkindle in them the fire of your love.

Roman Missal, Pentecost, Sequence

God communicates Himself to man in the Holy Spirit. The simplest and most common manner makes itself felt in prayer.

"... the Holy Spirit, who breathes prayer in the heart of man in all the endless range of the most varied situations and conditions.... Many times, through the influence of the Spirit, prayer rises from the human heart.... The Holy Spirit is the gift that comes into man's heart together with prayer.... The Holy Spirit not only enables us to pray, but guides us from within in prayer: he is present in our prayer and gives it a divine dimension.... Prayer through the power of the Holy Spirit becomes the ever more mature expression of the new man, who by means of this prayer participates in the divine life ... the Holy Spirit as he inspires in hearts a profound yearning for holiness."

St. Pope John Paul II - *Dominum et Vivicantem*

In God's Presence Consider ...

Do I allow the Holy Spirit to breathe prayer into my heart and allow Him to guide my prayer? How have I experienced the influence of the Holy Spirit when I pray?

Closing Prayer

Breathe in me O Breath of God, that my prayer may rise before the Father and I may participate in the divine life and become holy; a saint. St. Pope John Paul II, pray for me.

The Holy Spirit is the Master of Prayer and the Interior Life, who not only teaches us how to pray, but prays with us and through us as children of the Father.

"Paul also teaches us another important thing. He says that there can be no authentic prayer without the presence of the Spirit in us. In fact, he writes: 'In the same way, the Spirit too comes to the aid of our weakness; for we do not know how to pray as we ought, but the Spirit itself intercedes with inexpressible groaning. And the one who searches hearts knows what is the intention of the Spirit, because it intercedes for the holy ones according to God's will.' (cf. Rom. 8:26–27)

"It is as if saying that the Holy Spirit, namely, the Spirit of the Father and of the Son, becomes the soul of our soul, the most secret part of our being, from which rises incessantly to God a movement of prayer, of which we cannot even specify the terms. The Spirit, in fact, ever awake in us, makes up for our deficiencies and offers the Father our adoration, along with our most profound aspirations. Obviously, this calls for a level of great vital communion with the Spirit. It is an invitation to be ever more sensitive, more attentive to this presence of the Spirit in us, to transform it into prayer, to experience this presence and to learn in this way to pray, to speak with the Father as children in the Holy Spirit."

Pope Benedict XVI - *Paul's Teaching on the Holy Spirit*

In God's Presence Consider …

I might be a person of prayer, but is my prayer authentic and led by the Holy Spirit? Have I ever thought of the Holy Spirit as making up for my deficiencies in prayer? Do I live in communion with Him?

Closing Prayer

Come, Holy Spirit, Great Searcher of Hearts, awaken in me a sensitivity and attentiveness to Your transforming presence in me. Make my soul rise incessantly as a movement of prayer to the Father and the Son.

Salvation is the forgiveness of sins and the restoration of friendship with God, which the Catechism reminds us in # 16, can only be done by God alone.

"Only one thing is important—eternal salvation. Only one thing, therefore, is to be feared—sin. Sin is the result of ignorance, weakness, and indifference. The Holy Spirit is the Spirit of Light, of Strength, and of Love. With His sevenfold gifts He enlightens the mind, strengthens the will, and inflames the heart with love of God. To ensure our salvation we ought to invoke the Divine Spirit daily, for 'The Spirit helpeth our infirmity. We know not what we should pray for as we ought. But the Spirit Himself asketh for us.'"

Fr. Gabriel of St. Mary Magdalen, O.C.D. - *Divine Intimacy*

In God's Presence Consider ...

Do I fear sin, recognizing that sin jeopardizes my eternal salvation? Do I invoke the Holy Spirit daily to help ensure my salvation?

Closing Prayer

O Lord, I do not know how to pray the way I should. Please renew Your Holy Spirit within me, that He will enlighten, strengthen, and inflame my heart with Your love.

Mother John Marie Stewart, tells us how we can share in the missionary nature of the Church by proclaiming Jesus when we are filled with the Holy Spirit.

"I saw that this outreach and the ministry involved are rooted in the call to prayer. Indeed, the very nature of the charismatic spirituality is a constant sense of God's presence and of His intimate involvement in every aspect of our lives. Everything that we do—whether it be manual work on the farm or in the house, or evangelistic outreach of some kind—is contemplative in that we are working together with the Lord in an attitude of praise and worship. It is all for Him and is done through His power working in us….

"I had found that this intimacy with the Lord is one of the characteristic fruits of the baptism in the Holy Spirit. We usually associate these spiritual heights and depths, especially the gifts of the Spirit, with the saints. In this great outpouring of the Holy Spirit, these gifts and that fruitful intimacy are seen in multitudes of ordinary charismatics—wives, husbands, young people, and children. For surely in this day our sons and daughters are prophesying! (See Joel 3:1)"

Mother John Marie Steward, DLJC - *Laying the Foundation*

In God's Presence Consider …

Does my spirituality make full use of the Holy Spirit's charisms? Do I sense God's presence and intimate involvement in every aspect of my life? Do I seek the Holy Spirit's help in growing in my intimacy with God? Does my prayer include praise and worship?

Closing Prayer

Come, Holy Spirit, Master of Prayer, help me be rooted in You. Help me to see God's presence in all things and to grow in my intimacy with the Blessed Holy Trinity. Help me to develop an attitude of gratitude giving God the praise and worship due His Holy Name.

Fr. Michael O'Carroll says that the Holy Spirit was one of the dominant themes of St. Pope John Paul II's teachings. In speaking at the World Council of Churches on June 12, 1984, JPII speaks of the Holy Spirit giving us new ways to walk together in unity. One of those ways is prayer, which is the basis of ecumenical unity.

"There is another aspect of the Christian mystery which unites us more than in the past. We have together learned to understand better the entire role of the Holy Spirit. But this rediscovery which marks the renewal of Catholic liturgy has rendered us sensitive to a new dimension of our ecclesial life. The Spirit is the source of a liberty in faithfulness that we have received from the generations which have gone before us. He can find new ways when there is question of walking together towards a unity which is, at the same time, based on truth and yet is respectful of the rich diversity of really Christian values which spring from a common patrimony (Decree on Ecumenism #4).

"From the fact of this new attention to the presence of the Spirit, our prayer has taken on a special accent. It is more fully opened to the action of grace, in which we detach ourselves from our own preoccupations to fix our gaze on the work of God and the wonder of his grace.... Prayer has a special place in our options."

St. Pope John Paul II - *A Dictionary of His Life and Teachings*

In God's Presence Consider ...

The rediscovery of the Holy Spirit and His role in our lives, marks renewal. Have I undergone a rediscovery of the Holy Spirit in my spiritual life? Am I open for Him finding new ways for me to approach healing of relationships, moral difficulties, personal challenges in my life?

Closing Prayer

Come, Holy Spirit, help me to rediscover and be more sensitive to You in prayer, that I may be more fully opened to the action of grace, detached from my own preoccupations, and have my gaze fixed upon the mighty works and wonders of God. St. Pope John Paul II, pray for me.

Our Filial Prayer **Day 165**

"The more the Holy Ghost finds Mary, His dear and inseparable spouse, in any soul, the more active and mighty He becomes in producing Jesus Christ in that soul, and that soul in Jesus Christ." St. Louis DeMonfort, #20 of True Devotion to Mary

"In prayer the Holy Spirit unites us to the person of the only Son, in his glorified humanity, through which and in which our filial prayer unites us in the Church with the Mother of Jesus (Act. 1:14).

"By entrusting ourselves to her prayer, we abandon ourselves to the will of God together with her: 'Thy will be done.'

"When we pray to her, we are adhering with her to the plan of the Father, who sent his Son to save all men.... We can pray with and to her".

Cf. CCC #2673, 2675, 2677, 2679

In God's Presence Consider ...

Do I seek the help of Mary in developing an ever-deeper intimacy with the Holy Spirit her spouse? Do I seek God's will in all things in my life? Have I ever thought of being led to Jesus and the Holy Spirit by Mary and sustained in my union with them through her prayers?

Closing Prayer

Hail Mary, full of grace, the Lord is with thee. Blessed art thou among women and blessed is the fruit of thy womb, Jesus. Holy Mary, Mother of God, pray for us sinners, now and at the hour of our death.

True devotion to the Holy Spirit is about allowing Him to possess us with His gifts, to let ourselves be loved and moved according to His good pleasure, and to give Him our lives so that He may mold us into the divine image of Jesus, infusing us with new life.

"... under the influence of the Holy Spirit, souls are purified, illuminated, and enkindled until they are transformed into Jesus, who is the ultimate ideal of God's love and of the aspirations of the soul, the glorious summit of the mystical ascent where we find peace and happiness: where we find God.

"What is devotion to the Holy Spirit but a loving and constant cooperation with his divine influence, with his sanctifying work? To be devoted to the Holy Spirit is to open our soul for him to dwell there, to dilate our heart that he may anoint it with his divine charity, to deliver our whole being up to him that he may possess it with his gifts, to give him our life that he may transform it into a divine one, to put into his hands the shapeless block of our imperfection that he may mold it to the divine image of Jesus.

"To be devoted to the Holy Spirit is to possess him and to let ourselves be loved and moved according to his good pleasure ... let him infuse into us a new life, the marvelous participation in the life of God."

SOG Archbishop Louis M. Martinez - *The Sanctifier*

In God's Presence Consider ...

Where do I find peace and happiness? Do I loving and constantly cooperate with the divine influences of the Holy Spirit? Am I free with allowing the Holy Spirit to love and move me according to His good pleasure and not what I view as good or desirous?

Closing Prayer

Father, I desire to participate in Your life and be holy. Help me to accept the way You love me through the Holy Spirit that I will lovingly and constantly cooperate with His sanctifying work.

Desired to be Poured Out **Day 167**

The grand scale that St. Pope John XXIII prays, is for the Holy Spirit to help us search for truth, to have a devotion to truth, and a readiness for self-sacrifice for that truth so that the love God desires to pour out over the Church and the souls of men and nations will be accomplished.

"O Holy Ghost, Paraclete, perfect in us the work begun by Jesus; enable us to continue to pray fervently in the name of the whole world; hasten in every one of us the growth of a profound interior life; give vigor to our apostolate so that it may reach all men and all peoples, all redeemed by the Blood of Christ and all belonging to him. Mortify in us our natural pride, and raise us to the realms of holy humility, of the real fear of God, of generous courage. Let no earthly bond prevent us from honoring our vocation. No cowardly considerations disturb the claims of justice, no meanness confine the immensity of charity within the narrow bounds of petty selfishness. Let everything in us be on a grand scale; the search for truth and the devotion to it, and readiness for self-sacrifice, even to the cross and death; and may everything finally be according to the last prayer of the Son to his heavenly Father, and according to Your Spirit, O Holy Spirit of love, which the Father and the Son desired to be poured out over the Church and its institutions, over the souls of men and over nations. Amen. Amen. Alleluia, Alleluia!"

St. Pope John XXIII - *The Journal of a Soul*

In God's Presence Consider ...

Am I open for the Holy Spirit to perfect the work Jesus has begun in me? Do I seek the growth of a profound interior life apart from the Holy Spirit? Do I allow the bonds of earthly life to prevent me from following Christ and coming to full spiritual maturity?

Closing Prayer

O Holy Spirit the Great Paraclete, perfect in me the work begun by Jesus. Enable me to continue to pray fervently in the name of the whole world. Hasten in me the growth of a profound interior life, the seeking and acquiring of truth, and to be the means of Your pouring out Your love over the souls of all mankind. St. Pope John XXIII, pray for me.

Few Know How to Listen **Day 168**

An attitude of gratitude helps us to be more sensitive to the presence and workings of God. Servant of God Lubich encourages the Holy Spirit to look at our lack of finesse and make us receptive to His graces preparing us for our life ending and dissolving itself into the next.

"O Holy Spirit, we should be thankful to you so many times, and yet we thank you so rarely. Though we are consoled to know that you are one with Jesus and the Father, this does not justify us. We want to be near you….

"Greatest consoler, sweet guest of our soul, you refresh our lives. You are Light, Joy, Beauty. You attract us, inflame our hearts, and inspire our thoughts. You help us to live lives committed to holiness. You accomplish in us what many sermons would not have taught. You sanctify us.

"Holy Spirit, you are so gentle and at the same time strong and overwhelming. You blow like a light breeze which few know how to listen to. Look at our lack of finesse and make us receptive to your graces."

SOG Chiara Lubich - *From Heaven on Earth*

In God's Presence Consider …

Do I rarely thank the Holy Spirit for His presence, gifts, and the fruits in my life? Am I committed to living a life of holiness and the Holy Spirit's work of sanctifying? Do I know how to listen to the light breeze of the Spirit's presence and be receptive to His graces?

Closing Prayer

Holy Spirit, I ask for the grace that no day may pass in which I don't invoke You and thank You, adore You and love You, and listen to Your voice. Wrap me in the great light of Your love, especially in my darkest hour, when the vision of this life will come to a close and dissolve itself into the next.

Prayer of Servant of God Chiara Lubich

Prayers can give us insight into who the Holy Spirit is, what He has done, is doing, and what He seeks to do in our hearts.

"Come, Holy Spirit, replace the tension within us with a holy relaxation. Replace the turbulence with us with a sacred calm. Replace the anxiety within us with a quiet confidence. Replace the fear within us with a strong faith. Replace the bitterness within us with the sweetness of grace. Replace the darkness within us with a gentle light. Replace the coldness within us with a loving warmth. Replace the night with us with your light. Straighten our crookedness. Fill our emptiness. Dull the edge of our pride. Sharpen the edge of our humility. Light the fires of our love. Quench the flames of our lust. Let us see ourselves as You see us. That we may see You as You have promised, and be fortunate according to Your word: 'Blessed are the pure of heart, for they shall see God.'(Mt. 5:8)"

Association of Marian Helpers - Stockbridge, MA

In God's Presence Consider ...

Do I ever pray to the Holy Spirit this way asking Him to replace those things that are not of God? Do I ever ask the Holy Spirit to show me myself in the light of how He sees me?

Closing Prayer

Come, Holy Spirit, and purify my love that I may see God in the circumstances of my life and be joined to You forever.

"He asked his disciples, 'Who do people say that I am?' And they said, 'Some say John the Baptist, others say Elijah, and others Jeremiah or one of the prophets.' 'But who do you say that I am?' Simon Peter replied, 'You are the Christ, the Son of the living God.' And Jesus answered him, 'Blessed are you, Simon Bar-Jona! For flesh and blood has not revealed this to you, but my Father who is in heaven." Mt. 16:13–17

"Holiness is like salt; its usefulness to others must begin with self. As only the wise man can impart wisdom to others, so only the saintly can communicate sanctity. A man can bring forth to others only those treasures which he already has in his own heart.

"They who have not the Spirit call him 'a great man,' 'a teacher,' 'a master'; but to see Him as the Lord of heaven and earth, as the Son of the Living God, comes only through the Holy Spirit."

Ven. Fulton Sheen - *The Quotable Fulton Sheen*

In God's Presence Consider …

Who is Jesus to me? How can I salt the earth if I have lost my saltiness? What treasures from my heart do I share with others? How can I know Him as Son of God if I don't have a relationship with the Holy Spirit?

Closing Prayer

Mark me dear Lord, with the sign of your true disciples and animate me in all things with your Spirit.

The Holy Spirit Father's Novena to the Holy Spirit

Complete union with God is sanctity and it requires a perfect orientation towards Him. This perfect orientation exceeds our finite powers. Thus the need of the Holy Spirit.

"Although our soul is super naturalized by sanctifying grace, our powers strengthened by the infused virtues, and our actions preceded and accompanied by actual grace, still the manner of our acting always remains human, and is therefore incapable of uniting us perfectly with God, of bringing us to sanctity. In fact, our intellects, although invested with the virtue of faith, are always inadequate in regard to infinite Being, and are always incapable of knowing God as He really is.... The inadequacy of our knowledge of God extends equally to our ideas of sanctity ... complete union with God, which is sanctity, requires a perfect orientation toward Him ... we have seen that this perfect orientation exceeds our powers, precisely because our knowledge of God and of the way which leads to Him is far too imperfect.... God wants our sanctification, has provided us with the means of attaining it: He has given us the Holy Spirit."

Fr. Gabriel of St. Mary Magdalen, O.C.D. - *Divine Intimacy*

In God's Presence Consider ...

God desires my holiness. Do I write this off as impossible or non-attainable in this life? Do I anticipate, look toward, and seek the Holy Spirit's help in being united perfectly with God?

Closing Prayer

Holy Spirit, I am incapable of knowing who God really is, for my knowledge of God is so finite and inadequate. I continually fall short. Come, Holy Spirit, pour forth Your brilliance upon my intellect, dissipate the darkness which covers me and direct my soul in the way of sanctity.

He will teach you all things, and bring to your remembrance all that I have said to you. Jn. 14:26

"In what concerns sanctity, we are always like school children, apprentices who, having only a rudimentary knowledge of the art they are learning, are always in need of direction and suggestions from their teacher. Our Teacher in sanctity is none other than the Holy Spirit…. He teaches us what we must do in order to love God with all our strength; He teaches us all that we do not know, whether about God, or about the spiritual life; and to perfect His teaching, He guides us in the accomplishment of it. Actually, by directly influencing our wills, He strengthens them, attracts them, impels them forcefully to God, orientating them perfectly toward Him. In this way, the Holy Spirit 'helpeth our infirmity' (Rom. 8:26), which being constitutional—inherent in our human nature—causes us to be continually in need of Him. In truth, He never leaves us: our whole spiritual life is enveloped in His action…. That is why the whole work of our sanctification may be reduced to a question of docility to the divine Paraclete. The promptings of the Holy Spirit can come to us in the words of Sacred Scripture, preaching, the teachings of the Church, the various circumstances of life, good thoughts and holy inspirations. Let us cooperate with them at once, proving our good will by our ready acceptance of and obedience to them."

Fr. Gabriel of St. Mary Magdalen, O.C.D. - *Divine Intimacy*

In God's Presence Consider …

How docile am I to the Holy Spirit? Are there areas in my life that I just as soon the Holy Spirit did not have access to? Do I cooperate with the Holy Spirit, ready to accept and obey His actions in me? Why might I be hesitating to let the Holy Spirit envelope me completely?

Closing Prayer

Breathe in me, O Holy Spirit, that my thoughts may all be holy. Act in me O Holy Spirit, that my work, too, may be holy. Draw my heart O Holy Spirit, that I love but what is holy.

Prayer of St. Augustine of Canterbury

Not a Passing Visitor **Day 173**

St. Paul tells us that we are temples of God and speaks of the Holy Spirit dwelling in us, converting our bodies into those temples and dwelling places of God. His work is not transitory but permanent and intimate. He dwells in us as our soul's eternal Guest.

"Without this dwelling of the Holy Spirit in us we cannot 'become Christ.' 'If anyone does not have the Spirit of Christ, he does not belong to Christ' (Rom. 8:9). Grace and charity, which are the life of our souls, have relationship with the Spirit who dwells in us, because 'the charity of God is poured forth in our hearts by the Holy Spirit, who has been given to us' (Rom. 5:5).... And the Holy Spirit does not come to us in a transitory manner; infinite Love is not a passing visitor who pays us a call and then goes away. He establishes in us his permanent dwelling and lives in intimate union with our souls as their eternal Guest."

SOG Archbishop Louis M. Martinez - *The Sanctifier*

In God's Presence Consider ...

In order to have a relationship with Jesus, I must have the Holy Spirit dwelling within me. How intimate am I with the Holy Spirit? Do I treat Him as an eternal Guest? Have I ever thought that Infinite Love is not a passing visitor but permanent? Does Love dwell in me?

Closing Prayer

Jesus, my Lord and my God, pour out Your grace and charity into my soul, that I may receive Your Holy Spirit as a delightful and eternal Guest, and may You ever dwell in intimate union with me.

We often speak of the Holy Spirit being out there and we call Him down upon us. Fr. O'Sullivan uses the Scripture to remind us that the Holy Spirit isn't out there somewhere around us, but dwells in us as God's temple.

"... the Holy Ghost is in our very souls. St. Paul says, 'Do you not know that you are God's temple and that God's Spirit dwells in you?' (1 Cor. 3:16) And again: 'Do you not know that your body is a temple of the Holy Spirit within you, which you have from God.' (1 Cor. 6:19)

"And St. John: 'And I will ask the Father, and he will give you another Counselor, to be with you forever, even the Spirit of truth, whom the world cannot receive, because it neither sees him nor knows him; you know him, for he dwells with you, and will be in you.' (Jn. 14:16–17)"

Fr. Paul O' Sullivan, O.P. - *The Holy Ghost Our Greatest Friend*

In God's Presence Consider ...

These passages make it very clear that the Holy Spirit dwells in a soul that is in a state of grace. Do I ever think of my body as a temple that houses the Holy Spirit? The Holy Spirit is not merely with us but in us. Do I think of His indwelling in me?

Closing Prayer

Father, Jesus Your Son has asked You to send me the Counselor to be with me forever. Please help me to prepare my heart and soul for Him, that He may dwell in me as Your Temple.

Promoter of Sanctification **Day 175**

Just as the Holy Spirit dwelt in the most holy soul of Christ in order to bring it to God, so He abides in our souls for the same purpose.

"In Jesus, He (the Holy Spirit) found a completely docile will, one that He could control perfectly, whereas in us He often meets resistance, the fruit of human weakness; therefore, He desists from the work of our sanctification because He will not do violence to our liberty. He, the Spirit of love, waits for us to cooperate lovingly in His work, yielding our soul to His sanctifying action freely and ardently. In order to become saints, we must concur in the work of the Holy Spirit; but since effective concurrence is impossible without an understanding of the promoter's actions, it is necessary for us to learn how the divine Paraclete, the promoter of our sanctification, works in us.

"We must realize that the Holy Spirit is ever active in our souls, from the earliest stages of the spiritual life and even from its very beginning, although at that time in a more hidden and imperceptible way … it consisted especially in the preparing and encouraging of our first attempts to acquire perfection. By giving us grace, without which we could have done nothing to attain sanctity, the Holy Spirit inaugurated His work in us: He elevated us to a supernatural state. Grace comes from the Father, merited by the Son, and diffused in our souls by the Holy Spirit. But it is to the latter, to the Spirit of love, that the work of our sanctification is attributed in a very special manner…. Therefore, it is the Holy Spirit who has prepared and disposed our souls for the supernatural life by pouring forth grace in us."

Fr. Gabriel of St. Mary Magdalen, O.C.D. - *Divine Intimacy*

In God's Presence Consider …

Do I recognize the movement and work of the Holy Spirit in my soul? Do I avail myself to His loving presence? How can I dispose myself more to the Holy Spirit's work in me?

Closing Prayer

Come, Holy Spirit, teach me to recognize Your work within me and to cooperate with it.

Because the Holy Spirit is one with the Father and Son, He also is not subject to change and is always perfect and good. It is the Holy Spirit who brings about change in created things.

"The Holy Spirit, since He sanctifies creatures, is neither a creature nor subject to change. He is always good, since He is given by the Father and the Son; neither is He to be numbered among such things as are said to fail. He must be acknowledged as the source of goodness. The Spirit of God's mouth, the amender of evils, and Himself good. Lastly, as He is said in Scripture to be good, and is joined to the Father and the Son in baptism, He cannot possibly be denied to be good.

"The Holy Spirit is not, then, of the substance of things corporeal, for He sheds incorporeal grace on corporeal things; nor, again, is He of the substance of invisible creatures, for they receive His sanctification, and through Him are superior to the other works of the universe. Whether you speak of Angels, or Dominions, or Powers, every creature waits for the grace of the Holy Spirit. For as we are children through the Spirit, because God sent the Spirit of His Son into our hearts crying, Abba, Father; so that you are now not a servant but a son; Galatians 4:6–7 in like manner, also, every creature itself shall be changed by the revelation of the grace of the Spirit, and shall be delivered from the bondage of corruption into the liberty of the glory of the children of God.

St. Ambrose - *Book 1 On the Holy Spirit*

In God's Presence Consider …

Does my life reflect the goodness of the Holy Spirit? Do I see myself as a creature before God waiting for the grace of the Holy Spirit to deliver me from the bondage of corruption in order to live in the glory of being a child of God? Have I ever considered that even the angels are in need of the grace of the Holy Spirit?

Closing Prayer

Heavenly King, Consoler Spirit, Spirit of Truth, present everywhere and filling all things, treasure of all good and source of all life, come dwell in us, cleanse and save us, you who are All-Good.

Byzantine Liturgy, Pentecost Vespers, Troparion

Sharing in God's Infinity **Day 177**

To share in God's abundant life is as simple as being open and disposed to receive the Holy Spirit as He comes to us.

"The Holy Spirit is rightly called the Counselor. When the touches of the Spirit, enlightening us and impelling us to act, are well received, they pour into our hearts not just light and strength but solace and peace, that often fills us with consolations. This happens even when their object is something unimportant; because these touches proceed from the Holy Spirit they share in God's power to console and fulfill us…. Just a minute amount of the unction of the Holy Spirit can fill our hearts with more contentment than all the riches of the earth, because it shares in God's infinity."

Fr. Jacques Philippe - *In the School of the Holy Spirit*

In God's Presence Consider …

Am I disposed to receive the touches of the Holy Spirit? How can I foster these touches of the Holy Spirit in my spiritual life? Have I ever experienced the contentment of sharing in God's life?

Closing Prayer

Come, Holy Spirit, the Great Counselor, touch me with Your solace and peace, that I may be well received to work with and receive You. Fill me with a contentment that only You can bring about within me.

All four saints attest that the Church is holy in virtue of the Sanctifying Spirit.

"There is no holiness without the Holy Spirit."

St. Basil - *On the Holy Spirit, XVI, 38*

"The union of God with men is accomplished by the work of the Holy Spirit."

St. John Damascene -
Sermon for the Feast of the Nativity of the Theotokos, 3

"As the Spirit sanctified the humanity of Christ, so he continues to sanctify his mystical body, the Church.... Because the Spirit is holy by nature, sanctification belongs to him."

St. Cyril of Alexandria - *Commentary on the Gospel of John, XI, 11*

"The Church of Christ is holy. The temple of God is holy and this temple is you.... Temple and house alludes to the idea of habitation.

St. Thomas Aquinas, O.P. - *Commentary on "I Believe in God", Art. IX*

In God's Presence Consider ...

Do I avail myself to the working of the Holy Spirit that unites me to God and makes me holy? Do I see myself as a temple of God where holiness resides? Is holiness even a part of my desires or life?

Closing Prayer

Spirit of the Living God, fall afresh on me. Melt me, mold me, sanctify me, and use me. For You alone are the Holy One, the Sanctifier, the Spirit of communion. Sts. Basil, John Damascene, Cyril of Alexandria and Thomas Aquinas, pray for me.

Romans 8:29 tells us that we are to be made conformable to the image of Jesus. The Church teaches us that we shall be saints according to the degree we resemble Christ. It is the Holy Spirit's work to bring about this conformity.

"The Holy Spirit is given to us to sanctify us, but how will He accomplish His mission? The Encyclical Mystici Corporis, tells us that the divine Paraclete 'is communicated to the Church … so that she and each of her members may become more and more like to our Savior.' The Holy Spirit comes into our souls to make us conformable, and even assimilated to Christ: this is the immediate end of His action in us, this is the way by which He will lead us to sanctity…. The Holy Spirit has been given to us that He may imprint in us the traits of this divine resemblance (to Christ), and make us daily more and more like our Savior.

"Of ourselves, we are unable to reach such perfect conformity with Christ, but the divine Spirit is in us to bring it about…. In order to make us like Him, the Holy Spirit initially communicates to us Christ's sanctity by pouring grace into us; this grace penetrates our being, our activity, and our life in such a way that it makes of each one of us an another Christ."

Fr. Gabriel of St. Mary Magdalen, O.C.D. - *Divine Intimacy*

In God's Presence Consider …

Do I take time periodically to examine my life looking for the traits of my own divine resemblance to Christ? Am I responding positively to the graces the Holy Spirit is pouring out upon me to make me another Christ? Am I growing in sanctity?

Closing Prayer

O Holy Spirit, sanctify me and make me conformable to Jesus. Make me another Christ.

"Without Me you can do nothing." (Jn. 15:5) All glorification of the Father is done through Jesus. We participate in this marvelous work when we allow the Holy Spirit to transform us into Jesus.

"To fully glorify the Father, it is necessary to be transformed into Jesus because the glorification of the Father is his work and in order to do the work of Jesus it is necessary to be Jesus.

"The end of the sanctification of souls is the glory of the Father; the essence of that marvelous work is transformation into Jesus.... To be transformed into Jesus is to bear his image, uncreated Wisdom, graven in our souls with strokes of divine light....Through sanctifying grace itself, which is a participation in the divine nature, we resemble God and possess him, but the further, special assimilation with each one of the divine Persons and individual possession of them comes from supernatural gifts that have sanctifying grace as their origin.... The gifts of love make us resemble the Holy Spirit, who is infinite Love, and by opening the way to his mission, put us in the happiest possession of him."

SOG Archbishop Louis M. Martinez - *The Sanctifier*

In God's Presence Consider ...

Am I giving God glory by allowing myself to be transformed into Jesus by the Holy Spirit? Do I bear the image of Jesus graven on my soul? Do I participate and make use of sanctifying grace? Am I open to the mission of the Holy Spirit and allowing myself to be possessed by Him?

Closing Prayer

Father, glorify Your Name through me. Jesus, continue the work of transforming me into Your image through sanctifying grace. Holy Spirit, assimilate me into each of the Divine Persons through Your gifts of love. Open me, to allow You to complete Your mission through me. Please continue the work in me that You have begun.

Taking Us by the Hand **Day 181**

The Holy Spirit, who searches the deep things of God (1 Cor. 2:10) has a perfect knowledge of the divine nature and mysteries.

"He who penetrates all things and knows perfectly the delicacy and secrets of the highest virtue, as well as the needs and deficiencies of our souls, comes to take us by the hand and lead us to sanctity. As long as we advance by our own initiative, our orientation toward God will always be imperfect and incomplete, because we shall be acting in a human manner, but when the divine Spirit intervenes, He operates as God, in a divine manner: that is why He draws us and directs us completely toward Himself. In human actions, thought precedes the determination of the will, and since our capacity for thought is so limited, our actions are, of necessity, limited too. This is especially true in regards to divine things. But when the Holy Spirit intervenes, He acts directly on the will by drawing it to Himself. He inflames our heart and enlightens our mind. This is the genesis of that 'sense of God' which is impossible for us to express, but which makes us know God and taste Him; it directs us toward Him, more than any reasoning on our part could ever do … we feel that any sacrifice, even the greatest, is but a trifle when made for such a God. This is how the Holy Spirit guides us on the road to sanctity."

Fr. Gabriel of St. Mary Magdalen, O.C.D. - *Divine Intimacy*

In God's Presence Consider …

Determination, will power, and action on our part is limited and not enough. We need the intervention of the Holy Spirit. Am I advancing towards God in a human manner or a divine manner? Do I know and taste God? Am I willing to sacrifice anything in order to be drawn toward and have God more completely in my life?

Closing Prayer

Come, Holy Spirit, and penetrate me, leaving nothing inside of me untouched. Draw me to Yourself. Inflame my heart and enlighten my mind that I may know, love, and see God and become a saint.

Time Cannot Measure **Day 182**

The Holy Spirit is a mystery that is timeless and inexhaustible. We can add nothing to His fullness.

"We are compelled to direct our thoughts on high, and to think of an intelligent being, boundless in power, of unlimited greatness, generous in goodness, whom time cannot measure.

"All things thirsting for holiness turn to Him, everything living in virtue never turns away from Him. He waters them with His life-giving breath and helps them reach their proper fulfillment.

"He perfects all other things, and Himself lacks nothing; He gives life to all things and is never depleted.

"He does not increase by additions, but is always complete, self-established and present everywhere.

"He is the source of sanctity, spiritual light, who gives illumination to everyone using His powers to search for truth—and the illumination He gives us is Himself.

"His nature is unapproachable; only through His goodness are we able to draw near it. He fills all things with His power, but only those who are worthy may share it.

"He distributes His energy in proportion to the faith of the recipient, not confirming it to be a single share. He is simple in being; His powers are manifold; they are wholly present everywhere and in everything.

"He is distributed but does not change. He is shared, yet remains whole."

St. Basil - *Treatise on the Holy Spirit*

In God's Presence Consider …

In my meditations, do I ponder the boundlessness and unlimited greatness of the Holy Spirit? Do I ever think of the Holy Spirit as the enlightenment and illumination I seek?

Closing Prayer

Holy Spirit, You are timeless. Increase and perfect my faith that I may fully hold the love of the Father, the Son, and You in my heart. St. Basil, pray for me.

The action of the Holy Spirit in forming the image of Jesus into us is tied to the very creation of humanity, and after the fall, restores us to the original state. He helps us to endure.

"We were created in the divine image. Sanctification produced this image in us, that is, our participation in Christ in the Spirit. This image was deformed when human nature fell into perversion. We return to our original state thanks to the Holy Spirit, who once again fuses us to the image of him who created us or, as might be better said, to the Son from whom everything comes to us through the Father."

Cyril of Alexandria - *On the Trinity, VI*

"Above all the graces and gifts of the Holy Spirit, the one that Christ gives to his friends, is to conquer oneself and for love of Christ voluntarily to endure pain, injury, disgrace, and discomfort.

St. Francis of Assisi- *The Little Flower*

In God's Presence Consider …

It is through the gift of the Holy Spirit that I have been called to a friendship with God, which in some way allows me a participation in the very transcendence of the depths of God and restores me to my original state prior to the fall of my sin. Do I thank the Holy Spirit for such a work in me? Do I see opportunities to suffer as great graces and gifts of the Holy Spirit? How can I make my own self-martyrdom meritorious and pleasing to God?

Closing Prayer

Lord, grant to us the gifts of the Holy Spirit, and render us worthy to approach the holy of holies with a pure heart and with irreproachable consciences.

Prayer of Anaphora of the Twelve Apostles

The Holy Spirit urges and invites us to be conformed to Christ Crucified, and to take up our cross and to follow Jesus. He urges us to embrace our daily crosses not merely to endure them.

"We must be thoroughly convinced that if the Holy Spirit works in our souls to assimilate us to Christ, He can do so only by opening to us the way of the Cross. Jesus is Jesus Crucified; therefore, there can be no conformity to Him except by the Cross, and we shall never enter into the depths of the spiritual life except by entering into the mystery of the Cross … conformity to Jesus Crucified has more value and importance than all mystical graces … the acts of mortification and self-denial which we make are wholly insufficient to strip us of the old man and clothe us with Christ, with Christ Crucified. That is why the Holy Spirit, after setting us on the road of the Cross by His inspirations takes it upon Himself to complete our purification. He does this by sending us trials, both exterior and interior … suffering is necessary for our purification and our participation in the redemptive work of Jesus…. It is evident then, that in order to sanctify us the Holy Spirit cannot lead us by any way other than that of the Cross…. It is for us (to) willingly accept everything hard and painful that comes to us in our daily life … by the aid of the Holy Spirit who urges us to embrace these daily crosses, not merely endure them—to accept them and offer them willingly, saying with all our heart: 'Yes, I want this, even though it seems to crush me!' "

Fr. Gabriel of St. Mary Magdalen, O.C.D. - *Divine Intimacy*

In God's Presence Consider …

We can never enter into the depths of the spiritual life except by conformity to Jesus and the mystery of the Cross. Do I shrug away from and try to avoid suffering and sacrifices? Is mortification and self-denial something I do with the Holy Spirit's help? Is the Cross of Jesus a part of my spiritual life and do I regularly embrace the Cross?

Closing Prayer

Come, Holy Spirit, and teach me the value of suffering as a means of my sanctification and conformity to Christ. Help me to embrace and endure my crosses that they may be joined to Jesus' Cross of victory.

St. Hannibal di Francia was a priest and spiritual director for Venerable Luisa Piccarreta known as "The Little Daughter of the Divine Will." His comments on Luisa's work on Jesus' Passion give us insight to the work of the Holy Spirit and how to console Jesus for souls who reject Him.

"In this hour, abandoned by his eternal Father, Jesus Christ suffered such a burning fire of love that He was able to destroy all conceivable and imaginable sins, and enflame with his love all souls and the souls of those who (squander this love by) choosing to remain eternally obstinate in their evil and choosing to go to hell. Let us enter into Jesus and, after we have penetrated his whole interior—his most intimate recesses, his heartbeats of fire, his intelligence which was set ablaze—let us take this love and clothe ourselves on the inside and out with the fire of love with which Jesus burned. Then, emerging from him and pouring ourselves into his Will, we will there find all souls. Let us give Jesus' love to each one of these souls and, touching their hearts and minds with this love, transform them completely into love..... If we do this, we will offer Jesus true consolation, as he continually utters: 'I burn with love, and yet there is no one to receive My love. Oh please, comfort Me by accepting my love and, in exchange, grant me your love.'

St. Hannibal di Francia - *Divine Will Prayer Book*

In God's Presence Consider ...

Do I let myself be transformed into the image of Jesus by God's Fire of Love? Do I accept everything that happens to me that is not sinful as God's divine crafting? Do I see everything in human terms and as meaningless, thereby rejecting God's divine crafting? Do I seek to console the Heart of Jesus by accepting His Love?

Closing Prayer

O Jesus my love and my all, may Your Burning Fire of Love consume me and vanquish everything that opposes You. Let my love dispel all the sadness that others who reject Your Love bring to Your Heart. Help me to clothe myself with Your Fire and draw every soul into Your most Sacred Heart. St. Hannibal di Francia and Venerable Luisa Piccarreta, pray for me.

The inhabitation of the Holy Spirit within us brings about a renewed dignity as children of God and helps us to enter into a relationship with Him that is beyond mere gift.

"Who can be personally present at once with every Christian, but God Himself? Who but He, not merely ruling in the midst of the Church invisibly, as Michael might keep watch over Israel, or another Angel might be the 'Prince of Persia,' but really taking up His abode as one and the same in many separate hearts, so as to fulfill our Lord's words, that it was expedient that He should depart; Christ's bodily presence, which was limited to place, being exchanged for the manifold spiritual indwelling of the Comforter within us? This consideration suggests both the dignity of our Sanctifier, and the infinite preciousness of His Office towards us.

"The Holy Ghost, I have said, dwells in body and soul, as in a temple. Evil spirits indeed have power to possess sinners, but His indwelling is far more perfect, for He is all-knowing and omnipresent, He is able to search into all our thoughts, and penetrate into every motive of the heart. Therefore, He pervades us as light pervades a building, or as a sweet perfume in the folds of some honorable robe; so that, in Scripture language, we are said to be in Him, and He in us. It is plain that such an inhabitation brings the Christian into a state altogether new and marvelous, far above the possession of mere gifts, exalts him inconceivably in the scale of beings, and gives him a place and an office which he had not before."

St. John Henry Newman - *Sermon 19*

In God's Presence Consider ...

Jesus is fully human and divine. Have I ever pondered Jesus' bodily limitations before His resurrection? Do I see the Holy Spirit as omnipresent knowing all my thoughts and penetrating my every motive? Does the Holy Spirit dwell in me?

Closing Prayer

O Jesus, You send the Holy Spirit as my Comforter and Sanctifier. May He pervade me with His light and abide in me in a renewed way. Help me to allow Him to inhabit me freely and marvelously reign in the temple of my heart. St. John Henry Newman, pray for me.

St. Pope John Paul II often talked about the Holy Spirit's role in divinizing us. Here St. Athanasius points out that without the Holy Spirit dwelling and working in us we are strangers and far from God. With the Holy Spirit, we are participators and are divinized.

"Without the Spirit we are strangers and far from God. Instead, if we participate in the Spirit, we are united with Divinity.

"Through the Spirit we are all called participators of God.... We enter to form part of divine nature through participation in the Spirit.... This is why the Spirit makes divine all those in which he is present."

St. Athanasius - *Letter to Serapion, I, 23–24*

In God's Presence Consider ...

Is God a stranger in my life? Am I a participator of God? Do I allow the Holy Spirit to make me divine?

Closing Prayer

Father, I do not want to be a stranger to You. Send me Your Holy Spirit that I may be united to You and share in Your divine nature. St. Athanasius, pray for me.

Holiness is living in intimate, loving communion with God. It is the perfection of love. St. Joseph shows how we can grow in holiness in this earthly life.

"… With the exception of Our Lady's life, the Holy Spirit was more active in the life of St. Joseph than in any other saint. The earthly father of Jesus never did anything without seeking the direction of the Holy Spirit. St. Joseph's docility to the Holy Spirit made it possible for him to communicate with God even while he slept!

"What is holiness, anyway? Is it some unattainable spiritual summit you can never hope to reach? No, it is not. Holiness is living in intimate, loving communion with God. More specifically, holiness is observing the two great commandments of love of God and neighbor, avoiding sin, leading a life of virtue, and abiding in sanctifying grace. None of this is possible without the Holy Spirit in your life.

"… St. Joseph would tell you that if you want to be filled with the Holy Spirit there is one absolutely necessary thing: prayer. Without prayer, you will never be able to have intimacy with God. Without prayer, you will not be able to follow the direction of the Holy Spirit.

"After Jesus and Mary, St. Joseph is the holiest, most prayerful, and most virtuous person who has ever lived. He avoided anything and everything that displeased the Holy Spirit. How did he do it? Prayer."

Fr. Donald Calloway, MIC - *Consecration to St. Joseph*

In God's Presence Consider …

Have I ever thought of holiness as the perfection of love and therefore something I can work on in this life and attain? Do I avoid everything and anything that displeases the Holy Spirit? Am I a person of deep prayer?

Closing Prayer

St. Joseph, I seek your powerful intercession and ask that through your Son, Jesus, He would pour extraordinary graces into my heart, mind, and soul, so that I may become a saint! Holy Spirit, make me into another St. Joseph and fill me with graces similar to those You gave him. Help me to love God and neighbor.

A Secret of Sanctity **Day 189**

Withdrawing to our inner sanctuary and praying to the Holy Spirit can aid us in submitting to His work within us.

"I am going to reveal to you a secret of sanctity and happiness. If every day during five minutes, you will keep your imagination quiet, shut your eyes to all the things of sense, and close your ears to all the sounds of earth, so as to be able to withdraw into the sanctuary of your baptized soul, which is the temple of the Holy Spirit, speaking there to that Holy Spirit saying: O Holy Spirit, soul of my soul, I adore You. Enlighten guide, strengthen, and console me. Tell me what I ought to do and command me to do it. I promise to be submissive in everything that You permit to happen to me, only show me what is Your will.

"If you do this, your life will pass happily and serenely. Consolation will abound even in the midst of troubles. Grace will be given in proportion to the trial as well as strength to bear it, bringing you to the gates of Paradise full of merit.

"This submission to the Holy Spirit is the Secret of Sanctity"

Cardinal Désiré-Joseph Mercier

In God's Presence Consider …

Do I see my soul as a sanctuary, a temple of the Holy Spirit? Do I seek to know the will of the Holy Spirit in my life? Have I ever experienced consolation in the midst of troubles? Do I accredit this consolation to the Holy Spirit?

Closing Prayer

O Holy Spirit, soul of my soul, I adore You. Enlighten, guide, strengthen, and console me. Tell me what I ought to do and command me to do it. I promise to be submissive in everything that You permit to happen to me, only show me what is Your will.

Prayer of Cardinal Désiré-Joseph Mercier.

The whole purpose and mission of the Holy Spirit is to sanctify our hearts making us Temples for God to dwell. He brings us into intimacy with God.

"The mission of the Holy Spirit can be summed up in this way: he brings to the faithful the life of God and of Christ. He is the sanctifying Spirit whose personal activity is parallel to that of the Father and Son, but different from theirs. His role and his work are so well defined that we feel at once that it is no longer a question merely of a divine activity as in the Old Testament; he is a Person, a being who can be addressed, to whom divine qualities are ascribed. Christians are purified, sanctified, justified, 'in the name of the Lord Jesus, by the Spirit of the God we serve' (1 Cor. 6:11). The Trinitarian form of this verse puts the Spirit on the same level as the Lord Jesus (Titus 3:6).

"The body of a Christian has its own high dignity: it is the Temple of the Holy Spirit (1 Cor. 6:19). For this reason alone, St. Paul begs the Corinthians no longer to indulge in debauchery, for it is a sin against the body whose guest is the Holy Spirit.... We are given the assurance that the Kingdom of God will be established by rightness of heart (that is, by God's life).

Bernard Piault - *What is the Trinity?*

In God's Presence Consider ...

How do I experience the Holy Spirit's mission in me? Do I make decisions and live my life centered on the Holy Spirit dwelling in me as a guest? Does my life reflect the presence of the Blessed Trinity living in me?

Closing Prayer

Holy Spirit, Life of God, come and be my guest. Come with Your sanctifying power and pour into my heart the Love of God that I may be a dwelling place, a Temple fit for God the Almighty.

Holy Spirit on Mission in the Church

Sent on a Mission **Day 191**

The Catechism tells us the Holy Spirit has a mission. He is sent to continually sanctify the Church, giving various gifts to her in order to help her in proclaiming and establishing the Kingdom of God here on earth.

"When the work which the Father gave the Son to do on earth was accomplished, the Holy Spirit was sent on the day of Pentecost in order that he might continually sanctify the Church. As the convocation of all men for salvation, the Church in her very nature is missionary, sent by Christ to all the nations to make disciples of them.

"So that she can fulfill her mission, the Holy Spirit bestows upon the Church varied hierarchic and charismatic gifts, and in this way directs her. Henceforward the Church, receives the mission of proclaiming and establishing among all peoples the Kingdom of God, and she is on earth the seed and the beginning of that kingdom."

CCC #767–768

In God's Presence Consider …

Do I seek the Holy Spirit's gifts in order to help the Church fulfill her mission? Do I seek the gifts of the Holy Spirit in order to help the Church fulfill her mission of making disciples? How might the Holy Spirit be sending me to proclaim and establish God's Kingdom?

Closing Prayer

Come, Holy Spirit, enlighten my heart, to see the things which are of God; Come, Holy Spirit, into my mind, that I may know the things of God; Come, Holy Spirit, into my soul, that I belong only to God. Sanctify all that I think, say and do, that all will be for the glory of God. Amen.

Chaplet of Virtues prayer from 'In the End My Immaculate Heart Will Triumph.'

Quietly Opens Hearts to Receive **Day 192**

God's love for us is undeserved and unfathomable. We are so precious to Him that He sends His Son and the Holy Spirit to help us receive, hope in, and live the message of God's great love for you and me.

"For God, you have worth; you are not insignificant. You are important to him, for you are the work of his hands. That is why he is concerned about you and looks to you with affection. He does not keep track of your failings and he always helps you learn something even from your mistakes, because he loves you. Try to keep still for a moment and let yourself feel his love. Try to silence all the noise within, and rest for a second in his loving embrace. It is the love of the Lord: a daily, discreet, and respectful love; a love that is free and freeing, a love that heals and raises up. The love of the Lord has to do more with raising up than knocking down, with reconciling than forbidding, with offering new changes than condemning, with the future than the past. Beloved of the Lord, how valuable must you be if you were redeemed by the precious blood of Christ! You are priceless!

"The Holy Spirit is the one who quietly opens hearts to receive that message. He keeps alive our hope of salvation. When you receive the Spirit, he draws you ever more deeply into the heart of Christ, so that you can grow in his love, his life, and his power. Ask the Holy Spirit each day to help you experience anew the great message."

Pope Francis - *Christus Vivit*

In God's Presence Consider …

We often times don't feel worthy of the love God wants to give us. How can the Holy Spirit help me to receive God's love? Do I ask the Holy Spirit to daily be a part of my prayer life? Do I ask for His help to experience anew God's great love for me?

Closing Prayer

Spirit of Christ, stir me; Spirit of Christ, move me; Spirit of Christ, fill me; Spirit of Christ, seal me. Consecrate in me Your heart and will O Heavenly Father. Create in me a fountain of virtues. Seal my soul as Your own, that Your reflection in me may be a light for all to see.

From: In the End My Immaculate Heart Will Triumph

The Holy Spirit is given to the Church to flourish and to sanctify her members thus equipping them to carry on Jesus' mission. We encounter this grace of empowerment and transforming love through the Church's sacraments.

"... This fullness of the Spirit was not to remain uniquely the Messiah's, but was to be communicated to the whole messianic people.... Thus the Church's mission is not an addition to that of Christ and the Holy Spirit, but is its sacrament: in her whole being and in all her members, the Church is sent to announce, bear witness, make present, and spread the mystery of the communion of the Holy Trinity.... The Spirit is the source and giver of all holiness ... it is he who has endowed the Church with holiness."

Cf CCC #1287, 738, 749

In God's Presence Consider ...

Do I keep the fullness of the Holy Spirit poured out upon me bottled up and for myself or do I allow Him to flourish? Do I fear sharing my faith with others? Do I fear living a life of holiness in the Holy Spirit?

Closing Prayer

Come Breath of the Living God. Move me in the paths of holiness; flourish within me, that with holy boldness I may witness to others the mighty works of God.

In the Church, the communion of men with God is to govern everything, especially the Church's structure and activities. All is ordered to the holiness of her members.

"To say that Jesus merited the Holy Spirit for His Church is equivalent to saying that He merited Him for us; to say that Jesus, together with the Father, has sent and continues to send His Spirit to the Church is equivalent to affirming that He has sent and continues to send Him to us. The Encyclical Mystici Corporis asserts that the Holy Spirit 'is communicated to the Church abundantly, so that she herself and each one of her members may become, day by day, more like our Redeemer.' Thus the Holy Spirit exercises His influence not only in the Body of the Church, but also in each soul in which He dwells as the 'sweet Guest.' He is in us: to take possession of our souls, to sanctify them, to form them in the likeness of Christ, and to urge us to continue His redemptive mission; He is that impulse of love which urges us to do God's will, guides us towards the glorification of the Most Holy Trinity, and brings us to God."

Fr. Gabriel of St. Mary Magdalen, O.C.D. - *Divine Intimacy*

In God's Presence Consider ...

The Holy Spirit was not merely sent on the day of Pentecost to accomplish God's work of salvation, but is continually poured out and communicated in the Church. Do I see the Church as the work of God giving me access to the graces of the Holy Spirit? Do I seek to provide a dwelling place in my soul for the Divine Sweet Guest of the Holy Spirit?

Closing Prayer

Come Sweet Guest of God. Invade my soul and take possession of me forming me into the image of Jesus and making me holy.

In every liturgical action the Holy Spirit is sent in order to bring us into communion with Christ. He is "the sap of the Father's vine," the "soul of the Church," the "principle of unity."

"We have seen that the Holy Spirit was in Christ's soul to direct Him in the accomplishment of His redemptive mission. Jesus could have carried out this mission alone, but He wished the Church to participate in it. Since the Church continues Christ's work, she needs the same impetus which guided His soul, she needs the Holy Spirit. Jesus merited His Spirit for us on the Cross; by His death, He atoned for all sin, the chief obstacle to the action of the Holy Spirit, and when He has ascended into heaven, He sent Him to the Apostles, who represent the whole Church. Now, seated in glory at the right hand of the Father, He intercedes continually for us, He is always sending the Holy Spirit to the Church, as He promised.

"The Holy Spirit operates in the Church now, just as He once did in the blessed soul of Christ, He gives her impulse, moves her, and drives her to accomplish God's will, thus enabling her to fulfill His mission, the continuation down through the ages of the redemptive work of Christ…. As the soul vivifies the body, the Holy Spirit vivifies the Church. He is the impulse of love who kindles in her zeal for the glory of God and the salvation of souls. He gives light and strength to her shepherds, fervor and energy to her apostles, courage and invincible faith to her martyrs."

Fr. Gabriel of St. Mary Magdalen, O.C.D. - *Divine Intimacy*

In God's Presence Consider …

Jesus merited His Spirit for us on the Cross. To reject the Holy Spirit or want nothing to do with Him for a variety of reasons is to reject Jesus' saving work. Do I refuse to accept the Holy Spirit? Do I allow the very soul of the Church to be my very soul? Do I seek to accomplish the will of God by allowing the Holy Spirit to work in my life?

Closing Prayer

Come, Holy Spirit, You who deign to dwell in me, help me to open my soul completely to Your action that You may vivify my soul with divine life.

"I will ask the Father, and he will give you another to befriend you, one who is to dwell continually with you forever. It is the truth-giving Spirit, for whom the world can find no room, because it cannot see him, cannot recognize him." Jn. 14:16–17 (The Ronald Knox version of the Bible)

"Jesus will pray to the Father, and at his request 'another' will be sent to dwell forever among the faithful, with them and in them.

"The Father will send the Holy Spirit for Jesus' sake. The purpose of this mission is revealed: to make Jesus' message clear, because until then it had been unintelligible to the Apostles (Jn. 14:26). This is very revealing: it is useless to try to find the whole message in the words of Jesus by themselves. The truth is all there, but only as the stream is in its source. This source must be tapped by the Church in which it becomes a great river, thanks to the Holy Spirit who was promised and sent for this purpose. Without him the words of Jesus would be a dead letter, without further development, unfruitful. With him, the group of the apostles, and undoubtedly also their successors throughout history – since the mission of the Spirit was not confined to the time of the Church's foundation—possess what we now call the gift of infallibility in interpreting the words of Jesus."

Bernard Piault - *What is the Trinity?*

In God's Presence Consider …

In the Knox version of Scripture, the Holy Spirit is "befriender," an eternal dweller, giver of truth. He has been given to me. Is He unintelligible to me? Without Him, the words of Jesus are dead, lack development, unfruitful. Do I see Him as the "truth—giving Spirit" who gives meaning and life to Jesus' words? Do I see the Spirit's mission in the gift of infallibility?

Closing Prayer

Father, send Your Spirit upon me anew that His mission and presence in me would become a great river of grace helping me to understand and apply Your Son's words in my life.

Redemption through Sending **Day 197**

In the Last Supper discourse, Jesus tells the disciples that He must depart from them in order for them to receive the Holy Spirit.

"Thus there is established a close link between the sending of the Son and the sending of the Holy Spirit. There is no sending of the Holy Spirit (after the original sin of Adam and Eve) without the Cross and the Resurrection. 'If I do not go away, the Counselor will not come to you (Jn. 16:7).' There is also established a close link between the mission of the Holy Spirit and that of the Son in the Redemption. The mission of the Holy Spirit draws from the Redemption.... The Redemption is totally carried out by the Son as the Anointed One, who came and acted in the power of the Holy Spirit, offering himself finally in sacrifice on the wood of the Cross. And this Redemption is, at the same time, constantly carried out in human hearts and minds—in the history of the world—by the Holy Spirit, who is the other Counselor."

St. Pope John Paul II - *Dominum et Vivicantem*

In God's Presence Consider ...

Do I see my redemption as a onetime event or as an ongoing work? Do I see the Cross of Jesus guarantee the sending of the Holy Spirit into my life? Do I allow the Holy Spirit to constantly carry out the work of redemption in my heart?

Closing Prayer

Jesus, please continue to send Your Holy Spirit to me, so that my heart and mind will be open to the work of Your Redeeming love. St. Pope John Paul II, pray for me.

St. Elizabeth of the Trinity speaks to how necessary suffering is in order that God's work be done in a soul. St. Pope John Paul II speaks of Jesus' suffering through His Passion and death as the means of creating a new humanity; a restoring of our image to God.

"We know that 'God anointed Jesus of Nazareth with the Holy Spirit and with power,' as Simon Peter said in the house of the Centurion Cornelius (c.f. Acts 10:38). We know of the Paschal Mystery of his 'departure,' from the Gospel of John. The words of the Letter to the Hebrews now explains to us how Christ 'offered himself without blemish to God,' and how he did this 'with an eternal Spirit.' In the sacrifice of the Son of Man, the Holy Spirit is present and active, just as he acted in Jesus' conception, in his coming into the world, in his hidden life, and in his public ministry. According to the Letter to the Hebrews, on the way to his 'departure' through Gethsemane and Golgotha, the same Christ Jesus in his own humanity opened himself totally to this action of the Spirit-Paraclete, who from suffering enables eternal salvific love to spring forth….

"The Son of God Jesus Christ, as man, in the ardent prayer of his Passion, enabled the Holy Spirit, who had already penetrated the inmost depths of his humanity to transform that humanity into a perfect sacrifice through the act of his death as the victim of love … the Holy Spirit, acted in a special way in this absolute self-giving … in order to transform this suffering into redemptive love."

St. Pope John Paul II - *Dominum et Vivicantem*

In God's Presence Consider …

Suffering can help us to totally open ourselves to the transforming love of the Holy Spirit. Do I accept suffering in my life as a means of God's salvific love? Do I allow suffering to transform my humanity?

Closing Prayer

O Holy Spirit, penetrate the inmost depths of my heart, that I may embrace my sufferings as the means of transforming my humanity into a perfect sacrifice of love to the Father. St. Elizabeth of the Trinity and St. Pope John Paul II, pray for me.

No Distance **Day 199**

Often times we hear people being okay with a relationship with Jesus but want nothing to do with a relationship with the Holy Spirit. You cannot have one without the other.

"The notion of anointing suggests … that there is no distance between the Son and the Spirit. Indeed, just as between the surface of the body and the anointing with oil neither reason nor sensation recognizes any intermediary, so the contact of the Son with the Spirit is immediate, so that anyone who would make contact with the Son by faith must first encounter the oil by contact. In fact there is no part that is not covered by the Holy Spirit. That is why the confession of the Son's Lordship is made in the Holy Spirit by those who receive him, the Spirit coming from all sides to those who approach the Son in faith."

St. Gregory of Nyssa - *De Spiritu Sancto*

In God's Presence Consider …

Am I afraid of the Holy Spirit? Do I see my faith open to the reality of first encountering the Holy Spirit before encountering Jesus?

Closing Prayer

St. Gregory of Nyssa, pray that the Holy Spirit would take away any fear I have of Him. May He increase and perfect my faith so that with His help I may proclaim the Lordship of Jesus in my words and with the actions of my life.

The Pledge of Incorruptibility **Day 200**

The Holy Spirit is the invisible principle of the Church's communion.

"What the soul is to the human body, the Holy Spirit is to the Body of Christ, which is the Church. To this Spirit of Christ, as an invisible principle, is to be ascribed the fact that all the parts of the body are joined one with the other and with their exalted head; for the whole Spirit of Christ is in the head, the whole Spirit is in the body, and the whole Spirit is in each of the members. The Holy Spirit makes the Church the temple of the living God.

"Indeed, it is to the Church herself that the "Gift of God" has been entrusted.... For where the Church is, there also is God's Spirit; where God's Spirit is, there is the Church and every grace (St. Irenaeus)."

CCC #797

In God's Presence Consider ...

As a member of the Body of Christ, the Church, have I considered the Holy Spirit as a Gift entrusted to me? Do I see the Holy Spirit as the means for bringing about communion with other members of the Body of Christ? Do I live my spiritual life as a member of the Church recognizing the Holy Spirit as our very soul?

Closing Prayer

Come, Holy Spirit, Ladder of Ascent to God, fill my soul with Your presence that I may have a love for the members of the Body of Christ as the Father has a love for them. Strengthen my faith that I may see You in the Church, regardless of my sinfulness and the sinfulness of her members.

Jesus is both human and divine, therefore, His mission will be both visible and invisible. The Church, the body of Christ, shares in the nature and mission of her head, Jesus. He is aided by the Holy Spirit who is the fullness of grace.

"By the operation of the Holy Ghost, not only was the conception of Christ accomplished, but also the sanctification of His soul which, in Holy Scripture, is called His 'anointing' (Acts 10:38). Wherefore all His actions were performed in the Holy Ghost, and especially the sacrifice of Himself: Christ, through the Holy Ghost, offered Himself 'without spot to God' (Heb. 9:14). Considering this, no one can be surprised that all the gifts of the Holy Ghost inundated the soul of Christ. In Him resided the absolute fullness of grace … signified in that miraculous dove which appeared at the Jordan, when Christ, by His baptism, consecrated its water for a new sacrament…. Therefore, by the conspicuous apparition of the Holy Ghost over Christ and by His invisible power in His soul, the twofold mission of the Spirit is foreshadowed, namely, His outward and visible mission in the Church, and His secret indwelling in the souls of the just."

Pope Leo XIII - *Divinum Illud Munus*

In God's Presence Consider …

What does the Holy Spirit as a dove signify? Have you ever thought about how the Holy Spirit helped Jesus humanly and divinely in His conception and the sanctification of His soul? How can the Holy Spirit help me?

Closing Prayer

Come, Holy Spirit, dwell fully in me, that anointed with Your secret indwelling, I may share in the mission of the Church and may offer myself unblemished to God as a pleasing sacrifice.

God's indwelling abiding goes beyond His presence in the rest of creation. The degree of His presence depends on the proportion of our cooperation and acceptance of grace. I become a partaker of God's divinity through the Holy Spirit dwelling and working in me.

"While God is in everything in creation, He dwells in the just by grace. He is in all things; in the just He dwells. The same word actually is applied to the presence of God in the souls of those in grace as is used when speaking of God's presence in the Temple.... God has, over and above His ordinary presence in every single created thing, a further and special presence in the hearts of those in friendship with Him by grace, and this new presence is a fuller and richer presence whereby God's excellencies and perfections are more openly displayed.

"By God's indwelling, then, effected by grace, the Holy Spirit now present in the soul differently from the way in which He is present by creation ... there are again degrees of His presence, so that even among men He is more in one than in another. This gradation is in proportion to their grace. The more holy and sanctified they become, the more does the Holy Spirit dwell in them, the more fully is He sent, the more completely given.... In all the rest of creation God is present by His action; in the souls of the just He is present by their actions of faith, hope, and love ...we are made partakers of His divinity."

Fr. B. Jarrett, O.P. - *The Abiding Presence of the Holy Ghost in the Soul*

In God's Presence Consider ...

God creates all things and His existence is present in all created things. Yet He dwells not in all creation but in the souls of the just. Does God dwell in me? Are there obstacles that might stand in the way of His indwelling friendship? What actions in my life hinder or enhance the Holy Spirit dwelling in me? Do I display God's excellencies and perfections openly?

Closing Prayer

O Holy Spirit, sweet Guest of my soul, abide in me and grant that I may ever abide in You and become a partaker of God's divinity, openly displaying God's excellencies and perfections.

In the mystery of the incarnation, the work of the Holy Spirit reaches its highest point when God, in the Person of His Son, takes on human flesh. Through the mystery of the incarnation, a new way is open to humanity giving us access to the source of this divine life.

"The Spirit is precisely the personal place where humanity finds possible its encounter with Christ. The unique mediation of Christ, by which every human being can be introduced to the inaccessible intimacy of the Father, takes place through the experience of the Holy Spirit…. Knowing Christ, therefore, within the horizon of the Spirit means basing the wisdom of the faith on the experience, in the Spirit, of the mystery of the Word made flesh: 'No one can say, Jesus is Lord except by the Holy Spirit' (1 Cor. 12:3).

"The Spirit has been entrusted with the mission of updating throughout time the loving design of God … he progressively makes known and brings about the culmination of God's self-communication, with the humanizing of the Son of God in the womb of the Virgin Mary…. The design of God, that of uniting himself with humanity and making it divine, is fully realized in Jesus. Jesus, in the power of the Spirit, is the perfect union between God and humankind: in the mystery of the incarnation, the work of the Spirit who gives life reaches its highest point … the mystery of the incarnation opens in a new way the source of this divine life in the history of mankind: the Holy Spirit."

THC - *The Holy Spirit, Lord and Giver of Life*

In God's Presence Consider …

To encounter Christ is to first encounter the Holy Spirit. How do I experience this personal encounter with the Holy Spirit? Am I open to the new way and source of divine life that the Holy Spirit can bring to my life?

Closing Prayer

Jesus, relying on Your unique mediation, I ask for Your Spirit to lead me into intimacy with the Father, and open to me the mystery of the incarnation as the source of my divine life.

In the Gospel of John 14, we hear Jesus ask the Father to send the Paraclete to remain with the Apostles, teaching, bringing to remembrance, and to complete the work He began.

"It is precisely this Spirit of truth whom Jesus calls the Paraclete—and parakletos means counselor, and also intercessor, or advocate. And he says that the Paraclete is another Counselor, the second one, since he, Jesus himself is the first Counselor, being the first bearer and giver of the Good News. The Holy Spirit comes after him and because of him, in order to continue in the world, through the Church, the work of the Good News of salvation. Concerning this continuation of his own work by the Holy Spirit, Jesus speaks more than once during the same farewell discourse, preparing the apostles gathered in the Upper Room for his departure, namely for his Passion and Death on the Cross.

"The Holy Spirit will be the Counselor of the Apostles and the Church, always present in their midst—even though invisible—as the teacher of the same Good News that Christ proclaimed … he will continue to inspire the spreading of the Gospel of salvation … he will help people to understand the correct meaning of the content of Christ's message … he will ensure continuity and identity of understanding in the midst of changing conditions and circumstances … he will ensure that in the Church there will always continue the same truth which the Apostles heard from their Master."

St. Pope John Paul II - *Dominum et Vivicantem*

In God's Presence Consider …

How do I experience the Paraclete? Does the Holy Spirit play a role in my relationship with Jesus? Do I see the Holy Spirit working in the Church today?

Closing Prayer

Come O Paraclete, Spirit of Truth, come and be my advocate, my intercessor, my counselor. Help me to believe and live the Good News. St. Pope John Paul II, pray for me.

Theologically, the word economy means work. The work of salvation is a joint mission of the Son and the Spirit sent by the Father to restore us and giving us access to God and to be able to share in His divine life.

"Between the Holy Spirit and Christ there thus subsists, in the economy of salvation, an intimate bond, whereby the Spirit works in human history as 'another Counselor,' permanently ensuring the transmission and spreading of the Good News revealed by Jesus of Nazareth. Thus, in the Holy Spirit-Paraclete, who in the mystery and action of the Church unceasingly continues the historical presence on earth of the Redeemer and his saving work, the glory of Christ shines forth…. He will teach … will bring to your remembrance … will bear witness. The supreme and complete self-revelation of God, accomplished in Christ and witnessed to by the preaching of the Apostles, continues to be manifested in the Church through the mission of the invisible Counselor the Spirit of truth. How intimately this mission is linked with the mission of Christ, how fully it draws from this mission of Christ, consolidating and developing in history its salvific results, is expressed by the verb 'take': 'He will take what is mine and declare it to you (Jn. 16:14).'"

St. Pope John Paul II - *Dominum et Vivicantem*

In God's Presence Consider …

Why would a relationship with the Holy Spirit be beneficial to my spiritual life? How does the Holy Spirit continue the mission of Jesus in my life? How closely am I bonded to the joint mission of Jesus and the Holy Spirit?

Closing Prayer

Come, Holy Spirit, Paraclete, come. Make me know the continual presence and mission of Jesus to be carried out in my life. Help me to be a son or daughter of the Church. St. Pope John Paul II, pray for me.

The Holy Spirit is sent to each of us with the mission to guide and help us live our life in Christ and to be holy.

"In a special way, it is the mission of the Holy Spirit to guide us in our new life in Christ. He does so by the work of His gifts, the stirrings of His inspirations, and the growth of His love in our hearts. Scripture abounds in evidence of the Holy Spirit's mission to be with us and assist us in the work of our sanctification. St. Paul frequently reminded the early Christians and us too of this sublime mystery (Rom. 5:5; 2 Cor. 1:21–22).

"It is the Spirit of Life Who, as the Director of the interior life within our souls, is continuously at work in us, bringing to completion the dying to our sinfulness and self-centeredness, which began on the day of our Baptism. He will continue His work in us until we reach the fullness of the new life we have in Christ! This is the spiritual life, and the Holy Spirit has been given to us to bring it to completion for our sanctification."

Fr. Andrew Apostoli, C.F.R. - *The Gift of God: The Holy Spirit*

In God's Presence Consider …

What goals have I set in my life? Is becoming a saint and growing in sanctity one of my goals? Am I allowing the Holy Spirit to accomplish His mission in me?

Closing Prayer

Come, Holy Spirit, guide me in my life in Christ. Continue the work You have begun in me and bring it to completion. Make me holy. Make me a saint.

Looking at the Vatican II document on the apostolate of the laity, we find a surprising understanding of charisms.

"[The laity] exercise a genuine apostolate by their activity directed to the evangelization and sanctification of men, and to the penetrating and perfecting of the temporal sphere of things through the spirit of the Gospel. In this way their temporal activity can openly bear witness to Christ and promote the salvation of men. Since it is proper to the layman's state in life for him to spend his days in the midst of the world and of secular transactions, he is called by God to burn with the spirit of Christ and to exercise his apostolate in the world as a kind of leaven....

"For the exercise of this apostolate, the Holy Spirit who sanctifies the people of God through the ministry and the sacraments gives to the faithful special gifts as well (1 Cor. 12:7) 'allotting to everyone according as he wills (1 Cor. 12:11).... From the reception of these charisms or gifts ... there arise for each believer the right and duty to use them in the church and in the world for the good of mankind and for the up building of the church."

Vatican Council II - *Apostolicam Actuositatem* #2b, 3b, 3d

In God's Presence Consider ...

Do I burn with the Holy Spirit in order to be leaven to the world and my secular transactions? I have a right and duty to receive and use the Holy Spirit's gifts and charisms for the good of mankind and the up building of the Church. Do I take seriously this obligation?

Closing Prayer

All-powerful and ever-living God, in midmorning you poured out the Holy Spirit as a constant Friend and Guide for your apostles. Send that same Spirit of love to us to make us faithful witnesses to you in the sight of all mankind. Grant this through Christ our Lord.

Week 1 Tuesday Midmorning Prayer

In St. Augustine of Hippo's prayer we find the various titles of the Holy Spirit and work that He seeks to do in preparing our souls to be a dwelling place for the Holy Trinity.

"O Love of the eternal God, sacred communication between the omnipotent Father and His blessed Son, all-powerful Paraclete, most merciful Consoler of the afflicted, penetrate the innermost depths of my heart with Your powerful virtue; brighten with Your shining light any dark corners of that neglected dwelling of my soul … inflame it with Your salutary fire.

"I believe that each time You come into a soul, You prepare there a dwelling for the Father and the Son. Blessed is he who is worthy to have You as Guest! Through You, the Father and the Son establish their dwelling in him. Come then, most benign Consoler of suffering souls, Protector in all circumstances and Support in tribulations. Come, Purifier of faults, Healer of the wounded. Come, Strength of the weak, Restorer of those who fall! Come, Master of the humble, rejecter of the proud! Come, O charitable Father of orphans, merciful Judge of widows! Come, hope of the poor, strength of the weak! Come, guiding star of sailors, harbor of the shipwrecked! Come, O unique beauty of all the living, and only salvation of the dying! Come, O Holy Spirit, come and take pity on me! Clothe me with Yourself, and graciously hear my prayers. Amen!"

St. Augustine

In God's Presence Consider …

What title and what work of the Holy Spirit in St. Augustine's prayer, strikes a chord in me? Do I enter prayer by humbly proclaiming my littleness and weakness, seeking the strength of the Holy Spirit to clothe me with His greatness and prepare me for my time of prayer? Do I live the reality of God dwelling in me?

Closing Prayer

O Holy Spirit, inflame me in Your salutary fire making me docile to Your actions, always willing to be guided and directed by You so that I may become a dwelling place of the Most Holy Trinity. St. Augustine, pray for me.

What a Story! **Day 209**

To undergo the baptism of the Lord is to have unleashed within us the fullness of the Holy Spirit who helps us in our responding to the hunger and thirst of God we feel, and to the opening of the doors of our heart and letting God become a personal friend. It is the work of the Holy Spirit who sets us afire and unites us to the love of God.

"Within two years (1977–1978) our community doubled in size, including six novices and four postulants, and our first Mexican Sisters, by the Fall of 1978. It was amazing to look back over those five or six years since our beginnings and see the patterns of preparation that the Lord had led us into. Great was His work of leadership and guidance.

"What a story! Who would believe it? Only someone who hungered and thirsted for God and opened the door of his heart to let Him become a personal friend. This is the person who receives that fullness of the Holy Spirit which we call 'the baptism.' The Holy Spirit, the 'Finger of God,' is a great revealer. He shows us God, and He shows us ourselves. His truth sanctifies us and unites us to God and to each other and we are the living stones of the Church.

"What a story! The great and small gifts He gives us enable us to be His hands and feet, His heart and mind. Into our frail hands He places His own power to heal and restore and uplift. What a Church that would be: a beautiful Bride! Marvelous workmen in His vineyard, fulfilling His every will and command—going where He says go, doing what He says do. Loving community, united and afire with that love which alone can heal and restore humanity."

Mother John Marie Stewart, DLJC - *Laying the Foundation*

In God's Presence Consider...

Do I find myself at times experiencing a great hunger and thirst for something more in my spiritual life? Have I opened the doors of my heart to have Jesus become a personal friend? Do I earnestly believe and seek the Holy Spirit to sanctify and unite me to God?

Closing Prayer

Come, Holy Spirit, and fill the hunger and thirst I feel for God. Come and set me afire with Your love and renew Your Church.

The Holy Spirit is communion and gives this life of communion to and through the members of Christ's body, the Church.

"The Holy Spirit has been entrusted to the Church … that all members receiving it may be vivified; and the means of communion with Christ has been distributed throughout it, that is, the Holy Spirit."

St. Irenaeus - *Against Heresies*

In God's Presence Consider …

Do I believe that the Holy Spirit has been entrusted to the Church and to me? Do I accept this entrustment and how He vivifies me? Do I accept Christ's means of communion as He distributes it through the Holy Spirit or do I look for another way?

Closing Prayer

O Holy Spirit, You are the Spirit of unity and communion. Work within me, vivifying me with Your presence, Your work, and Your communion. Help me to accept that which Christ is entrusting me through You. St. Irenaeus, pray for me.

The Holy Spirit is the source of life, holiness, unity, and communion for the Church. Because the Spirit abides, He dwells in the Church until the end of time. It is within the Church that we come to know who the Holy Spirit is.

"The article concerning the Church also depends entirely on the article about the Holy Spirit, which immediately precedes it. 'Indeed, having shown that the Spirit is the source and giver of all holiness, we now confess that it is he who has endowed the Church with holiness.' The Church is, in a phrase used by the Fathers, the place 'where the Spirit flourishes ... he (the Holy Spirit) is the principle of the Church's unity. Unity is of the essence of the Church.... The Spirit, who is the Spirit of communion, abides indefectibly in the Church.... The Church, a communion living in the faith of the apostles which she transmits, is the place where we know the Holy Spirit: in the Scriptures he inspired, in the Tradition, in the Church's Magisterium, in the sacramental liturgy, in prayer, in the charisms and ministries by which the Church is built up, in the signs of apostolic and missionary life, and in the witness of the saints...."

Cf. CCC #749, 813, 1108, 688

In God's Presence Consider ...

The Church's existence depends on the Holy Spirit. How do I see this truth actualized in my own spiritual life? Is holiness of life something I seek after and try to live? How do I experience the Holy Spirit through the Church?

Closing Prayer

Breathe in me, O Holy Spirit, that my thoughts may all be holy. Act in me, O Holy Spirit, that my work, too, may be holy. Draw my heart, O Holy Spirit, that I live what is holy. Strengthen me, O Holy Spirit, to defend all that is holy. Guard me, then, O Holy Spirit that I always may be holy.

Prayer of St. Augustine of Hippo

Unity of Fellowship and Service **Day 212**

There is a whole patristic and theological tradition concerning the intimate union between the Holy Spirit and the Church, a union presented sometimes as analogous to the relationship between the soul and the body of man.

"The Spirit dwells in the Church and in the hearts of the faithful as in a temple (cf. 1 Cor. 3:16; 6:19). In them he prays and bears witness to the fact that they are adopted sons (cf. Gal. 4:6; Rom. 8:15–16:26). The Spirit guides the Church into the fullness of truth (cf. Jn. 16:13) and gives her a unity of fellowship and service. He furnishes and directs her with various gifts, both hierarchical and charismatic, and adorns her with the fruits of His grace (cf. Eph. 4:11–12; 1 Cor. 12:4; Gal. 5:22). By the power of the Gospel he makes the Church grow, perpetually renews her and leads her to perfect union with her Spouse."

Vatican Council II - *Lumen Gentium* #4

In God's Presence Consider …

Do I accept the fullness of truth that the Holy Spirit gives the Church? Do I see Church renewal as a program or as a perpetual deepening of union with Jesus?

Closing Prayer

Come, Holy Spirit, You who dwell in the Church as her very life. Help me be open to receive the fullness of truth, the varied gifts and fruits of Your grace, in order to be perfectly united to Jesus my Spouse.

The Holy Spirit is sent by the Father and the Son out of love for humanity. He is to give us access to the Father, bring about holiness of life, perfection of love, and is the principle of unity among those who believe.

"The Holy Spirit was sent on Pentecost in order that he might continually sanctify the Church, and that, consequently, those who belong might have access through Christ in one Spirit to the Father. He is the Spirit of life…. The Father gives life through him….

"God sent the Spirit of his Son, the Lord and Giver of Life. The Spirit is for the Church and each and every believer, the principle of their union and unity in the teaching of the apostles and fellowship, in the breaking of the bread, and prayer.

"For he (God the Father) sent the Holy Spirit to all to move them interiorly to love God with their whole heart … soul … understanding … and strength, and to love one another as Christ loved them.

Vatican Council II - *Lumen Gentium* #3b, 13a, 40a

In God's Presence Consider …

God sends His Holy Spirit upon me; pouring Him into my heart. Do I accept Him and allow Him to love me as God desires to? Is my love directed to God and others or to myself?

Closing Prayer

Come, Holy Spirit, You who are the Lord and Giver of Life, move me interiorly to love God and my neighbor forming a deep union with God and His Church.

Continually Sanctifying **Day 214**

To ensure His continuous work of sanctifying all men and drawing them into His divine life of unity, the Father sent His Son and the Holy Spirit to establish the Church; which holds out to all the elect the means of salvation.

"When the work which the Father gave the Son to do on earth (cf. Jn. 17:4) was accomplished, the Holy Spirit was sent on the day of Pentecost in order that he might continually sanctify the Church, and that, consequently, those who believe might have access through Christ in the Spirit to the Father (cf. Eph. 2:18). He is the Spirit of life, the fountain of water springing up to eternal life (cf. Jn. 4:47; 7:38–39). To men, dead in sin, the Father gives life through him, until the day when, in Christ, he raises to life their mortal bodies (cf. Rom. 8:10–11). The Spirit dwells in the Church and in the hearts of the faithful, as in a temple (cf. 1 Cor. 3:16; 6:19). In them he prays and bears witness to their adoptive sonship (cf. Gal. 4:6; Rom. 8:15–16, 26). Guiding the Church in the way of all truth (cf. Jn. 16:13) and unifying her in communion and in the works of ministry, he bestows upon her varied hierarchal and charismatic gifts, and in this way directs her; and he adorns her with his fruits (cf. Eph. 4:11–12; 1 Cor. 12:4; Gal. 5:22). By the power of the Gospel he permits the Church to keep the freshness of youth. Constantly he renews her and leads her to perfect union with her Spouse…."

Vatican Council II - *Lumen Gentium* #4

In God's Presence Consider …

Do I see myself as a temple for the Holy Spirit to dwell and reside within? Am I open to receive any and all the gifts from the Holy Spirit for the building up of the Body, or do I pick and choose, shutting off the ones I don't feel comfortable with or desire to have? Am I a source of unity or division in the Church?

Closing Prayer

Come, Holy Spirit, and dwell within the Temple of my heart. Adorn me with Your graces and fill me anew with Your many gifts.

For Archbishop Sheen, the Holy Spirit is key in giving order and life to the Church. It is through the sending of the Holy Spirit that the Church becomes a living organism, the Mystical Body of Christ. When we focus more on organization, structures, and things, we are not being open to the Holy Spirit to govern the Church. Our life in Christ is not merely a symbol to be copied, rather a life to be lived.

"Many have wished that Our Blessed Lord had remained on earth, that we might have heard His voice, seen His compassionate eyes, and brought our children to be blessed by His hands. But He said 'I can say truly that it is better for you I should go away, He who is to befriend you will not come to you unless I do go, but if only I make my way there, I will send him to you.' If our Lord remained on earth, He would have been only a symbol to be copied—not a life to be lived. By returning to his heavenly Father, He could then send both from the Father and Himself the Holy Spirit that would make Him live on earth in His new Body, which is the Church. So on Pentecost the Apostles, who were like the cells of a body, became Christ's Mystical Body, because vivified by His Holy Spirit, governed by one visible head, Peter, and presided over by one invisible head, Christ in heaven. Our glorious Church is not an organization, but an organism."

Archbishop Fulton Sheen - *Meditations on the 15 Mysteries of the Rosary; the Descent of the Holy Spirit*

In God's Presence Consider ...

Have I ever thought that Jesus sent the Holy Spirit so that He would not merely be a symbol to be copied, but a life to be lived? Do I try to live the life of Jesus within the Mystical Body without the help of the Holy Spirit? Do I see the Church as a living organism, or do I get caught up in the institutionalism and organization of the Church?

Closing Prayer

O Lord, may the light of the Holy Spirit come upon me from on high, and vivify my heart and mind so that I may be a living cell in the living organism of Your Church.

The Holy Spirit inspires in people's heart and under His inspiration we are impelled to proclaim the Gospel which, under His inspiration, penetrates to the heart.

"We live in the Church at a privileged moment of the Spirit. Everywhere people are trying to know Him better, as the Scripture reveals Him. They are happy to place themselves under His inspiration. They are gathering about Him; they want to let themselves be led my Him. Now if the Spirit of God has a preeminent place in the whole life of the Church, it is in her evangelizing mission that He is most active. It is not by chance that the great inauguration of evangelization took place on the morning of Pentecost, under the inspiration of the Spirit.

"It must be said that the Holy Spirit is the principal agent of evangelization. It is He who impels each individual to proclaim the Gospel, and it is He who in the depths of consciences causes the word of salvation to be accepted and understood. But it can be equally said that He is the goal of evangelization. He alone stirs up the new creation the new humanity of which evangelization is to be the result, with that unity in variety which evangelization wishes to achieve within the Christian community. Through the Holy Spirit the Gospel penetrates to the heart of the world...."

St. Pope Paul VI - *Evangelii Nuntiandi*

In God's Presence Consider ...

Am I trying to know the Holy Spirit better? Am I happy to be placed under His inspirations? Am I allowing the Holy Spirit to lead me? Am I allowing the Holy Spirit to penetrate my heart with the Good News of Jesus and to stir up in me a new humanity?

Closing Prayer

Holy Spirit, just as You have a preeminent place in the life and mission of the Church, so come and stir within me Your inspiration that I may truly live a relationship with Jesus that permeates and ushers in the new creation and humanity that You seek to bring about. St. Pope Paul VI, pray for me.

The Church is often seen by the world as an institution, a physical structure governed by rules and regulations that are archaic and out of touch with reality rather than the assembly of God's chosen, gathered around the Person of Jesus, His Son, and in intimate conversation with Him.

"The Fathers never gave specific definition of the Church. They understood the words of the Lord that the 'Kingdom is here' as referring to his Person encountered in his actions. This activity of the Son of God is, in fact, continually carried out by the presence of the sanctifying Spirit whom the Father sent to us when Christ withdrew his physical presence. Consequently, for Byzantine tradition, the Church is the life and the source of life. It is the plenitude of spiritual life in the risen Christ. As the stem is grafted to the branch and the two lives become one, so the baptized person is grafted onto Christ by the Holy Spirit, and the two become one Body and one Life.... The reality and essence of life in the Church is the conversation of peace and love in which God and man are involved. This conversation began from all eternity in the Trinity.... It came to its fullness in the Incarnation of the Word of God, and it will continue through space and time to the end of the world through the Holy Spirit. The Spirit, through the imparting of the life of the risen Christ through his mysteries, the sacrament ... the Holy Spirit sustains his presence in those who are united to Christ...."

Archbishop Joseph M. Raya - *The Face of God*

In God's Presence Consider ...

Do I see the Kingdom as a Person, place, or thing? Do I see myself grafted onto Christ and into Christ? Am I in a continual conversation of peace and love with God?

Closing Prayer

Come, Holy Spirit, the Sanctifier, the Source of all life. Come, and graft me to Jesus that I may be one with Him. Help me be more prepared and receptive to enter the Sacraments of the Church that the life of Jesus they impart may fill me in a fuller way, helping me to bear fruit pleasing to the Father.

We often fail to see that the Holy Spirit is the "same yesterday, today, and forever" (Heb. 13:8), and (Rm. 8:9) "The Holy Spirit dwells within us."

"Doubtless, the Holy Spirit was already at work in the world before Christ was glorified. Yet on the day of Pentecost, he came down upon the disciples to remain with them forever. On that day the Church was publicly revealed to the multitude, and the Gospel began to spread."

Vatican Council II - *Ad Gentes* #4

"Having accomplished the work that the Father had entrusted to the Son on earth (cf. Jn. 17:4), on the day of Pentecost the Holy Spirit was sent to sanctify the Church forever, so that believers might have access to the Father through Christ in one Spirit (cf. Eph. 2:18). He is the Spirit of life, the fountain of water springing up to eternal life (cf. Jn. 4:14; 7:38), the One through whom the Father restores life to those who are dead through sin.... At the same time, the teachings of this Council is essentially pneumatological (the study of the Person and works of the Holy Spirit): it is permeated by the truth about the Holy Spirit, as the soul of the Church … the Council has made the Spirit newly present in our difficult age."

St. Pope John Paul II - *Dominum et Vivificantem*

In God's Presence Consider...

How does the truth that the Holy Spirit came to remain forever, impact my spiritual life? Do I allow the Holy Spirit to raise me from sin to new life? Am I permeated with the truth about the Holy Spirit? How have I experienced the new presence of the Holy Spirit in times of difficulty?

Closing Prayer

O God, who by the mystery of today's great feast sanctify your whole Church in every people and nation, pour out, we pray, the gifts of the Holy Spirit across the face of the earth and, with the divine grace that was at work when the Gospel was first proclaimed, fill now once more the hearts of believers.

Collect from the Mass of Pentecost

Jesus and the Holy Spirit share in a joint mission. When Christ's work on earth was accomplished, the founding of the Church, the Holy Spirit was sent to bring life efficaciously to the institution which Jesus founded. The Spirit is the life and unity of the Church.

"There is an extremely intimate relation between the Holy Spirit and the Church which no explanation can bring out completely, no image perfectly illustrates and which no formula can adequately express. We can say that the Church is constituted efficaciously by the Spirit. 'Where the Church is,' says St. Irenaeus, 'there also is the Spirit of God; and where the Spirit of God is, there also is the Church and the plenitude of Grace.' According to the Apostles' Creed, creation is attributed to the Father, the work of redemption to the Son, and the Church to the Holy Spirit: 'I believe in the Holy Spirit, the Holy Catholic Church....'

"The Messiah came, filled with the Holy Spirit. He laid the foundations of the Church, defined its organization and instituted the sacraments. Then he sent the Spirit who, like the breath of Yahweh causing a commotion among the dry bones in Ezekiel's prophecy, gave life to the institution which Jesus founded.... The Spirit is within the Church; he is her life and unity.... As a life-giving wind which brings in its path dew, blessings, fruitfulness and makes the earth germinate, thus the wind of God, which is the Holy Spirit, brings spiritual fruitfulness to the humanity with which it comes in contact, namely the Church."

Bernard Piault - *What is the Trinity*

In God's Presence Consider ...

Where the Church is, there also is the Spirit of God. Have I ever thought of the intimate relationship between the Holy Spirit and the Church? Do I speak negatively about the Church and thus grieve the Holy Spirit who gives her life? Renewal is the work of the Holy Spirit. Is spiritual renewal a common occurrence in my life?

Closing Prayer

O Breath of God, Life Giving Wind, bring about within me a spiritual fruitfulness and love for the Church. Breathe upon my dry bones Your breath and may they be renewed with Your new life.

The Church, guided by the Spirit, is continually renewed and purified and has been given the task to study, evaluate, and discern the authentic fruits of the Holy Spirit so that they may be a lasting treasure for the People of God in our earthly pilgrimage.

"For theirs' is a community of men. United in Christ, they are led by the Holy Spirit in their journey to the Kingdom of their Father and they have welcomed the news of salvation which is meant for everyman. That is why this community realizes that it is truly and intimately linked with mankind and its history.... The Church truly knows that only God, whom she serves, meets the deepest longings of the human heart, which is never fully satisfied by what the world has to offer.... God's Spirit ... with a marvelous providence, directs the unfolding of time and renews the face of the earth....

"By the power of the Holy Spirit the Church is the faithful spouse of the Lord and will never fail to be a sign of salvation in the world; but it is by no means unaware that down through the centuries there have been among its members, both clerical and lay, some who were disloyal to the Spirit of God. Today as well, the Church is not blind to the discrepancy between the message it proclaims and the human weakness of those to whom the Gospel has been entrusted.... Guided by the Holy Spirit the Church ceaselessly 'exhorts her children to purification and renewal so that the sign of Christ may shine more brightly over the face of the Church."

Vatican Council II - *Gaudium et Spes* #1a, 43f

In God's Presence Consider ...

Is there a discrepancy in my life between the living out of my faith and the demands of life in the world? With what do I fill the longings of my heart? Do I see the Holy Spirit as leading me on a journey to the Kingdom of God?

Closing Prayer

Holy Spirit, help me to realize and experience that only God can fill the deepest longings of my heart. Come, Holy Spirit, and renew the face of the earth.

Christ's mission was to establish the Church, which was to make His work of salvation present for all generations to participate in. This mission is a joint mission between Jesus and the Holy Spirit.

"For He who is the Spirit of Truth, in as much as He proceedeth both from the Father, who is the eternally True, and from the Son, who is the substantial Truth, receiveth from each both His essence and the fullness of all truth. This truth He communicates to His Church, guarding her by His all-powerful help from ever falling into error, and aiding her to foster daily more and more the germs of divine doctrine and to make them fruitful for the welfare of the peoples. And since the welfare of the peoples, for which the Church was established, absolutely requires that this office should be continued for all time, the Holy Ghost perpetually supplies life and strength to preserve and increase the Church.

"... That the Church is a divine institution is most clearly proved by the splendor and glory of those gifts and graces with which she is adorned, and whose author and giver is the Holy Ghost. Let it suffice to state that, as Christ is the Head of the Church, so is the Holy Ghost her soul. 'What the soul is in our body, that is the Holy Ghost in Christ's body, the Church' (St. Augustine)."

Pope Leo XIII - *Divinum Illud Munus*

In God's Presence Consider ...

Do I allow the seed of divine doctrine, planted by the Holy Spirit, to germinate life within my soul? We often hear that we are the Body of Christ and are different members of that Body. Have I ever thought of the Holy Spirit as being the soul of the Church? As her soul, what does the Holy Spirit do for the Body of Christ? How does the Holy Spirit offer me protection in my spiritual life?

Closing Prayer

Come, O Spirit of Truth, protect me from the errors of the evil one that I may grow in the mysteries and doctrines of the faith, so that I may bear fruit for the welfare of all those I come in contact with today.

The Church perseveres in prayer with the Apostles and with Mary, awaiting in prayer the coming of the Holy Spirit anew.

"While it is an historical fact that the Church came forth from the Upper Room on the day of Pentecost, in a certain sense one can say that she has never left it. Spiritually the event of Pentecost does not belong only to the past: the Church is always in the Upper Room.... The Church perseveres in prayer with Mary. This union of the praying Church with the Mother of Christ has been part of the mystery of the Church from the beginning: we see her present in this mystery as she is present in the mystery of her Son.... Imitating the Mother of the Lord, and by the power of the Holy Spirit, she preserves with virginal purity an integral faith, a firm hope, and a sincere charity.

"For the Spirit is given to the Church in order that through his power the whole community of the People of God, however widely scattered and diverse, may persevere in hope: that hope in which we have been saved (Rom. 8:24).... The Holy Spirit, given to the Apostles as the Counselor, is the guardian and animator of this hope in the heart of the Church.... The Church wishes to prepare ... in the Holy Spirit, just as the Virgin of Nazareth in whom the Word was made flesh was prepared by the Holy Spirit."

St. Pope John Paul II - *Dominum et Vivicantem*

In God's Presence Consider ...

Do I believe that the Holy Spirit was only given at Pentecost and we no longer need Him as the early Church did? Do I pray with Mary as closely as the Church does?

Closing Prayer

Come, Holy Spirit, let Your Fire fall. Pour out on me a new outpouring of Your graces and gifts that I may grow in an integral faith, a firm hope, and a sincere charity. You, Spouse of the Virgin Mary, join me with Mary, that I, too, may imitate her virtues and be constantly seeking You in my life.

Pope Benedict XVI credits the Charismatic Renewal for bringing to the forefront the need for the Church to look at and encourage the Holy Spirit's charisms among the faithful.

"What we learn in the New Testament on charisms, which appeared as visible signs of the coming of the Holy Spirit, is not a historical event of the past, but a reality ever alive. It is the same divine Spirit, soul of the Church, that acts in every age and those mysterious and effective interventions of the Spirit are manifest in our time in a providential way.

"The Movements and New Communities are like an outpouring of the Holy Spirit in the Church and in contemporary society. We can, therefore, rightly say that one of the positive elements and aspects of the Community of the Catholic Charismatic Renewal is precisely their emphasis on the charisms or gifts of the Holy Spirit and their merit lies in having recalled their topicality in the Church."

Pope Benedict XVI - *Catholic Fraternity of Charismatic Covenant Communities and Fellowships, 2008*

In God's Presence Consider ...

Do I see the Holy Spirit as an archive of past historical events in the life of the Church or an ever-present reality that is ever alive? How do I understand and cultivate the use of charisms in my life? Am I open to receive and use them?

Closing Prayer

O God, whose Son, at his Ascension to the heavens, was pleased to promise the Holy Spirit to the Apostles, grant, we pray, that, just as they received manifold gifts of heavenly teaching, so on us, too, you may bestow spiritual gifts. Through our Lord Jesus Christ, your Son, who lives and reigns with you in the unity of the Holy Spirit, God, forever and ever.

Collect from Saturday of the 6th Week of Easter

Holy Spirit Empowering through Sacraments

The Church is the mystery of communion of the members of the Body of Christ with God; for the work of the Holy Spirit is to build the Church in unity. It is He who takes the many members and makes them one in Christ.

"Where there is the Church there is also the Spirit of God; and where there is the Spirit of God there is also the Church and every grace. The gift of God has been confided to the Church, as breath to the molded creature, so that all its members, participating in it, are given life. In it has been placed communion with Christ, that is, the Holy Spirit, guarantee of incorruptibility, confirmer of our faith, and the ladder of our ascent to God."

St. Irenaeus - *Against Heresies, III, 24, 1*

In God's Presence Consider …

Where do I see the intimate union of the Holy Spirit with the Church? Do I see the graces of the Holy Spirit being given to me through the Church? Do I see my incorruptibility as coming from the Holy Spirit giving me life and living within me?

Closing Prayer

Thank You, Father, for Your gifts confided to the Church and the access to them that You offer to me. Continue the work of making me incorruptible that I may ascend to You and live in communion with You here on earth and in the world to come.

It is by the Holy Spirit freely distributing special graces and charisms among every rank of the faithful that we are made fit and ready to renew and build up the Church.

"However, now we must add that the Holy Spirit, the giver of every gift and the first principle of the Church's vitality, does not only work through the Sacraments. According to St. Paul he distributes to each his own gifts as he wills (1 Cor. 12:11) pouring out into the People of God a great wealth of graces both for prayer and contemplation and for action. They are charisms: lay people receive them too, especially in relation to their mission in the Church and society … as it is written in St. Paul, 'the manifestation of the Spirit is given to everyone for profit' (1 Cor. 12:7 and LG #12).

St. Pope John Paul II - *A Dictionary of His Life and Teachings*

In God's Presence Consider …

Do I lack spiritual vitality? Do I see the Holy Spirit working through the sacraments and His gifts? Do I know the Church's mission and am I committed to prayer, contemplation, and for action in fulfilling her mission?

Closing Prayer

Come, Holy Spirit, with Your vitality and pour out Your graces on me that I may contribute to the building up of the Church and may participate in her mission by using the charisms You manifest in my life.

Sacraments are powers which are ever-living and life-giving actions of the Holy Spirit. They are the masterwork of God. In every sacrament, the Church prays, asking for the sanctifying power of God's Holy Spirit. This prayer invoking the Spirit is an epiclesis.

"Celebrated in faith, the sacraments confer the grace that they signify.... sanctify men, to build up the Body of Christ, and finally, to give worship to God. They are efficacious because in them Christ himself is at work: it is he who acts in his sacraments in order to communicate the grace that each sacrament signifies. The Father always hears the prayer of his Son's Church which, in the epiclesis of each sacrament, expresses her faith in the power of the Spirit. As fire transforms into itself everything it touches, so the Holy Spirit transforms into the divine life whatever is subjected to his power.

"The Church affirms that for believers the sacraments of the New Covenant are necessary for salvation.... Sacramental grace is the grace of the Holy Spirit, given by Christ and proper to each sacrament. The Spirit heals and transforms those who receive him by conforming them to the Son of God. The fruit of the sacramental life is that the Spirit of adoption makes the faithful partakers in the divine nature by uniting them in a living union with the only Son, the Savior."

Cf. CCC #1123, 1127, 1129

In God's Presence Consider ...

Do I see the sacraments as necessary for my salvation and as a means of nourishment and strength to help me be holy, to build up the Body of Christ, and to give God worship? Do I allow myself to be touched by the Holy Spirit and set on fire in order to be transformed into the divine life?

Closing Prayer

Come, Holy Spirit, and touch me with the Fire of Your Love. Transform me into the divine life, heal me of my sinfulness and pride, and help me to live the sacramental graces You pour out through each of the sacraments.

Making Mystery Present **Day 227**

It is the work of the Holy Spirit through the Pascal Mystery; the Passion, Death, Resurrection, and Ascension of Christ, that makes every liturgical action full of grace and opportunities for intimate cooperation with Him.

"Christian liturgy not only recalls the events that saved us but actualizes them, makes them present. The Paschal mystery of Christ is celebrated, not repeated.... In every liturgical action the Holy Spirit is sent in order to bring us into communion with Christ and so to form his Body.... The most intimate cooperation of the Holy Spirit and the Church is achieved in the liturgy. The Spirit, who is the Spirit of communion, abides indefectibly in the Church. For this reason, the Church is the great sacrament of divine communion which gathers God's scattered children together. Communion with the Holy Trinity and fraternal communion are inseparably the fruit of the Spirit in the liturgy."

Cf. CCC #1104, 1108

In God's Presence Consider ...

Christ died once for our salvation. It is a real event that happened in a particular place at a particular time in human history, and is not intended to be repeated. Do I see each Mass as a celebration of the event of the Paschal Mystery? Do I see the fruit of the Holy Spirit each time I participate in the Mass?

Closing Prayer

Father, send Your Holy Spirit to make my life a living sacrifice to You. Through the spiritual transformation that Your Spirit works within me, make me into the image of Your Son, uniting me to Him and helping me to share in His mission through a life of witness and service of charity.

Sacramental grace requires faith, active cooperation, and interior disposition. Disposition is not mere external performance but a readiness to change and become more like Christ and closer to God.

"Grace is at once the fruit of God's acting upon us and a free supernatural gift of God to help us attain eternal life. Grace empowers our intellect and wills to understand God's will and obey it, yet at the same time it leaves us free to resist if we choose.

"St. Thomas Aquinas taught that grace heals the soul by helping us recognize the good while empowering us to desire the good, do the good, persevere in good, and reach glory. Sanctifying grace—the saving grace that makes us participants in the life of the Blessed Trinity and members of the body of Christ—is normally received … through a properly disposed reception of the sacraments (cf. CCC #1131).

"… But the validity of a sacrament does not guarantee that the grace made available has been actively received and is bearing fruit in a person's life…. Positive disposition means we are prepared to change and we actively seek the grace of God in order to do so."

Sherry Weddell - *Forming Intentional Disciples*

In God's Presence Consider …

Grace is a free gift from God that acts upon us. Do I choose to accept and cooperate with God's graces or do I resist them? Am I disposed and prepared to change my life to be more like Jesus? Do I actively receive and bear fruit with the graces God sends me?

Closing Prayer

St. Thomas Aquinas, I ask that through your intercession I may freely choose to actively receive the graces God desires to pour into my life, and that with the Spirit's help I may bear fruit pleasing to the Father.

Thwarted Grace **Day 229**

Sherry Weddell reminds us that it is not the quantity of receiving the sacraments that is helpful to our soul, but rather the quality of our disposed heart that is key. Not being properly disposed and participating in the graces of the sacraments could tie the grace preventing a sacrament's effectiveness.

"The grace we receive is directly related to the personal faith, spiritual expectancy, and hunger with which we approach the sacrament.... It is meaningless to increase the frequency with which a sacrament is received if there is no growth in the personal moral participation by the individual in the accomplishment of the sacrament, i.e., in his disposition.

"Father Raniero Cantalamessa ... points out that when someone receives without proper disposition, the grace of God can be tied. 'A sacrament is called tied if the fruit that should accompany it remains bound because of certain blocks that prevent its effectiveness'.... If we don't intentionally seek to continue to grow in our faith, the initial grace we received can be thwarted."

Sherry Weddell - *Forming Intentional Disciples*

In God's Presence Consider ...

Do I intentionally seek to grow in my faith? Do I thwart graces received through the improper reception of the sacraments? How serious do I take preparing and being properly disposed to receive Jesus in the Eucharist? Are any of the sacraments that I have received "tied"; especially the sacraments of Confirmation or Matrimony?

Closing Prayer

O Mary, Undoer of Knots, I entrust myself into your hands and ask that you would help me to be properly disposed and to actively enter into and receive with active faith the graces God desires to pour into my life. Untie any knots that prevent the fruits of the sacraments from being effective. Mary, Undoer of Knots, pray for me.

Every liturgical action, especially the celebration of the Eucharist and the other sacraments is an encounter between the Church and her Lord. The Church's unity comes from the Holy Spirit who gathers the assembly as the children of God and makes them the Body of Christ.

"In the liturgy, the Holy Spirit is teacher of the faith of the People of God and artisan of God's masterpieces, the sacraments of the New Covenant. The desire and work of the Spirit in the heart of the Church is that we may live from the life of the risen Christ. When the Spirit encounters in us the response of faith which he has aroused in us, he brings about genuine cooperation. Through it, the liturgy becomes the common work of the Holy Spirit and the Church.

"... he prepares the Church to encounter her Lord; he recalls and makes Christ manifest to the faith of the assembly. By his transforming power, he makes the mystery of Christ present here and now. Finally, the Spirit of communion unites the Church to the life and mission of Christ."

CCC #1091–1092

In God's Presence Consider ...

The desire and work of the Holy Spirit in the Church is to help her members live from the life of the risen Christ. Do I treat the sacraments as something I do or as the means of sharing in the divine life of Jesus? Do I believe Jesus is really present in the sacraments or are they merely symbols, memories of what He has done for me?

Closing Prayer

Come, Holy Spirit, with Your transforming power and make me aware of Jesus present in the here and now through the liturgy and especially the sacraments.

The Paschal Mystery—the Passion, Death, Resurrection, and Ascension of Jesus, is a new definitive revelation of the Holy Spirit as a Person who is the "gift". The celebration of the Paschal Mystery in the Mass makes present and re-presented to us the work of your salvation to participate in.

"The Paschal events are also the time of the new coming of the Holy Spirit, as the Paraclete and the Spirit of truth. They are the time of the 'new beginning' of the self-communication of the Triune God to humanity in the Holy Spirit through the work of Christ the Redeemer. This new beginning … expresses the most profound essence of God who, as Love, is the inexhaustible source of the giving of gifts…. The Holy Spirit, who in the inscrutable depths of the divinity is a Person-Gift, through the work of the Son … is given to the Apostles and to the Church in a new way, and through them is given to humanity and the whole world.

"The definitive expression of this mystery reaches its zenith in the Resurrection. It can be said therefore that the messianic 'raising up' of Christ brings to the Apostles the Holy Spirit. He brings him at the price of his own departure; he gives them this Spirit as it were through the wounds of his crucifixion. It is in the power of this crucifixion that he says to them: Receive the Holy Spirit.'"

St. Pope John Paul II - *Dominum et Vivicantem*

In God's Presence Consider …

Jesus brings us the Holy Spirit but at the price of his own death. Do I accept the Gift or do I reject it for any reason? Do I see God's love as full of power and an inexhaustible source, or do I limit God's power in my life by unbelief or by personal restrictions? Do I seek to grow and perfect the virtue of faith God has given me?

Closing Prayer

Father, I thank You for Your inexhaustible love for me. Help me to appreciate the sacrifice Your Son made in order to send me the Holy Spirit. Help me to receive Your great Gift of the Holy Spirit with humility and gratitude and to participate fully in the events of my salvation in the Paschal Mystery.

Everything He Touches **Day 232**

The Holy Spirit's presence in the Eucharist makes the celebration of this sacrament a Pentecost, and an efficacious descent of the Spirit. We could say that there is a Pentecostal character in the Eucharist.

"Then, we too, sanctified through these spiritual hymns (the chant of the Trisagion, that is, the Sanctus), ask the all-giving God to send the Holy Spirit over the gifts placed here to make the bread the body of Christ and the wine the blood of Christ. Everything that the Holy Spirit touches becomes sanctified and transformed.

St. Cyril of Jerusalem - *Catechesis, V, 7*

In God's Presence Consider …

In the Mass, we pray: "We ask you to make these gifts holy by the power of your Spirit, so that they may become the body and blood of your Son, our Lord Jesus Christ…." Do I believe in the real presence of Jesus in the Eucharist? Do I believe that everything the Holy Spirit touches becomes sanctified and transformed?

Closing Prayer

St. Cyril of Jerusalem, pray that I may be so touched by the Holy Spirit that I may come to believe in the presence of Jesus in the Eucharist with a new love and expectation. Help me be attentive to the Spirit's transforming actions in the Liturgy and to participate fully at every Mass.

Baptism is necessary for salvation for it is the source of new life in Christ from which the entire Christian life springs forth.

"Holy Baptism is the basis of the whole Christian life, the gateway to life in the Spirit, and the door which gives access to the other sacraments.

"Through the Holy Spirit, Baptism is a bath that purifies, justifies, and sanctifies.... The power of the Holy Spirit is sent upon the water, so that those who will be baptized in it may be born of water and the Spirit.... The anointing with sacred chrism, perfumed oil consecrated by the bishop, signifies the gift of the Holy Spirit ... a Christian, anointed by the Holy Spirit and incorporated into Christ.... Thus the two principal effects are purification from sins and new birth in the Holy Spirit ... giving them the power to live and act under the prompting of the Holy Spirit through the gifts of the Holy Spirit.... The Holy Spirit has marked us with the seal of the Lord for the day of redemption. Baptism indeed is the seal of eternal life."

Cf. CCC #1213, 1215, 1227, 1238, 1241, 1262, 1265, 1274

In God's Presence Consider ...

Baptism is the basis of my whole Christian life which is a life in the Spirit. Does my life reflect being a life lived in the Spirit? Do I use the power of the sacrament to live and act under the promptings of the Holy Spirit?

Closing Prayer

Almighty ever-living God, who sent your Son into the world to drive out from us the power of Satan, the spirit of evil, and bring the human race, rescued from darkness, into the marvelous Kingdom of Your light: I humbly beseech You to help me renew my baptismal promises, cleanse me as a temple of Your glory, and grant that Your Holy Spirit may continually dwell in me.

Based on the Rite of Baptism

Supreme Gift **Day 234**

The beginning of our regeneration and renovation is the sacrament of Baptism.

"In this sacrament, when the unclean spirit has been expelled from the soul. The Holy Ghost enters in and makes it like to Himself.... The same Spirit gives Himself more abundantly in Confirmation, strengthening and confirming Christian life; from which proceeded the victory of the martyrs and the triumph of the virgins over temptations and corruptions.... For He not only brings to us His divine gifts, but is the Author of them and is Himself the supreme Gift, who, proceeding from the mutual love of the Father and the Son, is justly believed to be and is called Gift of God most High....

".... charity is the special mark of the Holy Ghost, is shared in only by the just. In harmony with this, the same Spirit is called Holy, for He, the first supreme Love, moves souls and leads them to sanctity, which ultimately consists in the love of God."

Pope Leo XIII - *Divinum Illud Munus*

In God's Presence Consider ...

Is the gift you received at your Baptism and Confirmation lying dormant and unused? Do you ever seek the Gift of all gifts: the Holy Spirit? Do you take seriously your personal holiness?

Closing Prayer

O Holy Spirit, the Gift of all gifts; come with the Fire of Your love. Move my soul and lead me to be holy as my Heavenly Father is holy.

Simeon the New Theologian says that without the Holy Spirit dwelling in and allowed to work with us, all our labor to do good or do spiritual works for God are in vain.

"The aim of all those who live in God is to please our Lord Jesus Christ and become reconciled with God the Father through receiving the Holy Spirit, thus securing their salvation, for in this consists the salvation of every soul. If this aim and this activity is lacking, all other labor is useless and all other striving is in vain. Every path of life which does not lead to this is without profit.

Simeon the New Theologian - *Orthodox Church Quotes*

In God's Presence Consider …

Is my aim in life to please God or myself? Do I make use of the Holy Spirit in reconciling me to God? Do I seek the activity of the Holy Spirit within me so that I can profitably bear fruit that pleases God? Do I take time throughout my day to reflect on whether I am on the path of life or have strayed, walking by my own counsel?

Closing Prayer

O Holy Spirit, I so often times have many dreams and goals for my life that do not include God. I ask for Your aid to reconcile me with the Father. Help me to reform my thinking in order that I may aim to please Jesus in all things, and for Your guidance to discern and walk with You the path of life.

The Catholic Charismatic Renewal had its humble origins on the university campus of Duquesne in Pittsburgh in 1967. The retreatants prayer was for God to deepen the grace of their confirmation. They were all flooded with the glory of God and immersed in His great love.

"This view of baptism in the Spirit—as an activation, or a coming alive, of what was already given through faith and the sacrament of baptism—understands baptism in the Spirit to occur at the moment of regeneration (for Catholics, in the sacrament of Baptism). It recognizes, however, that most people do not experience this reality at the time, either because they were baptized as infants or because they were not in an environment of expectant faith. It is not that nothing occurred, but rather the gift of the Spirit is dormant in the person's life. Later, often in the context of receiving prayer to be filled with the Holy Spirit, this gift is activated. The later experience is not a receiving of the Spirit, but a stirring up or a release of the Holy Spirit, who was already present in the individual.

"Many Christians are not living in the Kingdom they have inherited. Their lives are not showing forth what are meant to be the normal effects of these sacraments. In such cases, there is need for a fresh outpouring of the Holy Spirit in order to experience the fullness of what God has for us."

Randy Clark & Mary Healy - *The Spiritual Gifts Handbook*

In God's Presence Consider …

Do I shy away from or have reservations about the term: "baptism in the Spirit?" Is the Holy Spirit lying dormant in my life? Do I desire and seek a fresh outpouring of the Holy Spirit in order to experience the fullness of what God has for me?

Closing Prayer

Come, Holy Spirit, come alive within me. Awaken and activate within me the graces of Your dormant presence. Stir into flame the fire of Your love, that I may live the fullness of what God has planned for me.

The sacrament of Confirmation is necessary for the completion of baptismal grace and binds us to the Church enriching us with the special strength of the Holy Spirit to live out our baptismal promises.

"By Confirmation Christians … share more completely in the mission of Jesus Christ and the fullness of the Holy Spirit with which he is filled, so that their lives may give off the aroma of Christ. By this anointing (with sacred chrism) a sign of consecration, the confirmand receives the mark, the seal of the Holy Spirit. A seal is a symbol of a person, a sign of personal authority, or ownership of an object. Hence soldiers were marked with their leader's seal and slaves with their master's…. Christians are also marked with a seal: 'It is God … who has commissioned us; he has put his seal on us and given us his Spirit in our hearts as a guarantee' (2 Cor. 1:21–22, Eph. 1:13, 4:30).

"… the effect of the sacrament is a special outpouring of the Holy Spirit as once granted to the apostles on the day of Pentecost … brings an increase and deepening of the baptismal grace, roots us more deeply in the divine filiation, unites us more firmly to Christ, increases the gifts of the Holy Spirit in us, renders our bond with the Church more perfect, gives us a special strength of the Holy Spirit to spread and defend the faith by word and action as true witnesses of Christ, to confess the name of Christ boldly, to never be ashamed of the Cross"

Cf. CCC #1285, 1287, 1294–1296, 1303–1305

In God's Presence Consider …

Do I spread and defend the faith by word and deed? Am I a true ambassador and soldier of Christ defending and professing Him boldly in public? Do I see myself as sealed by the Holy Spirit? Does this seal make a difference in my life?

Closing Prayer

All-powerful God, Father of our Lord Jesus Christ, send Your Holy Spirit upon me anew to be my helper and guide. Stir the fire of Your love within me and increase and perfect the Spirit's gifts in my life, that I may be a bold witness of Christ in all of my life.

The sacrament of Confirmation, St. Pope Paul VI, reminds us, expresses the dynamic life of a Catholic Christian. It is the Holy Spirit who helps us participate in the very functions of Christ for the building of the civilization of love by being witnesses, ambassadors, and soldiers of Christ.

"With the sacrament of Confirmation, those who are reborn in Baptism receive an ineffable gift, the Holy Spirit himself, through which they are enriched with a special power.... They are more perfectly linked to the Church, while they are more strictly obliged to spread and defend, through word and deed, their faith, as authentic witnesses of Christ. Finally, Confirmation is so tied to the sacred Eucharist that the faithful, already marked by sacred Baptism and Confirmation, are inserted fully in the body of Christ through participation in the Eucharist."

St. Pope Paul VI - *Divine Consortium Naturae*

In God's Presence Consider ...

Do I ever ask the Holy Spirit to stir up or rekindle in me the special power He gave me at my Confirmation? Do I see myself linked to the Church with a special obligation to evangelize? Do I receive devoutly and reverently the Holy Eucharist that fully inserts me into the body of Christ?

Closing Prayer

Come Spirit of the Living God, and stir in me anew Your ineffable gifts that You poured upon me at my Confirmation. Help me as a fully incorporated member of the Church to spread, defend, and witness to Christ, thus building the civilization of love.

A Continual Giving **Day 239**

"If anyone loves Me, we will come to him and will make our abode with him." Jn. 14:23

"The gift of the Holy Spirit is not a temporary gift, but a permanent one; in fact, for a soul who lives in charity, He is the sweet Guest who dwells within it.... However, this indwelling of the Trinity—and hence of the Holy Spirit—in the soul which is in the state of grace, is a gift which can and should increase; it is a continual giving. The first donation was made when we were baptized; it was renewed later, confirmed, in a special way, by the Sacrament of Confirmation, the Sacrament that is, so to speak, the Pentecost of every Christian soul. Progressive renewals of this gift were made with every increase in charity. And what of the present? The Holy Spirit, in union with the Father and the Son, continues to give Himself to the soul more completely, more profoundly and possessively."

Fr. Gabriel of St. Mary Magdalen, O.C.D. - *Divine Intimacy*

In God's Presence Consider ...

Do I progressively seek to renew the Holy Spirit's indwelling in me and His life of grace? Do I seek an increase and perfection of charity in my life thus enabling me to live a life in the Spirit?

Closing Prayer

Come, Holy Ghost, Creator Blest, and in our hearts take up Thy rest. Come with Thy grace and heavenly aid, to fill the hearts which Thou has made.

Written by Rabanus Maurus; translated by Edward Caswall

The Sacrifice Directed to Communion **Day 240**

The Eucharist is the source and summit of the Christian life because it contains the whole Christ who is made present through the Holy Spirit who is the principle of the Church's unity.

"The Eucharist is the efficacious sign and sublime cause of that communion in the divine life and that unity of the People of God by which the Church is kept in being. It is the culmination both of God's action sanctifying the world in Christ and the worship men offer to Christ and through him to the Father in the Holy Spirit.

"At the heart of the Eucharistic celebration are the bread and wine that, by the words of Christ and the invocation of the Holy Spirit, become Christ's Body and Blood.... The Mass is at the same time, and inseparably, the sacrificial memorial in which the sacrifice of the cross is perpetuated and the sacred banquet of communion with the Lord's body and blood. But the celebration of the Eucharistic sacrifice is wholly directed toward the intimate union of the faithful with Christ through communion. To receive communion is to receive Christ himself who has offered himself for us.

"Communion with the flesh of the risen Christ, a flesh given life and giving life through the Holy Spirit, preserves, increases, and renews the life of grace received at Baptism."

Cf. CCC #1325, 1362, 1333, 1353, 1382, 1392, 1405

In God's Presence Consider ...

Eucharist is not merely a symbol or nice idea. It is receiving the body, blood, soul, and divinity of Christ. Do I believe that in receiving the Eucharist I am receiving Christ Himself? Do I see the work of my redemption as an ongoing process that the Mass represents, manifests, and makes present for me to receive?

Closing Prayer

Holy Spirit, You transform simple elements of bread and wine into the Body and Blood of Jesus. Prepare me to receive Jesus worthily and to worship God in thanksgiving for such a wonderful gift.

The Mass is the highest prayer for Catholics. Because of the intimate encounter and communion that takes place between the Trinity and the believer, those attending Mass should prepare for this encounter and exchange with God.

"In every liturgical action the Holy Spirit is sent in order to bring us into communion with Christ and so to form his Body. The Holy Spirit is like the sap of the Father's vine which bears fruit on its branches....

"When the Church celebrates the Eucharist, she commemorates Christ's Passover, and it is made present: the sacrifice Christ offered once for all on the cross remains ever present (Heb. 7:25–27). As often as the sacrifice of the Cross by which Christ our Pasch has been sacrificed is celebrated on the altar, the work of our redemption is carried out (LG #3, 1 Cor. 5:7).

"The assembly should prepare itself to encounter its Lord and to become a people well disposed. The preparation of hearts is the joint work of the Holy Spirit and the assembly, especially of its ministers. The grace of the Holy Spirit seeks to awaken faith, conversion of heart, and adherence to the Father's will. These dispositions are the precondition both for the reception of other graces conferred in the celebration itself and the fruits of new life which the celebration is intended to produce afterward."

CCC #1108, 1364, 1098

In God's Presence Consider …

Do I have the sap of the Holy Spirit flowing through me? Do I see myself actively engaged during the Mass? How do I prepare and make myself disposed for the new life that is offered to me at each Mass?

Closing Prayer

May the grace of the Lord Jesus Christ and the love of God our Father bring me into fellowship with the Holy Spirit and make my life a living sacrifice to the Father, spiritually transforming me into the image of Jesus His Son, and leading me to take my part in the mission of the Church through my witness and service of charity.

A Living Tabernacle **Day 242**

Jesus, Our Lord is in the Blessed Sacrament on the altar and in our tabernacles, whereas, the Holy Spirit is in our very souls.

"Every soul in the state of grace is a living tabernacle of the Holy Ghost, and as we are obliged to adore and honor Jesus Christ on the altar, so too are we obliged to honor the Holy Ghost in our souls.

"The Presence of Our Lord in the Blessed Sacrament in millions and millions of Sacred Hosts in the cities and towns of the whole world, and even in the wild deserts of Africa and Asia, day and night, is indeed a proof of the boundless love of God for us. But the Presence of the Holy Ghost in our souls is still more amazing, because God's Presence in the Blessed Sacrament will cease on the last day; whereas, the presence of the Holy Ghost in our souls will never cease. It will last for all Eternity."

Fr. Paul O' Sullivan, O.P. - *The Holy Ghost Our Greatest Friend*

In God's Presence Consider …

Just as I am obliged to adore and honor Jesus on the altar, I also am obliged to honor the Holy Spirit who dwells in my soul. Do I honor and adore Jesus really present in the consecrated and sacred host? Do I honor and adore the Holy Spirit present in the tabernacle of my heart?

Closing Prayer

Holy Spirit, God of Love, I adore You really and truly dwelling in my soul. Increase and perfect in me Your holy Love.

Jesus is alive and acting today in the world through His Church. Jesus spoke of His death as the necessary condition for the Spirit's coming (Jn. 16:7) and for His own new way of coming and remaining with us in the sacraments.

"... by the power of the Holy Spirit, who makes it possible for Christ, who has gone away, to come now and forever in a new way. This new coming of Christ, by the power of the Holy Spirit, and his constant presence and action in the spiritual life are accomplished in the sacramental reality. In this reality, Christ, who has gone away in his visible humanity, comes, is present, and acts in the Church in such an intimate way as to make it his own Body. As such, the Church lives, works, and grows.... All this happens through the power of the Holy Spirit.

"In every celebration of the Eucharist, his coming, his salvific presence, is sacramentally realized: in Sacrifice and in Communion. It is accomplished by the power of the Holy Spirit.... The Holy Spirit is the principle of the Church's unity.... The Son ... who is continuously present in the mystery of the Church ... happens in a sacramental way through the power of the Holy Spirit ... who constantly gives life.... For the sacraments signify grace and confer grace: they signify life and give life. The Church is the visible dispenser of the sacred signs, while the Holy Spirit acts in them as the invisible dispenser of the life they signify. Together with the Spirit, Christ Jesus is present and acting."

St. Pope John Paul II - *Dominum et Vivicantem*

In God's Presence Consider ...

Do I see Jesus alive, present, and acting in the Church today? Knowing the Holy Spirit is the invisible dispenser of the divine life through the sacraments, how can I better prepare to receive Him, with Jesus, in the Eucharist? Do I see the Holy Spirit constantly present and acting in my spiritual life through the sacraments?

Closing Prayer

Come, Holy Spirit, come. Constantly be present in me, giving me Your life through sacramental realities and uniting me with other members of Jesus' Body.

Those in the state of Sanctifying Grace carry the Holy Spirit within their hearts as a pyx or a tabernacle holds the Blessed Eucharist.

"Pope Alexander had an intense devotion to Our Lord in the Blessed Eucharist, and to satisfy this great love, he caused to be made a beautiful golden pyx in which he placed the Blessed Sacrament every morning and wore it on his breast during the day. This perpetual adoration obtained for the Holy Pontiff the greatest graces and consolations. He felt that he was always in the presence of Our Lord.

"Now each one of us [in the state of Sanctifying Grace] carries the Holy Ghost Himself in us—not in a golden pyx on our breast, but in our very souls.

"What an immense joy and consolation for those who realize this wonderful fact!"

Fr. Paul O' Sullivan, O.P. - *The Holy Ghost Our Greatest Friend*

In God's Presence Consider …

Do I believe that the Holy Spirit is really in my soul? Do I adore and Love Him? Do I make time throughout my day to take brief moments to offer prayers of thanksgiving and praise to the Holy Spirit?

Closing Prayer

O Holy Spirit, fill me with Your joy and consolation that I may always live with an intense devotion to You.

Jesus has willed that His Church would continue His work of mercy and forgiveness. The power of the Holy Spirit given to continue this work is one of healing, salvation, and especially for our new life as a child of God weakened and even lost by sin. This work is called the sacrament of Penance and Reconciliation.

"It is called the sacrament of conversion because it makes sacramentally present Jesus' call to conversion, the first step in returning to the Father from whom one has strayed by sin….

"… the Holy Spirit who brings sin to light is also the Consoler who gives the human heart grace for repentance and conversion: namely contrition, confession, and satisfaction…. Contrition is sorrow of the soul and detestation for the sin committed, together with the resolution not to sin again … contrition is also a gift of God, a prompting of the Holy Spirit.

"The whole power of the sacrament of Penance consists in restoring us to God's grace and joining us with him in an intimate friendship … the sacrament repairs and reconciles us with the Church."

Cf. CCC #1423, 1426, 1433, 1448, 1451, 1453, 1468–1469

In God's Presence Consider …

Even though all sins are forgiven and washed away with the waters of Baptism, the reality of our inclination to sin (concupiscence) is not abolished and our new life in Christ becomes a constant struggle with the forces of the world, the flesh, and the devil that break our intimate communion with God. Do I see this struggle of conversion directed to my personal holiness and eternal life? Do I see the Holy Spirit's role in bringing me to conversion and restoring the fraternal communion I have damaged through my sins?

Closing Prayer

God, the Father of mercies, through the death and the resurrection of his Son has reconciled the world to himself and sent the Holy Spirit among us for the forgiveness of sins; I beg You Father to bring me to true contrition and conversion, that through receiving the sacrament of Penance I may be restored to an intimate friendship with You.

Based on the Prayer of Absolution in the Sacrament of Penance

Sin is a rejection of God's love; a rejection of the ways God loves us. The Holy Spirit is sent by the Father, at the Son's request, to convict the world of its sin and to give man the capacity for a restored personal relationship with his Creator.

"Sin in its original reality … is as opposition of the will of man to the will of God … a disobedience … a direct transgression of a prohibition laid down … at the root of human sin is the lie which is a radical rejection of the truth contained in the Word of the Father.... The Spirit of God is … the direct witness of their (God the Father and the Son) mutual love from which creation derives, but he himself is this love. He himself, as love, is the eternal uncreated gift … the gift of the Spirit ultimately means a call to friendship, in which the transcendent depths of God become, in some way, opened to participation on the part of man.... Man cannot decide by himself what is good and what is evil—cannot know good and evil like God.... It is the Holy Spirit who gives the gift of conscience … and who at the same time is for man, the light of conscience and the source of the moral order.... And the Spirit does not cease convincing the world of it (sin) in connection with the Cross of Christ on Golgotha."

St. Pope John Paul II - *Dominum et Vivicantem*

In God's Presence Consider …

Have I ever asked the Holy Spirit to see and convict me of my sins? How do I handle the gift of conscience that the Holy Spirit has given me? Do I see the presence of the Holy Spirit in me as a call to friendship with God?

Closing Prayer

Come, Holy Spirit, the Light of Conscience, convict me of my sins, my rejections of God's love, and help me to know what is good and evil; that I may fully participate in a friendship with God.

Blasphemy against the Holy Spirit deals with rejecting God's mercy. Origin views this blasphemy as ultimately rejecting the Trinity of which the Holy Spirit is One with the Father and the Son. The Catechism says, "There are no limits to the mercy of God, but anyone who deliberately refuses to accept his mercy by repenting, rejects the forgiveness of his sins and the salvation offered by the Holy Spirit. Such hardness of heart can lead to final impenitence and eternal loss." CCC #1864

"Now, what the Holy Spirit is, we are taught in many passages of Scripture, as by David in the Psalm 51, when he says, "And take not Thy Holy Spirit from me;" and by Daniel, where it is said, 'The Holy Spirit which is in thee.' And in the New Testament we have abundant testimonies, as when the Holy Spirit is described as having descended upon Christ, and when the Lord breathed upon His apostles after His resurrection, saying, 'Receive the Holy Spirit;' and the saying of the angel to Mary, 'The Holy Spirit will come upon thee;' the declaration by Paul, that no one can call Jesus Lord, save by the Holy Spirit. In the Acts of the Apostles, the Holy Spirit was given by the imposition of the apostles' hands in baptism.... Who, then, is not amazed at the exceeding majesty of the Holy Spirit, when he hears that he who speaks a word against the Son of man may hope for forgiveness; but that he who is guilty of blasphemy against the Holy Spirit has not forgiveness, either in the present world or in that which is to come?"

Origen - *De Principiis, Book I Chapter IV*

In God's Presence Consider …

Do I use the Scriptures to teach me more about who the Holy Spirit is and what He does? Do I seek and accept God's forgiveness? Do I live in God's mercy? Have I ever considered the "unforgivable sin" against the Holy Spirit as a rejection of God's merciful love?

Closing Prayer

Come, Holy Spirit, in all Your majesty; melt my hardness with Your love. Come, and set my heart on fire, that I may embrace God's mercy and forgiveness with great joy and thanksgiving.

Lost in the Divine Essence **Day 248**

Union with the Divine is a co-effort on the part of the Holy Spirit and the man or woman called to Divine Intimacy with God.

"The Holy Ghost is the spiritual love who resides in the will as a bond and as a divine impetus which inspires and urges us on; he is the charity of God.... In him are transformed those who love God and are attracted to the light, and this in so intimate a manner that is neither known nor understood except by experience.... To be united with him you must prepare your spirit and your body, renouncing flesh and sensuality, subjecting the senses, seeking after the things of the spirit, and persevering in recollection and prayer. Such is the way to arrive at the higher Spirit, who is God, and to be united to him. Then you will feel this divine Spirit inspires you, calls you, invites you, and attracts you ... resign yourself on him with loving trust and remain buried in him, forgetting yourself and losing yourself quite completely ... and when you are thus elevated, lost in the immensity of the divine essence, you will then be united and transformed in the Spirit of God."

Blessed Henry Suso – *Union*

In God's Presence Consider ...

Do I take serious my efforts to prepare myself for union with God through cooperating with the Holy Spirit? Do I see my love for God as being lost in the immensity of His divine essence? Am I attached to the light of the Holy Spirit and drawn to renouncing all for God?

Closing Prayer

Blessed Suso, pray that the Holy Spirit, the Fire of God's Love, attract me, transform me, and help me prepare to enter into deep union with our God.

***AUTHOR'S NOTE:** Over the next three days, we will be looking at what the Holy Spirit does through the sacraments of Marriage and Holy Orders. Because not all are called to live out their lives in the married or ordained state, we are called to bear witness and serve. In articles #897–933 of the Catechism, we see how we are all called to personal intimacy with Jesus, holiness of life, witnessing life in Christ, mission, and service. In #901 we see that the Holy Spirit is sent to anoint all those who are baptized and fully incorporated into the Church and thus sealed with His power and strength are sent out. My encouragement to you, if you are not married or ordained, is that you would read the text provided to see how the Holy Spirit acts in these two sacraments; then read through it a second time, looking for how the text might affect you in the vocation that you have been called. I have included questions that would pertain to your call in the section "In God's Presence Consider."

A Bond Perpetual and Exclusive **Day 249**

God is the author of marriage. The intimate union and bond which marriage brings about is unbreakable. Even though this kind of union seems humanly impossible, it is the work of the Holy Spirit that gives marriage its dignity and fruitfulness.

"The various liturgies abound in prayers of blessing and epiclesis asking God's grace and blessing on the new couple, especially the bride. In the epiclesis of this sacrament the spouses receive the Holy Spirit as the communion of love of Christ and the Church. The Holy Spirit is the seal of their covenant, the ever available source of their love and the strength to renew their fidelity.... From a valid marriage arises a bond between the spouses which by its very nature is perpetual and exclusive; furthermore, in a Christian marriage the spouses are strengthened and, as it were, consecrated for the duties and the dignity of their state by a special sacrament. Thus the marriage bond has been established by God himself in such a way that a marriage concluded and consummated between baptized persons can never be dissolved.

Cf. CCC #1605, 1608, 1609, 1615, 1624, 1638, 1640

In God's Presence Consider ...

For those married: Marriage as a perpetual union can seem impossible and scary. How do I avail myself to the graces of the sacrament to live marriage as God intends? Do I make use of the ever available source of love and strength of the Holy Spirit to daily renew my fidelity and love to my spouse?

For those not married: How do I avail myself to the graces of the sacraments to live faithfully my vocation? Do I make use of the ever available source of love and strength of the Holy Spirit to daily anoint and renew my fidelity to love God and neighbor? Do I give thanks to God and seek to live out fully my vocational call with the help of the Holy Spirit?

Closing Prayer

Pour out upon these gifts (my vocation) the blessing of your Spirit, we pray, O Lord, so that through them your Church may be imbued with such love that the truth of your saving mystery may shine forth for the whole world.

Prayer over the gifts of the Vigil Mass for Pentecost

Indissoluble Unity **Day 250**

To bind oneself for life to another human being is not only difficult, but impossible without God's help.

"God who created man out of love also calls him to love—the fundamental and innate vocation of every human being.... The vocation to marriage is written in the very nature of man and woman as they came from the hand of the Creator. Marriage is not a purely human institution....

"... man and woman need the help of the grace that God in his infinite mercy never refuses them. Without his help man and woman cannot achieve the union of their lives for which God created them.... The grace proper to the sacrament of Matrimony is intended to perfect the couple's love and to strengthen their indissoluble unity. By this grace they help one another to attain holiness in their married life and in welcoming and educating their children. The Holy Spirit is given to the married couple as the communion of love of Christ and the Church. The Holy Spirit is the seal of their covenant, the ever available source of their love and the strength to renew their fidelity."

Cf. CCC #1604, 1603, 1608, 1617, 1641, 1624

In God's Presence Consider ...

For those married: Do I ever refuse God's infinite mercy when it comes to living out my vocation of marriage? Do I see myself as a means for my spouse to attain holiness and get to heaven? Do I ever look at the Holy Spirit's role in my marriage covenant?

For those not married: The fundamental and innate vocation of every person is love. Do I ever refuse God's infinite mercy when it comes to loving? Do I see myself as a means for others to attain holiness and get to heaven? Do I ever look to the Holy Spirit helping me live out faithfully my vocation and to bear witness to others? The Holy Spirit is given as a seal to all the baptized as a source of love, strength, and renewed fidelity. What do I do with the seal that has been entrusted to me?

Closing Prayer

Come, Holy Spirit, of love and unity. Help me to live my vocation fully under Your guidance, grace, and love.

Instrument for His Church **Day 251**

The faithful all share in the common priesthood through Baptism, but through the Sacrament of Holy Orders, a man is called, invited, and set apart for ecclesial service. They activate the graces available in the sacraments. It is Christ Himself who is present to the Church through His ordained ministers. The ordained acts in persona Christi.

"Holy Orders is the sacrament through which the mission entrusted by Christ to his apostles continues to be exercised in the Church until the end of time.... The laying on of hands by the bishop, with the consecratory prayer, constitutes the visible sign of this ordination ... for it confers a gift of the Holy Spirit that permits the exercise of a sacred power which can come only from Christ himself through his Church ... with the grace of the Holy Spirit being given, and a sacred character is impressed.

"This sacrament configures the recipient to Christ as Priest, Teacher, and Pastor by a special grace of the Holy Spirit, so that he may serve as Christ's instrument for his Church.

Cf. CCC #1536, 1538, 1558, 1581, 1585

In God's Presence Consider ...

For the ordained: The sacrament of Holy Orders configures the recipient to Christ by a special grace of the Holy Spirit, so that he may serve as Christ's instrument for his Church. How do I exercise the sacred power of the Holy Spirit imparted to me? Do I make it a constant practice to invoke the Holy Spirit to stir up the gifts of my ordination and make me a clean instrument?

For the non-ordained: How do I talk about or treat my parish deacon, priest, bishop, and pope? Do I see my parish priest as an instrument of service, a channel of grace conformed to be another Christ? Do I know the mission Christ has entrusted to me? Do I seek the Holy Spirit to configure me to Christ the servant?

Closing Prayer

Father, You know all hearts. Choose shepherds from among Your sheep and through the Holy Spirit give them the grace of holy priesthood. Clothe them with the Power from on High making them holy priests; priests after Your own heart. Help me to treat all deacons, priests and bishops with respect.

The Touch That Heals **Day 252**

Illness and suffering are among the gravest problems facing us and are the consequences of original sin. In illness, we experience our powerlessness, limitation, and finitude. Every illness can make us glimpse death and very often provokes a search for God and a return to Him.

"Christ has come to heal the whole man, soul and body … so in the sacraments Christ continues to touch us in order to heal us.… The first grace of the sacrament is one of strengthening, peace and courage to overcome the difficulties that go with the condition of serious illness or the frailty of old age. This grace is a gift of the Holy Spirit, who renews trust and faith in God and strengthens against the temptations of the evil one, the temptation to discouragement and anguish in the face of death. This assistance from the Lord by the power of his Spirit is meant to lead the sick person to healing of the soul, but also of the body if such is God's will. Furthermore, if he has committed sins, he will be forgiven."

Cf. CCC #1499, 1503–05, 1520

In God's Presence Consider …

Do I seek to join my discomforts, suffering, and illnesses to the Cross with Jesus? Do I seek the Holy Spirit's help in embracing God's will for me in my sickness and aging?

Closing Prayer

Through this holy anointing may the Lord in his love and mercy help you with the grace of the Holy Spirit. May the Lord, who frees you from sin save you and raise you up.

Adapted from the Roman Rite

The Redemptive work Jesus did and continues to do in the Paschal Mystery celebrated at every Mass would be useless without the Holy Spirit.

"The Holy Ghost is like a gardener cultivating our souls.... The Holy Ghost is our servant.... There is a gun; well you load it, but someone must fire it and make it go off.... In the same way, we have in ourselves the power of doing good ... when the Holy Ghost gives the impulse, good works are produced. The Holy Ghost reposes in just souls like the dove in her nest. He brings out good desires in a pure soul, as the dove hatches her young ones. The Holy Ghost leads us as a mother leads by the hand her child of two years old, as a person who can see leads one who is blind.

"The Sacraments which Our Lord instituted would not have saved us without the Holy Ghost. Even the death of Our Lord would have been useless to us without Him. Therefore Our Lord said to His Apostles, 'It is good for you that I should go away; for if I did not go, the Consoler would not come.' The descent of the Holy Ghost was required, to render fruitful that harvest of graces. It is like a grain of wheat—you cast it into the ground; yes, but it must have sun and rain to make it grow and come into ear. We should say every morning, 'O God, send me Thy Spirit to teach me what I am and what Thou art."

St. John Vianney - *Catechism on the Holy Spirit,* Chapter 3

In God's Presence Consider ...

Do I recognize the impulses of the Holy Spirit? Do I allow these impulses to cultivate my soul to do good? Have I ever thought the reason for fruitlessness in my life is not allowing the presence of the Holy Spirit to dwell in me?

Closing Prayer

O God, send me Your Spirit to teach me what I am and who You are. Fill me with Your good desires and purity.

Holy Spirit as God's Gift: Gifts, Virtues, Fruits

Body Building

The Holy Spirit is given to the Church in order to renew and build up the Body of Christ.

"The Holy Spirit is the principle of every vital and truly saving action in each part of the Body. He works in many ways to build up the whole Body in charity, by God's Word which is able to build you up, by Baptism, through which he forms Christ's Body, by the sacraments, which give growth and healing to Christ's members; by the grace of the apostles, which holds first place among his gifts, by the virtues, which make us act according to what is good; finally, by the many special graces (called charisms). By which he makes the faithful fit and ready to undertake various tasks and offices for the renewal and building up of the Church."

CCC #798

In God's Presence Consider …

Do I use all the means God has given me through the Church to be made fit and ready to build up the Body of Christ, the Church? Do I see my personal and continual renewal as important for the renewal of the Church?

Closing Prayer

May your Spirit, O Lord, we pray, imbue us powerfully with spiritual gifts, that he may give us a mind pleasing to you and graciously conform us to your will.

Collect from Thursday of the 7th week of Easter

Person as Love and Gift **Day 255**

In John's Gospel, the three Members of the Trinity are called Persons, distinct from one another yet coming from one another. Jesus Himself speaks of the Holy Spirit using the personal pronoun "He."

"At the same time, the Holy Spirit, being consubstantial with the Father and the Son in divinity, is love and uncreated gift from which derives as from its source all giving of gifts (visible and invisible) … the gift of grace to human beings through the whole economy of salvation. As the Apostle Paul writes: 'God's love has been poured into our hearts through the Holy Spirit which has been given to us (Rom. 5:5).'

St. Pope John Paul II - *Dominum et Vivificantem*

In God's Presence Consider …

Love is an uncreated gift. How do I experience the Holy Spirit as God's love poured into my heart? How Can I share in the intimate life of God?

Closing Prayer

Come, Holy Spirit, Gift of Love, fill me with Your grace that I may be capable of sharing in the great gift of love and grace that You are.

Sustained by the grace of the Holy Spirit, we are mobilized, purified, and called to follow His promptings to live a moral life.

"The moral life of Christians is sustained by the gifts of the Holy Spirit. These are permanent dispositions which make man docile in following the promptings of the Holy Spirit.

"Human virtues … are purified and elevated by divine grace. With God's help, they forge character and give facility in the practice of the good. It is not easy for man, wounded by sin, to maintain moral balance. Christ's gift of salvation offers us the grace necessary to persevere in the pursuit of the virtues. Everyone should always ask for this grace of light and strength, frequent the sacraments, cooperate with the Holy Spirit, and follow his calls to love what is good and shun evil."

Cf. CCC #1769, 1810–1811, 1830

In God's Presence Consider …

Do I seek to forge my character by practicing the virtues and seeking the Holy Spirit's help in elevating them with His grace? How do I maintain moral balance in my life? Do I ask for and cooperate with the Holy Spirit to love what is good and shun evil?

Closing Prayer

Come, Great Holy Mobilizer, and conform me to Christ's virtuous life. Forge my character in the Fire of Your divine love. Sustain me along the paths to heaven and help me to follow Your promptings.

As Anointing **Day 257**

Jesus is the Messiah, the promised One from God. The word "messiah" literally means Christ, or the Anointed One. Historically it means the one anointed by the Father with the Holy Spirit.

"The Prophet (Isaiah) presents the Messiah as the one who comes in the Holy Spirit, the one who possesses the fullness of this Spirit in himself and at the same time for others, for Israel, for all nations, for all humanity. The fullness of the Spirit of God is accompanied by many different gifts, the treasures of salvation, destined in a particular way for the poor and suffering, for all those who open their hearts to these gifts … through that interior availability which comes from faith."

St. Pope John Paul II - *Dominum et Vivicantem*

In God's Presence Consider …

Do I see Jesus and the Holy Spirit so intimately united? Am I interiorly available, having an open heart for the Holy Spirit's presence and gifts to live in me?

Closing Prayer

Come, Holy Spirit, come. Fill me with Your fullness as You filled Jesus my Messiah.

The Eyes of the Soul **Day 258**

The Holy Spirit as the breath of God, breathes into our souls understanding, new life, and an awareness of the presence of the Lord.

"When the Holy Spirit begins to breathe upon the soul, and to melt the frozen waters with His Spirit, through the gift of understanding, he lays open the hidden meaning of things. Through the breath of his charity, which he places in the soul, there is an interior sense and taste of the sweetness of the Lord. Then, surely as a torrent in the south (Psalm 125:4), he ends the captivity of the mind, just as a torrent frozen solid is loosed by warm air. Clouds are dispersed, and the aroma of the mysteries of faith, like the odor of a ploughed field, is spread abroad. The eyes of the soul are as doves, dwelling not in the barren and arid land, but alongside a full stream. The soul is filled with marrow and fatness by the light which is poured into it, and its prayer is like incense in the sight of God. All these things are results of the gift."

John of St. Thomas - *The Gifts of the Holy Spirit*

In God's Presence Consider …

Have I ever connected the sweetness of the Lord I find in prayer with the breath of the Holy Spirit breathing on me? Do I seek sending my roots deep into the Holy Spirit as a tree sends its roots towards a full stream or do I allow the aridness I sometimes experience discourage me from praying?

Closing Prayer

Come, Holy Spirit, true source of light and fountain of wisdom, grant me a penetrating mind to understand the hidden meaning of Your mysteries and release their aroma within me, that I may spread Your great love, as incense before God.

The Holy Spirit is given as a Counselor to guide us into all truth, for He does not speak on His own authority but only speaks what He hears from the Father and takes from the Son.

"We receive the Spirit of truth so that we can know the things of God. In order to grasp this, consider how useless the faculties of the human body would become if they were denied their exercise. Our eyes cannot fulfill their task without light, either natural or artificial; our ears cannot react without sound vibrations, and in the absence of any odor our nostrils are ignorant of their function. Not that these senses would lose their own nature if they were not used, rather, they demand objects of experience in order to function. It is the same with the human soul. Unless it absorbs the gift of the Spirit through faith, the mind has the ability to know God but lacks the light necessary for that knowledge.

"This unique gift which is in Christ is offered in its fullness to everyone. It is everywhere available, but it is given to each man in proportion to his readiness to receive it. Its presence is the fuller, the greater a man's desire to be worthy of it. This gift will remain with us until the end of the world, and will be our comfort in the time of waiting. By the favors it bestows, it is the pledge of our hope for the future, the light of our minds and the splendor that irradiates our understanding."

St. Hilary - *Treatise on the Trinity*

In God's Presence Consider …

How does my life reflect the absorbing of the Holy Spirit who seeks to help me know God beyond a mere knowledge of Him? Am I open to the fullness of the Holy Spirit? How do I prepare each day to make myself ready for receiving a fresh outpouring of the Holy Spirit?

Closing Prayer

Come, Holy Spirit, Pledge of our Hope for the future, fill my mind with Your light and splendor that I may have an intimate abiding relationship with God and that You irradiate my understanding.

Constant Work in Our Souls **Day 260**

It is the Holy Spirit who makes us capable of responding to God's desires for us and sharing in His divine life. He gives us access to Him, helps us to know Him better, and of loving Him far beyond our own natural ability.

"... in order to enable us to perform supernatural acts, the Holy Spirit comes to strengthen our powers—the intellect and the will—by the infused virtues: charity, together with the other theological virtues of faith and hope, and the moral virtues. Thus, through His intervention, we become capable of performing supernatural acts. But the Holy Spirit does not stop there; like a good teacher, He continues to help us in our work, urging us to do good and sustaining our efforts. He invites us by His interior inspirations, as well as by exterior means, especially Sacred Scripture and the teachings of the Church ... the activity of the soul is entirely permeated and sustained by the action of the Holy Spirit. We give too little attention to this truth and therefore, in practice, we tend to ignore the constant work of the divine Spirit in our souls. Let us give thought to this, lest His inspirations and impulses go unheeded."

Fr. Gabriel of St. Mary Magdalen, O.C.D. - *Divine Intimacy*

In God's Presence Consider ...

Have I ever pondered the Holy Spirit as the source from whom I can perform supernatural acts? Am I sensitive to the Holy Spirit working in my soul or am I ignoring His constant efforts of inspiring me to do good and performing acts of love and service? Do I recognize His gentle movements in my heart or do they go unheeded?

Closing Prayer

Come, Holy Spirit, and strengthen my will and intellect, permeating and sustaining my soul with Your work.

Just as we did not choose God first, but He chose us, so in the order of grace, we can only possess God because God first gives Himself to us. He does this through giving us the Holy Spirit.

"We possess God because he gives himself to us, but his first Gift is the Holy Spirit. Our first intimacy, then, is with the Holy Spirit. This does not mean that we can possess one divine Person without possessing the others, because they are inseparable. We possess the Father and the Son because we possess the Holy Spirit, who is the first Gift of God.

"To live spiritually is to have our affections and our actions in order. St. Augustine defined virtue by saying that it is order in love. Order in love produces order in our actions, in our thoughts, and in our faculties.... If we desire to obtain the fruits of the Spirit, we need to work, to try to purify our souls little by little, to advance little by little on the road to perfection.... The plants that produce the fruits of the Holy Spirit are the virtues and especially the gifts of the Holy Spirit.... Accordingly, there are three things that we must do to possess those celestial delights. We must pray; we must purify our soul; eliminating all that hinders us from perceiving the sweetness and mildness of the heavenly fruits; then, by also working ceaselessly and struggling against our interior and exterior enemies, we can be assured that the precious fruits will fill our souls with sweetness."

SOG Archbishop Louis M. Martinez - *The Sanctifier*

In God's Presence Consider ...

Because of the inseparable relationship of the Blessed Trinity, we cannot possess one Divine Person without possessing the others. Do I understand the Holy Spirit as the First Gift and how my intimacy with the Father and the Son is possible only through my relationship with the Holy Spirit? Do I have a habit of prayer, purifying my soul, and persevering in my struggles to overcome my interior and exterior enemies?

Closing Prayer

O First Gift of God, fan the flame of Your Love within me, that I may be inseparably possessed by all Three Person of the Blessed Trinity and be filled with the sweetness of Your celestial delights.

St. Padre Pio writes that self-conceit is an enemy that never grows weary and wars against us in all our actions. If we are not aware of its presence, he says, we become its victim. It is the work of the Holy Spirit and our pursuit of holiness that effectively combats this enemy.

"Vainglory, or self-conceit, is the true enemy of souls who are consecrated to the Lord and are committed to spiritual life. That is precisely why it can be said to be the devouring worm of any soul that aims for perfection. The saints have called it the worm that destroys holiness ... the vice is even more to be feared because there is no opposing virtue to counter it. Every vice actually has its remedy in an opposite virtue. Anger is overcome through meekness, envy through charity, pride through humility, and so on. Only the vice of self-conceit does not have a contrary virtue to counteract it. It insinuates itself into the holiest of actions, and, if it is not recognized, it haughtily sets up its tent even in humility.

"The apostle Paul tells us, 'If we live by the Spirit, let us also walk by the Spirit' (Gal. 5:25).... Do we want to live spiritually, that is, moved and led by the Holy Spirit? We are instructed to mortify the self, which puffs us up, which makes us impetuous, which makes us spiritually dry. In brief, we need to take concern to resist self-conceit, anger, and envy. These three malignant spirits have enslaved the majority of human beings and are extremely opposed to the Spirit of the Lord."

St. Padre Pio, O.F.M. Cap. - *Padre Pio's Spiritual Direction for Every Day*

In God's Presence Consider ...

Am I committed to the spiritual life? Am I aiming for spiritual perfection? Do I live by the Spirit declaring war on those vices and sins that distract me and are opposed to the Lord?

Closing Prayer

Come, Holy Spirit, and help me to counter my self-conceit, anger, and envy with Your help, that freed from their slavery I may, like St. Padre Pio, seek holiness in all my actions. St. Padre Pio, pray for me.

To Be in Touch **Day 263**

Although the Holy Spirit is the last of the Persons of the Holy Trinity to be revealed, He is the One who reveals and puts us in touch with the Father and Son. Without Him we would never know Them.

"This knowledge of faith is possible only in the Holy Spirit; to be in touch with Christ, we must first have been touched by the Holy Spirit. He comes to meet us and kindles faith in us. By virtue of our Baptism the first sacrament of the faith, the Holy Spirit in the Church communicates to us, intimately and personally, the life that originates in the Father and is offered to us in the Son.... And it is impossible to see God's Son without the Spirit.... Through his grace, the Holy Spirit is the first to awaken faith in us and to communicate to us the new life, which is to know the Father and the one whom he has sent, Jesus Christ (cf. Jn. 17:3)."

Cf. CCC #683–684

In God's Presence Consider ...

To touch Christ, we must first touch the Holy Spirit. Have I ever thought that without a relationship with the Holy Spirit, I would have no relationship with Jesus? Do I shut myself off to the ways the Holy Spirit communicates His life to me?

Closing Prayer

O God, who never cease to bestow the glory of holiness on the faithful servants you raise up for yourself, graciously grant that the Holy Spirit may kindle in us that fire with which he wonderfully filled the heart of Philip Neri, that we may be devoted to you with all our heart and united in purity of intent.

Collect from the Memorial of St. Philip Neri

Man can fully discover who he is only in a sincere giving of himself. This comes about through the working and guidance of the Holy Spirit.

"It is by the gift of the Holy Spirit that man, through faith, comes to contemplate and savor the mystery of God's design.... For it is the function of the Church to render God the Father and his incarnate Son present and as it were visible, while ceaselessly renewing and purifying herself under the guidance of the Holy Spirit. This is brought about chiefly by the witness of a living and mature faith, one namely that is so well formed it can see difficulties clearly and overcome them.... This faith should show its fruitfulness by penetrating the whole life, even the worldly activities, of those who believe, and by urging them to be loving and just especially towards those in need....

"The social order and its development must constantly yield to the good of the person, since the order of this must be subordinate to the order of persons and not the other way around.... The Spirit of God, who, with wondrous providence, directs the course of time and renews the face of the earth, assists at this development."

Vatican Council II - *Gaudium et Spes,* #15d, 21e, 26c–d

In God's Presence Consider ...

Have I ever thought of how the Holy Spirit directs the course of time and is the source of renewal? Do I ceaselessly seek to renew and purify myself under the guidance of the Holy Spirit, or do I seek these things on my own? Does my faith penetrate my whole life, even my worldly activities and desires?

Closing Prayer

Father, I beg that You continue to renew and purify the face of the earth, through my witness and the maturing of my faith. Help me to find myself in the giving of myself to the good of other persons.

Buoyed Up by Hope **Day 265**

The human virtues are rooted in the theological virtues which adapt man's faculties for participation in the divine nature. They dispose Christians to live in a relationship with the Holy Trinity, become the foundation of Christian moral activity, and makes us capable of acting as His children, meriting eternal life. Hope anchors our soul in God, helping us to hold fast to Him, despite the many trials and challenges of life.

"Hope is the theological virtue by which we desire the kingdom of heaven and eternal life as our happiness, placing our trust in Christ's promises and relying not on our own strength, but on the help of the grace of the Holy Spirit.... The virtue of hope responds to the aspiration to happiness which God has placed in the heart of every man; it takes up the hopes that inspire men's activities and purifies them so as to order them to the Kingdom of heaven; it keeps man from discouragement; it sustains him during times of abandonment; it opens up his heart in expectation of eternal beatitude. Buoyed up by hope, he is preserved from selfishness and led to the happiness that flows from charity.

"Hope does not disappoint ... is the sure and steadfast anchor of the soul ... a weapon that protects us in the struggle of salvation.... It affords us joy even under trial ... is expressed and nourished in prayer."

Cf. CCC #1817–1818, 1820

In God's Presence Consider ...

Do I rely more upon my own strength, goodness, and merits to gain eternal life or on the graces of the Holy Spirit? Have I ever related my desire for happiness with the aspirations of the theological virtue of hope? Do I see and feel hope buoy me up in the struggles of my salvation?

Closing Prayer

Come, O Spirit of hope, unite me with Christ and bring me to the glory and happiness of heaven.

Taking on the Virtues of Christ — Day 266

By pondering the life and writings of St. Thomas Aquinas, Edward Sri comes to know himself and his need for the Holy Spirit's help in cultivating the virtues which heal, perfect, and elevate his fallen human nature.

"My reading … helped me see more clearly my certain tendencies, fear, attachments, patterns of behavior, weaknesses, vices, and sins – were inhibiting my ability to give the best of myself to Beth (wife) and our children … these were problems for … me, my spiritual life, and were roadblocks in the relationships with the people I wanted to love most.

"But Aquinas also offered me a lot of hope and a road map for how to grow…. Through the virtues, we see the beauty of an integrated human person whose intellect, will, and passions are working harmoniously together to bring about what is truly good in his own life, and in the lives of the people around him. We see a human person who possesses interior freedom that enables him to love. We catch a glimpse of what the ideal can look like in a Catholic home that is built on a virtuous marriage and family life … a picture of good friendship, work relationships, dating, and life in community … the more we are sanctified and take on the virtues of Christ—the more grace heals, perfects, and elevates our fallen human nature to participate in the divine life of Christ…."

Edward Sri - *The Art of Living*

In God's Presence Consider …

We are often times quick at knowing our shortcomings, but do I really identify my tendencies, my fears, attachments, patterns of behavior, weaknesses, and vices which cause my shortcomings? Am I frustrated with my inability to give my best to the ones I love? Do I seek to be an integrated harmonious person through the Holy Spirit by the cultivation of virtues?

Closing Prayer

St. Thomas Aquinas, please pray for me that I may come to a clear knowledge of myself seeking the light and help of the Holy Spirit to live a virtuous life and to bring about what is truly good in my life and the lives of those around me.

St. John tells us that God is love (1 Jn. 4:16) and that when one abides in love, they abide in God and God abides in him. To assure us of this abiding, God gives us the gift of the Holy Spirit (1 Jn. 4:13) who helps us return to the Father where we are complete, perfected, and happy.

"The first gift of love is love itself, and all the other gifts emanate from this supreme gift, as from their source. Therefore, the Gift of the love of God is the Holy Spirit.... But of all the gifts that God gives us through his Gift, the most excellent and precious, the created gift that cannot be separated from the uncreated, is charity, the image of the Holy Spirit.... God loves us through the Holy Spirit. So that we may correspond to that infinite love with a love created, to be sure, but also supernatural and divine, when giving himself to us the Holy Spirit pours into our souls the likeness of himself, which is charity.

"The Holy Spirit does not give himself to us without pouring charity into our hearts, nor can there be the love of charity in us without the Holy Spirit's coming to us by the very act of loving.

"In the supernatural order, love leads to light; the Holy Spirit leads us to the Word, and through the Word we go to the Father, in whom all life is completed and all movement is converted into rest. And in him every creature finds its perfection and its happiness, because all things are completed when they return to their principle."

SOG Archbishop Louis M. Martinez - *The Sanctifier*

In God's Presence Consider ...

God's great gift to me is His Holy Spirit. Have I unwrapped His Gift or have I placed It on a shelf in my heart? Without the Holy Spirit active in our hearts there can be no charity. Do I allow God to love me as He desires to? Do I allow God to love me through the Holy Spirit Who is Love?

Closing Prayer

Come, O Gift of God's Love; come, and dwell in me. Consume me in Your sweet flame of charity that I may come to love You and find my completion, perfection, and happiness in Your Love.

St. Thomas Aquinas is looking at the two personal titles of the Holy Spirit as Love and Gift. He says that to be gratuitous in giving a gift is directly related to how the giver loves and desires the well-being of another.

"A gift, properly speaking, is a giving without anything in return, i.e. a giving without the hope of reward. A true gift implies gratuity. Now, for what reason do we give gratuitously unless it be that we love? If, in fact, we do give something gratuitously to another, it is because we desire his well-being, which is another way of saying we love him. So the first thing we give him is love in as much as we desire its well-being. Thus love is the first gift in virtue of which all gratuitous gifts are given. And since it is established that the Holy Spirit proceeds as Love, he proceeds also as a first gift. St. Augustine says; 'The particular gifts which are distributed to the members of Christ come from the gift which is the Holy Spirit.'"

St. Thomas Aquinas, O.P. - *Summa Theol. Qu. 45, art. 6, ad 2*

In God's Presence Consider ...

God loves us so much and desires our well-being so much that He gratuitously gives us His most beloved gift: the Holy Spirit. Do I accept the Gift and His Love, giving Him thanks? In accepting the Holy Spirit, I am accepting God's Love. How am I doing in my acceptance of such a gift?

Closing Prayer

Father, You desire that I have access to You and share in Your divine life. Help me to accept the ways You love me, and to accept the Gift of Your Love in the Holy Spirit. St. Thomas Aquinas, pray for me.

Infusing Supernatural Habits **Day 269**

The Very Reverend Adolphe Tanquerey makes the point that man can work on human virtues developing himself to habitual good acts, but it is through the Holy Spirit's infusion of the moral virtues and man's active cooperating that helps him to conquer his passions and vices, thus acquiring the divine docility which the gifts of the Holy Spirit confer, which leads to the cultivating of the fruits of the Holy Spirit and is seen lived out in the beatitudes.

"In order to act and develop the supernatural life engrafted into our souls by habitual grace.... God has given us in the form of infused virtues and gifts of the Holy Ghost.

"The Holy Ghost dwells in our soul and infuses, besides habitual grace, supernatural habits which perfect our faculties and enable them to perform supernatural acts under the impulse of actual grace. These habits are the virtues and the gifts....

"The virtues with the help of the grace we receive, we inquire, reason and work as we do in actions of a purely natural order. The virtues are therefore energies that are primarily and directly active. The gifts on the contrary, impart to us a docility and receptiveness that enables us to receive and follow the motions of operating grace. This grace moves our faculties to act, without however taking away their liberty, so that the soul, as St Thomas tells us, is more passive than active...."

Very Reverend Adolphe Tanquerey - *The Spiritual Life*

In God's Presence Consider ...

Do I allow the Holy Spirit's energies to actively dwell in me helping me to work on living a virtuous life? Do I prepare myself for the cultivating of the gifts of the Holy Spirit by actively practicing virtues? What virtues am I currently working on?

Closing Prayer

Melt the frozen, warm the chill; give me virtue's sure reward (from the Sequel of Pentecost). Fill me with Your energies, guide my steps when I go astray, and incline me to act always under the impulse of Your graces.

The gifts of the Holy Spirit sustain the moral life and are essential tools for Christians. They make man docile in recognizing and following the promptings of the Holy Spirit. They complete and perfect the virtues and prepare one for the fruits of the Holy Spirit.

"In the Pentecost sequence, just before the Gospel, the Church sings, 'On the faithful, who adore and confess you ever more, in your sevenfold gift descend.' Rooted in Scripture, Catholic tradition identifies seven gifts of the Holy Spirit: wisdom, understanding, counsel, fortitude, knowledge, piety, and fear of the Lord (Is. 11:2–3).

"Much more than items on a list, however, these are essential tools for the spiritual life. 'The moral life of Christians is sustained by the gifts of the Holy Spirit. These are permanent dispositions which make man docile in following the promptings of the Holy Spirit.... They complete and perfect the virtues of those who receive them. They make the faithful docile in readily obeying divine inspirations (CCC #1830–31)' If the soul is a boat, then the gifts are the sails, the means whereby the breath of God takes control of us and blows where it wills (Jn. 3:8) ... the gifts have a myriad of manifestations....

If one wishes to see the gifts in action and understand them in one's own life, it is also fruitful to ponder the lives of the saints.... Here we find the one light of the Spirit displayed in unique patterns of beauty."

The Magnificat - June 2022, Vol.24, No. 4

In God's Presence Consider ...

Do I look on the gifts of the Holy Spirit as a list of items I receive at Confirmation, or as essential tools for my spiritual life? How do I prepare myself to being docile in following the promptings of the Holy Spirit? Is pondering the lives of the saints and looking for the presence of the 'gifts' in their lives something that I do on a regular basis?

Closing Prayer

Beloved Spirit of God, pour upon me anew Your seven-fold gifts that I may become more docile to Your promptings and fortified to live the moral life as a true disciple of Jesus.

The Holy Spirit is the director of the seven gifts. The human faculties could not receive the motion of the Spirit without the gifts that the Spirit Himself places at the fountainhead of our activity to receive His sanctifying motion and divine inspiration. We could not receive His breath, without His first working in us.

"The virtues in the supernatural order are without doubt divine; as to their origin, God infuses them; as to their end, they lead to God; as to their object, they produce the work of sanctification. But the virtues are managed by men and they have consequently a human mark … the gifts, on the contrary, bear the stamp of him who is called the Finger of God's right hand. Without the gifts the work of perfection is impossible … the finest, most exquisite part of the work of sanctification belongs to them … the activity of the soul is more intense and complete under the impulse of the gifts than when it is exercising the virtues. The soul does not move itself through the gifts; it is moved by the Holy Spirit … the soul is a mother, fruitful under the divine fecundity of the Holy Spirit.

"The spiritual life in its most exalted and perfect sense consists in the adaptation of the soul to the divine norm, to the ideal of the Father. The Holy Spirit is the Artist, who unites in a kiss of love, the Father and the transformed soul."

SOG Archbishop Louis M. Martinez - *The Sanctifier*

In God's Presence Consider …

Are virtues a part of my life? Do I allow the exquisite work of sanctification, the Gifts of the Holy Spirit, to move me to perfection? Have I ever thought of my soul as a mother awaiting the divine fecundity of the Holy Spirit, the kiss of love from the Father?

Closing Prayer

O Finger of God's hand, make me fruitful under Your divine working in me with Your gifts. I cannot move myself, I must be moved by You. Help me adapt to Your divine norm and be transformed.

Whole and Uncorrupted **Day 272**

The temperate person directs their sensitive appetites toward what is good and maintains a healthy discretion. As followers of Jesus, we ought to live sober and upright lives.

"Temperance is the moral virtue that moderates the attraction of pleasures and provides balance in the use of created goods. It ensures the will's mastery over instincts and keeps desires within the limits of what is honorable.... Temperance ... is called 'moderation' or 'sobriety.'

"To live well is nothing other than to love God with all one's heart, with all one's soul and with all one's efforts: from this it comes about that love is kept whole and uncorrupted (through temperance). No misfortune can disturb it (and this is fortitude). It obeys only [God] (and this is justice), and is careful in discerning things, so as not to be surprised by deceit or trickery (and this is prudence)."

CCC #1809

In God's Presence Consider ...

Do I exercise balance and control over created things, or do I tend to be controlled and dictated to by created goods? Do I seek to cultivate the virtue of temperance in helping me to love God with my whole being? Temperance can help me to be more self-disciplined in living the Christian life. Do I exercise the virtue in living within honorable limits or do I seek the life of comfort and ease?

Closing Prayer

All good things come from You O Heavenly Father. Send Your Spirit upon me that I may live in moderation and love You with a single heart.

Justice is recognizing the rights of others and giving them what is their due. The highest form of justice is rendered to God. We call this the virtue of religion.

"St. Thomas Aquinas once said, 'The work of divine justice always presupposes the work of mercy. Indeed, God's Justice is founded upon His Mercy'.... All the various virtues related to justice perfect our will, enabling us to recognize the rights of other people and institutions ... in every area where we find a question of what is owed, some kind of justice will be involved.... The domain of justice is quite broad, for it involves all the various social bonds that link people together.... Justice presupposes that things exist and have their particular natures. We owe something to someone because of who that person is or is not ... we owe a debt to other people because they are persons. They have rights merely because of what they are at their most fundamental level ... through justice, our wills are turned away from egoism and made ready to recognize the rights of others ... the virtue of religion is an example of justice.... The very first debt of justice which we owe is a debt of devotion, recognition, gratitude, and prayer to God.... Merciful bounty pours forth the gifts of existence and of grace. We respond, yes, out of love, but also out of a true kind of justice, given that we owe all things to God."

Matthew Minerd - *Made by God; Made for God*

In God's Presence Consider ...

Do I respect the dignity and rights of others regardless of their race, color, gender, or political views, or am I more concerned about my rights and what is in it for me? What do I owe God and why do I owe Him, in justice, anything?

Closing Prayer

Lord, I am not worthy that You should come to me. Have mercy on me a sinner. Fill my heart with Your graces, Holy Spirit, that I may in gratitude and in love, give to God and others what is their due.

Before His death, Jesus instructs His disciples to exercise manly courage. "In the world you will have trouble, but take courage, I have conquered the world." Jn. 16:33

"The root word of courage is 'cour,' meaning 'heart.' To be courageous is to love the good more than you fear evil and suffering. The courageous man is stouthearted, bold, and brave in the midst of trials.... It took courage for St. Joseph to take his family into enemy territory (Egypt). He knew that he might need to defend his wife and Child against physical assaults, and he was willing to do it. No man who is easily intimidated would embark on such a journey.

"To be a saint, you must be courageous. If you imitate St. Joseph, you will not hesitate to enter enemy territory or undergo spiritual combat. Egypt was a land notorious for thieves, pagan rituals, idols, and sorcerers. St. Joseph fears no man because God is with him.... Jesus himself learned courage from the example of St. Joseph.... St. Joseph gave his Son an example of manly love, courage, strength, and fortitude."

Fr. Donald Calloway, MIC - *Consecration to St. Joseph*

In God's Presence Consider ...

What am I afraid of? How do I face trials and difficulties? Am I more concerned about what others think of me or what God thinks of me? Do I cower under the pressures of being politically correct or under the pressure of peers who hold worldly views and practices?

Closing Prayer

O Lord Jesus Christ, who, before ascending into heaven, did promise to send the Holy Spirit to finish your work in the souls of your apostles and disciples, deign to grant the same Holy Spirit to me that he may perfect in my soul, the work of your grace and your love. Holy Spirit Father's Novena to the Holy Spirit

The natural law states that we are to do good and avoid evil. Prudence helps our conscience and reason to choose and do the right and good and to avoid evil.

"St. Thomas Aquinas taught that prudence is the 'principal of all the virtues.' Its role is to govern the other cardinal (preeminent) virtues: temperance, justice, and fortitude. Without prudence, a person will be either too lenient or too harsh. Prudence serves as a guide and a 'charioteer,' helping the soul to avoid erroneous extremes.... Without prudence, no leader can exercise temperance, justice, and fortitude.

"Supernatural prudence is different from human prudence. Human prudence guides a person to avoid difficulty, suffering, and hardship. Supernatural prudence, on the other hand, does not seek to avoid suffering. Supernatural prudence embraces the cross out of love and always strives for the greater good."

Fr. Donald Calloway, MIC - *Consecration to St. Joseph*

In God's Presence Consider ...

Do I avoid erroneous extremes in my soul being too lenient or too harsh? Do I embrace the Cross out of love? Do I seek the greater good for others or myself? Do I take the time to use the virtue of prudence to discern the true good in every circumstance I encounter?

Closing Prayer

Come, Holy Spirit, and grant me the charioteer of all virtues that embracing the Cross of Christ, I may always strive for the greater good.

Virtues are important in preparing our heart for the gifts of the Holy Spirit by helping us be in tune with the Holy Spirit. This demands a total effort on our part that is guided by the Spirit. It demands fostering a life like Jesus who lived a life in the Spirit. Fr. Hauser challenges us to get out of the way and to allow the Holy Spirit to transform our attitudes and activities.

"Growth in union with the Lord demands the total effort of our being. We have the challenge of arranging patterns in our life in such a way that we live in habitual contact with the Spirit and allow the Spirit to guide all our activities. The effort is difficult because of many pressures moving us away from the Spirit toward self-centered actions. Rather than respond to the Spirit we often find ourselves responding to these pressures.... Daily we experience our self-centered drives ... dominating our lives blocking our responsiveness to the Spirit.

"The solution to this problem ... is to build rhythms into daily life that foster living in tune with the Spirit and so counteract the evils which surrounds us.... To be like Jesus, we ... must always seek to know and to do the Father's will by allowing the Spirit to direct our lives. God's Spirit ... will be as effective in us as we permit him to be.... The goal of the spiritual life is to allow the Spirit of Christ to influence all our activity.... Our role in this process is ... getting out of the way and allowing his Spirit to transform all our activities. Christ will do the rest."

Fr. Richard Hauser, S.J. - *In His Spirit*

In God's Presence Consider ...

What fears do I have that prevent me from a total surrender to the Holy Spirit? Do I experience a self-centered drive for popularity, money, power, prestige or pleasure? What kind of conditions can I provide that enables me to live in tune with the Spirit?

Closing Prayer

In the beginning Father, Your life-giving Spirit brought order to the chaos. Please speak to the chaos of my life. Send Your Spirit that I many build a rhythm of life in tune with You. Help me to get out of the way and be transformed to be like Jesus, Your Son.

In the "Great Commission" found in Mt. 28:16–20, Jesus gives the Church her mission. We are to go and make disciples. In order to fulfill this great task, He tells the apostles before they go, to "Stay in the city until you have been clothed with power from on high" (Luke 24:49). We need to be clothed with the power of the Holy Spirit in order to carry out our mission of making disciples.

"How are Christians supposed to carry out the gargantuan task of making disciples of all nations? There is only one way: by divine empowerment—by the power of the Holy Spirit and His gifts.... The evidence of being Spirit-filled, according to Luke, is the receiving of power—power to serve; power to love; power to heal, deliver, or work a miracle; power to suffer persecution; power to preach the Gospel; power to comprehend the Gospel.... It is clear that for Luke, when the Spirit comes on people, there is a visible manifestation ... there always seems to be a verbal manifestation.... Fulfilling the Gospel is more than preaching, more than the words we speak. It is also what Christ has done through us.

"When the Holy Spirit comes powerfully into a person's life, the manifestation of charisms is not the only result. Often, there is also an experience of being so overwhelmed by God's power and love that the person starts to feel, and act, inebriated—they are beside themselves (2 Cor. 5:13)."

Randy Clark & Mary Healy - *The Spiritual Gifts Handbook*

In God's Presence Consider ...

Do I seek divine empowerment, the power of the Holy Spirit, before I go out to do God's work or ministry? Have I been clothed with His power? Have I ever felt overwhelmed by God's love and power?

Closing Prayer

Come powerfully, Holy Spirit, into my life. Inebriate me with Your love, that clothed with Your power, I might give evidence to the mighty works that God is about doing. Prepare me for the task.

Fr. Garrigou Lagrance, OP, writes about the three ways of the spiritual life: purgative, illuminative, and unitive; and the importance of the Holy Spirit in these three ways. His work was published in 1938. In this quote, he is speaking of the interior life of man as it is in need of supernatural helps in the purgative or conversion stage.

"Finally, in order to supply the deficiencies of these virtues (theological and moral) which, in the twilight of faith and under the direction of prudence, still act in too human a fashion, we are given the seven gifts of the Holy Ghost, who dwells in us. These are like the sails on a ship; they dispose us to receive obediently and promptly the breathing that comes from on high, the special inspirations of God; inspirations which enable us to act, no longer in merely human fashion, but divinely, with the alacrity (a quick and cheerful readiness to do something) which we need in order to run in the way of God, undismayed by any obstacles.... In this way the whole of the spiritual organism develops simultaneously, though it may manifest its activity under various forms. And, from this point of view, since the infused contemplation of the mysteries of faith is an act of the gifts of the Holy Ghost, an act which disposes the soul to the beatific vision, must we not admit that such contemplation is in the normal way of sanctity?"

Fr. Garrigou Lagrance, O.P. - *The Three Ways of the Spiritual Life*

In God's Presence Consider ...

How do the seven gifts of the Holy Spirit act like sails on a ship? How does the Holy Spirit help me in living the spiritual life? How does He prepare me for the beatific vision? Do I continue to follow God even amidst obstacles? Do I abandon various spiritual activities when I run into difficulty or do I see them as means to grow in my spiritual life and seek the Spirit's aid in pressing through them?

Closing Prayer

Help me, Holy Spirit, to receive You as the guiding wind in my sails, that I may be disposed to receive obediently and promptly God's inspiring breath and act more divinely in running the ways of God.

Breathing of the Coming Breeze **Day 279**

Often times we want to grow in our spiritual life and in prayer with God, but we don't cultivate the gifts and virtues of the Holy Spirit thus making it difficult for us to hear the words the Spirit utters to our hearts in secret and in silence.

"The fullness of divine gifts is in many ways a consequence of the indwelling of the Holy Ghost in the souls of the just … through the gift, which is the Holy Ghost, many other special gifts are distributed among the members of Christ. Among these gifts are those secret warnings and invitations, which from time to time are excited in our minds and hearts by the inspiration of the Holy Ghost. Without these there is no beginning of a good life, no progress, no arriving at eternal salvation. And since these words and admonitions are uttered in the soul in an exceedingly secret manner, they are sometimes aptly compared in Holy Writ to the breathing of a coming breeze, and the Angelic Doctor (St. Thomas Aquinas, O.P.) likens them to the movements of the heart which are wholly hidden in the living body.

"More than this, the just man, that is to say he who lives the life of divine grace, and acts by the fitting virtues as by means of faculties, has need of those seven gifts which are properly attributed to the Holy Ghost. By means of them the soul is furnished and strengthened so as to obey more easily and promptly His voice and impulse."

Pope Leo XIII - *Divinum Illud Munus*

In God's Presence Consider …

Do I know what the gifts of the Holy Spirit are? Do I seek them? Do I cultivate growing in virtue? Have I ever felt the secret warnings, invitations, and inspirations of the Holy Spirit as a gentle breeze?

Closing Prayer

O Ruah, Breath of God, breathe on me that I may recognize Your movements in my heart and promptly obey Your voice and impulse.

After the Resurrection, Jesus confers on the Apostles and their successors, the power to forgive sins. This power presupposes and includes the saving action of the Holy Spirit.

"By becoming the light of hearts, that is to say the light of consciences, the Holy Spirit 'convinces concerning sin' which is to say, he makes man realize his own evil and at the same time directs him towards what is good. Thanks to the multiplicity of the Spirit's gifts, by reason of which he is invoked as the 'sevenfold one,' every kind of human sin can be reached by God's saving power. In reality—as St. Bonaventure says—'by virtue of the seven gifts of the Holy Spirit all evils are destroyed and all good things are produced.' Thus the conversion of the human heart, which is an indispensable condition for the forgiveness of sins, is brought about by the influence of the Counselor."

St. Pope John Paul II - *Dominum et Vivicantem*

In God's Presence Consider …

Does the influence of the Holy Spirit play an active, ongoing part in my life? Do I do a daily examination of conscience aided and led by the Holy Spirit who convinces concerning sin?

Closing Prayer

Come, Holy Spirit, the Sevenfold One. Let Your light shine in my conscience convincing me of my sin and bringing about in me a true and ongoing conversion and repentance.

Stupendous Prodigy of Love **Day 281**

Love is a process of being possessed by the Lover and possessing the Lover. God is the Great Lover who desires to love us and be loved by us. Our joy comes in the mutual possession of each other in love.

"The Holy Spirit lives in us not only to possess us, but also to be possessed by us, to be ours. For love must possess, as well as be possessed. He is the Gift of God-Altissimi Donum Dei. Now, the gift that belonged to the giver becomes the possession of the one who receives it. The Gift of God is ours through the stupendous prodigy of love.

"The words 'give' and 'gift' have a meaning proper to the Holy Spirit.... It is characteristic of love to give gifts, but the first gift, the gift par excellence, is love itself. The Holy Spirit is the Love of God; therefore, he is the Gift of God.... Possession is proper to love. In its first stage it is a desire of possession; perfect love is the joy of possession, and love that is consummated is the abyss of possession."

SOG Archbishop Louis M. Martinez - *The Sanctifier*

In God's Presence Consider ...

Have I ever thought about what it means to possess the Gift of God while at the same time to being possessed by the Gift? Do I ever think about the divine significance that the Holy Spirit is mine and that I am His?

Closing Prayer

O Gift of God, come and possess me and help me to possess You, that I may live the joy of being perfectly loved and possessed by You.

In looking at the broader picture of charisms, we find the framework laid out for us by the Second Vatican Council's Lumen Gentium.

"It is not only through the sacraments and church ministries that the same Holy Spirit sanctifies and leads the People of God and enriches it with virtues. Allotting his gifts 'to everyone according as he will' (1 Cor. 12:11), he distributes special graces among the faithful of every rank. By these gifts he makes them fit and ready to undertake the various tasks or offices advantageous for the renewal and building up of the church, according to the words of the apostle: 'The manifestation of the Spirit is given to everyone for profit' (1 Cor. 12:7). These charismatic gifts, whether they be the most outstanding or the more simple and widely diffused, are to be received with thanksgiving and consolation, for they are exceedingly suitable and useful for the needs of the church."

Vatican Council II - *Lumen Gentium* #12b

In God's Presence Consider …

The Holy Spirit allots His gifts to everyone according as He wills. Do I fear accepting them or seeking them? In my refusal to accept or seek them, am I also rejecting and not accepting the Holy Spirit? Do I seek to undertake various tasks in up building the Church apart from seeking the Holy Spirit and His charisms?

Closing Prayer

Graciously grant to your Church, O merciful God, that, gathered by the Holy Spirit, she may be devoted to you with all her heart and united in purity of intent. Collect from Wednesday of the 7th Week of Easter

St. Teresa of Jesus liked to insist that God does not force anyone; He takes what we give Him; but He does not give Himself wholly to us, until we give ourselves wholly to Him.

"But if the Holy Spirit is an impulse of love that comes into us to sanctify us and bring us to God, why do we not all become saints? The mystery of human responsibility enters here. The Holy Spirit, with the Father and the Son, has created us free beings and He wishes us so; therefore, in coming to us, He respects our liberty and does no violence to it. Although He is eager to enter our souls and to possess it, He will not act thus unless we give Him free access.... If we do not become saints, it is not because the Holy Spirit does not will it—He was sent to us and comes to us for this very purpose—but it is because we do not give full liberty to His action. This is the point in which we fail: we do not use our liberty to wholly yield our soul to His powerful, loving invasion. If our will would open the doors wide, the Holy Spirit would take us under His direction, and, with His help, we would become saints."

Fr. Gabriel of St. Mary Magdalen, O.C.D. - *Divine Intimacy*

In God's Presence Consider ...

Do I open wide the doors of my heart to give the Holy Spirit free access to my soul? Do I yield to His powerful loving invasion? Is one of my life goals to become a saint?

Closing Prayer

To You, O Holy Spirit, do I open wide the doors of my heart. Take me under Your direction and help me to become a saint.

Man is called to communion, to beatitude with God. Wounded by sin, man walks the ways of evil that turn us away from God and His love. We are in need of God's help for our salvation and justification. The Holy Spirit effects cleansing us from sin, sanctifying us, and reuniting us to living God's will.

"The grace of the Holy Spirit has the power to justify us, that is, to cleanse us from our sins and to communicate to us the 'righteousness of God through faith in Jesus Christ' (Rom. 3:22, 6:3–4) and through Baptism.... Through the power of the Holy Spirit we take part in Christ's Passion by dying to sin, and in his Resurrection by being born to a new life.... The first work of the grace of the Holy Spirit is conversion, effecting justification ... moved by grace, man turns toward God and away from sin....

"Justification is the most excellent work of God's love made manifest in Christ Jesus and granted by the Holy Spirit.... The Holy Spirit is the master of the interior life. By giving birth to the inner man (Rom 7:22, Eph. 3:16), justification entails the sanctification of his whole being...

"Grace is a participation in the life of God ... (man) receives the life of the Spirit who breathes charity into him.... The grace of Christ is the gratuitous gift that God makes to us of his own life, infused by the Holy Spirit into our soul to heal it of sin and to sanctify it."

Cf. CCC #1987–89, 1995, 1997, 1999

In God's Presence Consider ...

The call to conversion is a continual process and mutual work between God and man. God calls and man responds to the movement of grace and turns back to Him. Do I take serious my daily Examination of Conscience and seek the promptings and helps of the Holy Spirit? Do I fully participate in the life of God that the Holy Spirit offers to my soul?

Closing Prayer

Heavenly King, Consoler Spirit, Spirit of Truth, present everywhere and filling all things, treasure of all good and source of all life, come dwell in us, cleanse and save us, you who are All-Good.

Byzantine Liturgy, Pentecost Vespers, Troparion

Sunbeam **Day 285**

The Holy Spirit comes to us individually while always, at the same time, giving Himself to all other persons in the same personal way without depleting Himself.

"Consider the analogy of the sunbeam; each person upon whom its kindly light falls rejoices as if the sun existed for him alone, yet it illumines land and sea, is master of the atmosphere. In the same way, the Spirit is given to each one who receives Him as if He were the possession of that person alone, yet he sends forth sufficient grace to fill all the universe.

"Everything that partakes of His grace is filled with joy according to its capacity—the capacity of its nature, not of His power."

St. Basil - *On the Holy Spirit Capt. IX*

In God's Presence Consider ...

The Holy Spirit was given to me at Baptism and in His fullness at Confirmation. Do I receive Him, allowing Him full access to my life? Do I experience and live the joy of the Holy Spirit's working and living in me?

Closing Prayer

St. Basil, pray for me that the Holy Spirit, Light from the Father, will illumine me and be the Master of my spiritual and corporal life.

Bought with a Price **Day 286**

We are nothing, have nothing, and can do nothing that is good without the assistance of the Holy Spirit.

"… Anyone who attempts to resist the world, or to do other good things by his own strength, will be sure to fall. We can do good things, but it is when God gives us power to do them. Therefore we must pray to Him for the power.

"Our Lord, when He was going away, promised to His disciples a Comforter instead of Himself; that was God the Holy Ghost, who is still among us (though we see Him not), as Christ was with the Apostles.

"He has come in order to enlighten us, to guide us in the right way, and in the end to bring us to Christ in heaven.

"And He came down, as His name 'Comforter' shows, especially to stand by, and comfort, and strengthen those who are in any trouble, particularly trouble from irreligious men.

"When, then, religious persons are in low spirits, or are any way grieved at the difficulties which the world puts in their way, when they earnestly desire to do their duty, yet feel how weak they are, let them recollect that they are 'not their own,' but 'bought with a price,' and the dwelling-places and temples of the All-gracious Spirit."

St. John Henry Newman - *Sermon 19*

In God's Presence Consider …

Do I rely on my own gifts and abilities to get me out of difficulties or to solve issues and challenges that face me? Have I ever asked God to give me the Holy Spirit who is the power to do good?

Closing Prayer

You, Holy Spirit, are the invisible presence of God; enlighten and guide me in the right way and in fulfilling my duties. Bring me, when my life here on earth ends, to be with Jesus in heaven.

Love: Enduring Abiding **Day 287**

Who the Holy Spirit is, what He does, and the effects of His works, can be summed up in the word: love. Love shows itself in being enduring and in abiding. Something abides when there is an eternity.

"The gift of God is the Holy Spirit. The gift of God is love—God shares himself as love in the Holy Spirit.... The presence of the Holy Spirit makes itself known in the manner of love. Love is the criterion of the Holy Spirit, as against unholy spirits; indeed, it is the presence of the Holy Spirit himself and, in that sense, the presence of God. The essential and central concept summing up what the Holy Spirit is and what he effects is in the end, not 'knowledge' but love.... The basic criterion of love, its 'proper work,' so to speak—and, thereby, the 'proper work' of the Holy Spirit—is this, that it achieves abiding. Love shows itself by being enduring. It can by no means be recognized at a given moment and in the moment alone; but in abiding, it does away with uncertainty and carries eternity within it. And thus in my view the relationship between love and truth is also thereby given: love, in the full sense, can be present only where something is enduring, where something abides. Because it has to do with abiding, it can occur, not just anywhere, but only there where eternity is."

Pope Benedict XVI - *Pilgrim Fellowship of Faith*

In God's Presence Consider ...

Do I see God sharing with me His love which is the Holy Spirit? Do I know the Holy Spirit and His work as God's gift of love for me? Is eternity present in me allowing the gift of the Holy Spirit to abide in me?

Closing Prayer

Father, You are Love. Continue to share Your gift of love, the Holy Spirit, with me. Do away with all my uncertainty about Your love and help me to endure, to abide in You and You in me.

The Holy Spirit restores us as children of God and makes us capable of receiving the fullness of His graces and gifts.

"Through the Holy Spirit comes our restoration to paradise, our ascension into the kingdom of heaven, our return to the adoption of sons, our liberty to call God our Father, our being made partakers of the grace of Christ, our being called children of light, our sharing in eternal glory, and, in a word, our being brought into a state of all 'fullness of blessing,' both in this world and in the world to come, of all the good gifts that are in store for us, by promise hereof, through faith, beholding the reflection of their grace as though they were already present, we await the full enjoyment."

St. Basil the Great - *Treatise on the Holy Spirit*

In God's Presence Consider ...

Do I ever thank the Holy Spirit for restoring and making me fit to enter paradise, or do I take my salvation and heaven for granted? Am I a child of the light reflecting the love of God? Do I have my eyes focused on God and heaven, or am I too caught up in the things of this world?

Closing Prayer

O God my Father, thank You for sending the Holy Spirit, my liberty, who makes me a partaker in the graces of Your Son and allows me to call You Father. Fill me with holy hope for sharing in eternal glory with You as one of Your children of light. St. Basil the Great, pray for me.

Willing Instruments **Day 289**

The manifestations of God's grace and power is not meant to be rare in the life of the Church, or for a certain past history, but a part of the normal Christian life.

"From the Day of Pentecost onward, Christ has been pouring out His Holy Spirit to equip all believers with supernatural gifts for their mission of spreading the Gospel and building up the Church. These gifts are not just for specially qualified people or extraordinarily holy people. They are for every member of the Body of Christ, every 'little ole me.' They are available to all who are willing to let the Lord use them however He chooses, to be the instruments of His love in a needy world."

Randy Clark & Mary Healy - *The Spiritual Gifts Handbook*

In God's Presence Consider …

How has the Holy Spirit equipped me with His gifts for my mission of spreading the Gospel? Do I trust God and am I willing to let the Lord use me as the instrument of His love as He chooses?

Closing Prayer

Make me, O Holy Spirit, available and a willing instrument of God's love. Increase and perfect the gift of trust in me that I may allow God to use me however He chooses.

All of us have a common mission. We are to become saints by becoming as holy as possible. Holiness is only possible for us through the Holy Spirit and the exercise of His seven gifts.

"You have a mission: to become holy, loving God truly and your neighbor mercifully. You need the gifts of the Holy Spirit in your life. They will help you resemble your spiritual father (St. Joseph) and reach heaven.

"What specifically do the seven gifts of the Holy Spirit do for us though? Well, the Holy Spirit Fathers provided the answer for us. The Holy Spirit Fathers (also called Spiritans) are the religious community responsible for promulgating throughout the world a very powerful novena to the Holy Spirit that contains an excellent summary of what the gifts are and what they do for us."

Fr. Donald Calloway, MIC - *Consecration to St. Joseph*

In God's Presence Consider...

Do I know that my mission is to be holy, loving God and neighbor above all? Do I seek the intercession of St. Joseph and try to imitate his virtuous life? Do I seek the perfection of the seven gifts of the Holy Spirit?

Closing Prayer

Lord Jesus Christ, who, before ascending into heaven, did promise to send the Holy Spirit to finish your work in the souls of your apostles and disciples, deign to grant the same Holy Spirit to me that he may perfect in my soul, the work of your grace and your love. Holy Spirit Father's Novena

Wisdom embodies all the other gifts, as charity embraces all the other virtues.

"Wisdom is the most perfect of the gifts. Of Wisdom it is written 'all good things came to me with her, and innumerable riches through her hands.' It is the Gift of Wisdom that strengthens our faith, fortifies hope, perfects charity, and promotes the practice of virtue in the highest degree. Wisdom enlightens the mind to discern and relish things divine, in the appreciation of which earthly joys lose their savor, while the Cross of Christ yields a divine sweetness."

Holy Spirit Father's Novena

In God's Presence Consider …

Do I seek God's wisdom to enlighten my mind and to relish things that are divine? Do I spend time meditating on the Cross of Jesus? Do I find a divine sweetness in suffering and the Cross or do I dread and avoid the Cross in my life?

Closing Prayer

Lord Jesus, grant me the Spirit of Wisdom that I may despise the perishable things of this world and aspire only after the things that are eternal. Holy Spirit Father's Novena to the Holy Spirit

From this loving knowledge of Christ springs the desire to proclaim him to "evangelize," and to lead others to the "yes" of faith in Jesus Christ. But at the same time the need to know this faith better makes itself felt. CCC #429

"The gift of understanding helps us to grasp the meaning of the truths of our holy religion. By faith we know them. But by understanding we learn to appreciate and relish them. It enables us to penetrate the inner meaning of revealed truths and, through them, to be quickened to newness of life. Our faith ceases to be sterile and inactive, but inspires a mode of life that bears eloquent testimony to the faith that is in us."

Holy Spirit Father's Novena

In God's Presence Consider …

Knowledge should lead us to seek understanding of the things of God. Do I seek the gift of understanding in order to appreciate and relish the truths of my Catholic faith? Is my faith sterile and inactive or is it alive and bearing eloquent testimony to Jesus? Do I have a desire to proclaim Jesus, leading others to faith?

Closing Prayer

Lord Jesus, grant me the Spirit of Understanding to enlighten my mind with the light of your divine truth.

Holy Spirit Father's Novena to the Holy Spirit

The Gift of Counsel **Day 293**

Counsel helps develop a supernatural common sense in order to apply the principles we gain through knowledge and understanding.

"The gift of counsel endows the soul with supernatural prudence, enabling it to judge promptly and rightly what must be done, especially in difficult circumstances. Counsel applies the principles furnished by knowledge and understanding to the innumerable concrete cases that confront us in the course of our daily duty as parents, teachers, public servants, and Christian citizens. Counsel is supernatural common sense, a priceless treasure in the quest of salvation."

Holy Spirit Father's Novena

In God's Presence Consider …

Do I find myself exercising a supernatural common sense? Do I seek the Holy Spirit's gift of counsel in confronting and dealing with the circumstances and challenges I face living in this world?

Closing Prayer

Lord Jesus, grant me the Spirit of Counsel that I may ever choose the surest way of pleasing God and gaining heaven.

Holy Spirit Father's Novena to the Holy Spirit

The Gift of Fortitude **Day 294**

Fortitude is the holy boldness that came upon the Apostles at Pentecost enabling them to face all dangers and even martyrdom for the love of Jesus.

"The gift of fortitude strengthens the soul against natural fear and supports us in the performance of duty. Fortitude imparts to the will an impulse and energy which move it to undertake without hesitancy the most arduous tasks, to face dangers, to trample underfoot human respect, and to endure without complaint slow martyrdom of even lifelong tribulation.

Holy Spirit Father's Novena

In God's Presence Consider...

Do I live my life and make decisions based on fear? Do fears paralyze me and cause me to complain of the crosses I am to carry? Do I seek the Holy Spirit's gift of fortitude to help me perform my duties in a way that pleases God?

Closing Prayer

Lord Jesus, grant me the Spirit of Fortitude that I may bear my cross with you and that I may overcome with courage all the obstacles that oppose my salvation.

Holy Spirit Father's Novena to the Holy Spirit

The gift of knowledge helps us to discern all that is profitable to prize and grow in the friendship with God.

"The gift of knowledge enables the soul to evaluate created things at their worth— in their relation to God. Knowledge unmasks the pretense of creatures, reveals their emptiness, and points out their only true purpose as instruments in the service of God. It shows us the loving care of God even in adversity, and directs us to glorify him in every circumstance of life. Guided by its light, we put first things first, and prize the friendship of God beyond all else."

Holy Spirit Father's Novena

In God's Presence Consider ...

Do I take life and the things of the world around me for face value, or do I seek to find the spiritual worth of all created things? Do I see created things as instruments in the service of God? Do I see God's loving hand upon me even in adversity?

Closing Prayer

Grant me Lord Jesus the Spirit of knowledge that I may know God and know myself and grow perfect in the science of the saints.

Holy Spirit Father's Novena to the Holy Spirit

The Gift of Piety **Day 296**

Through the gift of piety, the Holy Spirit fosters a filial affection for God that inspires a proper love and respect for people and things.

"The gift of piety begets in our hearts a filial affection for God as our most loving Father. It inspires us to love and respect for his sake persons and things consecrated to him, as well as those who are vested with his authority, his mother, St. Joseph, the saints, the Church and its visible head, our parents and superiors, our country and its rulers. He who is filled with the Gift of Piety finds the practice of his religion not a burdensome duty, but a delightful service."

Holy Spirit Father's Novena

In God's Presence Consider …

Do I love and show respect for the dignity of all human life from the moment of conception until natural death and the created things of this world? Do I see religion as a duty that is very burdensome or as a delightful service?

Closing Prayer

Lord Jesus, grant me the Spirit of Piety that I may find the service of God sweet and amiable.

Holy Spirit Father's Novena to the Holy Spirit

Fear of the Lord arises from our love of God not from a dread of punishment. Fear of the Lord is based on the truth that God is Holy, we are not, and we respect and honor Him because He is God.

"The gift of Fear fills us with a sovereign respect for God, and makes us dread nothing so much as to offend Him by sin. It is a fear that arises, not from the thought of hell, but from sentiments of reverence and filial submission to our heavenly Father. It is the fear that is the beginning of wisdom, detaching us from worldly pleasures that could in any way separate us from God. 'They that fear the Lord will prepare their hearts, and in His sight will sanctify their souls.'"

Holy Spirit Father's Novena

In God's Presence Consider ...

What separates me from God? Do I fear God, and if so, what is the basis of my fear, love? Do I dread offending God by my sin? Do I see the gift of Fear of the Lord detaching me from worldly pleasures?

Closing Prayer

Come, O blessed Spirit of Holy Fear, penetrate my inmost heart, that I may set You, my Lord and God, before my face forever; help me to shun all things that can offend You, and make me worthy to appear before the pure eyes of Your Divine Majesty in heaven, where You live and reign in the unity of the ever Blessed Trinity, God world without end.

Holy Spirit Father's Novena to the Holy Spirit

The fundamental and supreme principle of all knowledge of God is always found in the theology of the Spirit. Knowing God means knowing Him in the Spirit.

"What is, in fact, the key to knowledge if not the grace of the Holy Spirit given through faith, which truly illuminated knowledge and full understanding? If the Holy Spirit is called key it is because, through him and in him, first of all, we have our spirit enlightened, and once purified we are illuminated with the light of knowledge and baptized from on high, born again, and made sons of God."

Simeon the New Theologian - *Catechesis, XXXIII*

In God's Presence Consider ...

How is the Holy Spirit key in my life? If my knowing God hinges on the work of the Holy Spirit, might my lack of understanding God be proportionate to my lack of knowing and cooperating with the presence and work of the Holy Spirit?

Closing Prayer

Heavenly Sovereign, Paraclete, Spirit of truth who are present everywhere and who fills all, treasure chest of every good and giver of life, come, live in us, cleanse us of every stain and, you who are good, save our souls.

Byzantine Liturgy, Troparion of the Pentecost Vespers

St. Bernard of Clairvaux speaks of the mysterious presence of God within that is beyond our detection of arriving or departing.

"… As often as he would enter into me, I didn't perceive the different times when he came. I perceived he was present; I remembered that he had been there. Now and then I would be able to get a premonition of his coming, but never perceive it, nor sense when he left (Ps. 120:8). Where he came from when he entered my soul, or where he went to when he left it again, and whatever the means were of his entry and exit, I must confess I'm still quite ignorant of, for, as it says, 'You do not know whence he comes or goes' (Jn. 3:8). You need not wonder about this, because he is the one of whom it is said, 'Your footsteps are not to be known' (Ps. 76:20). Surely he did not enter through the ears, since he does not make a sound. He does not enter through the nose, because he who created air does not mix with it, or mix it up, but mixes with the mind. Nor does he enter through the mouth, being neither eaten nor drunk; not explored by touch since he is not of that nature. How then does he enter? But perhaps he does not have to enter because he is already within? He is not something on the outside (1 Cor. 5:12).

"As an avid investigator, I descended to my lowest depths, and nevertheless discovered him to be far beyond everything that was mine; if I looked within, he was more interior than I was! Then I knew the truth of what I had read, that 'In him we live, and move, and have our being' (Acts 17:28)."

Saint Bernard of Clairvaux - *Sermon on the Song of Songs*

In God's Presence Consider...

Do I ever reflect upon how God knows me so intimately and is closer to me than I am to myself; and despite such closeness and intimacy, He deeply loves me? Could this be the work of the Holy Spirit St. Bernard speaks of?

Closing Prayer

Come, Holy Spirit, enter my soul and reside in me. Invisible as You are, help me to be open and perceive Your presence working in me. St. Bernard, pray for me.

The gifts and fruits of the Holy Spirit are needed in order for man to grow to the highest level of sanctity.

"These gifts are of such efficacy that they lead the just man to the highest degree of sanctity; and of such excellence that they continue to exist even in heaven though in a more perfect way. By means of these gifts the soul is excited and encouraged to seek after and attain the evangelical beatitudes, which, like the flowers that come forth in the spring time, are the signs and harbingers of eternal beatitude. Lastly there are those blessed fruits, enumerated by the Apostle (Gal. 5:22) which the Spirit, even in this mortal life, produces and shows forth in the just; fruits filled with all sweetness and joy, in as much as they proceed from the Spirit … the Divine Spirit, proceeding from the Father and the Word in the eternal light of sanctity, Himself both Love and Gift."

Pope Leo XIII - *Divinum Illud Munus*

In God's Presence Consider …

Do I view the gifts and fruits of the Holy Spirit as a means to attain perfect union with God? How do I cultivate and use the gifts of the Holy Spirit for the good of all and my personal growth in holiness?

Closing Prayer

Come, Holy Spirit, You who are Love and Gift. Increase and bring to perfection Your multitude of gifts within me, helping me to seek You, the Giver of the gifts, and not merely the gifts You bring.

In chapter 13 of St. Paul's first letter to the Corinthians, we have the great hymn of love. The chapter on love provides the foundational principle that orders all exercise of the charisms. Paul refers to charisms as "manifestations of the Spirit" (1 Cor. 12:7).

"What are charisms? First, it is important to distinguish them from another kind of gift mentioned in Scripture. The prophet Isaiah foretells that the Messiah will be endowed with seven qualities bestowed by the Spirit: wisdom, understanding, counsel, fortitude, knowledge, piety, and fear of the Lord (Is. 11:1–3). Catholic tradition has come to call these the seven sanctifying gifts of the Spirit. They are given to every Christian at baptism and confirmation, and their purpose to make us holy, forming in us the character of Jesus the Messiah.

"… No one has all the charisms, precisely because we need one another…. Charisms are also distinct from human talents. A charism is not a natural ability but a supernatural gift of the Holy Spirit. It either enables one to do what is humanly impossible (such as prophecy or healings) or elevates a natural endowment (such as teaching or hospitality) to a supernatural level of efficacy for building up the body of Christ."

Dr. Mary Healy - *Healing*

In God's Presence Consider...

Am I making use of the seven sanctifying gifts to grow in holiness and forming me in the character of Jesus or am I allowing them to lie dormant? Do I recognize my personal charisms? Do I allow the Holy Spirit to raise me to a supernatural level of prayer and living?

Closing Prayer

Come, Holy Spirit of Love. Fan the fire of Your love within me that I may be raised to the supernatural level of efficacy You desire of me so I may help build up the body of Christ, the Church.

Unity Not Uniformity **Day 302**

The Holy Spirit brings about unity, not uniformity. A unity that brings together diverse elements and makes them into the Body of Christ, united and given a unified purpose and mission.

"The Greek word is charis, which is used in the New Testament for the 'grace' or 'favor' of God to heal and save us. The gifts that come from the Spirit are called 'charisma,' free expressions of God's charis toward us, which enable us to be channels of God's charis to others … not for the glory of the individual, but for the common good (1 Cor. 12:7).

"In 1 Corthinians 12, Paul lists nine examples of the Spirit's manifestation…. Gifts of Grace (charis): the power to speak, sometimes called Word Gifts: Prophecy, Tongues, Interpretation of Tongues. Gifts of Service (diakonia): the power to know, the ability to express and understand various aspects of God's nature or plan: Wisdom, Knowledge, Discernment…. Gifts of Works (energema): the power to do: Faith, Miracles, Healing…. These are not all the charisms illustrated in the New Testament…. At least 27 gifts are listed covering a broad range from gifts like prophecy and healing, to teaching and almsgiving. Charismatic gifts are as important for the Church today as they were in apostolic times. These gifts work to bring unity, to empower, and serve the Church's needs."

Kay Murdy - *Charisms*

In God's Presence Consider...

Any gift we receive from God is not for our glory but for the common good and the building up of the Kingdom. Do I know the gifts that I have been given? Do I see my gifts and talents as gifts from the Holy Spirit and do I use them for the common good? Do I fear the Charismatic gifts?

Closing Prayer

Father, continue to pour out Your Holy Spirit and His charisms upon Your Son's Body, the Church. Forgive me for not accepting these gifts or misusing them for my glory rather than the common good and Your glory. Let Your Spirit freely flow through me to unify, empower, and serve the Church's needs.

Straightjacket or Freedom to Move **Day 303**

Since the Spirit "breathes where He wills" (Jn. 3:8) we are to respond spontaneously to the free flowing of the Holy Spirit and not seek to control, stifle, extinguish or confine Him to a program, a structure, or personal ownership.

"'... an obsession with planning could render the Church impervious to the action of the Holy Spirit, to the power of God by which they live. Not everything should be fitted into the straightjacket of a single uniform organization; what is needed is less organization and more Spirit' (Joseph Ratzinger [Benedict XVI], The Ecclesial Movements).

"The gifts are by definition spontaneous manifestations of the Holy Spirit. The Spirit is the initiator; we follow. To attempt to control the gifts or force them into a preexisting structure is to stifle them ... charisms must never be used independently. No one is the owner of his or her charism; 'no charism dispenses a person from reference and submission to the Pastors of the Church'" (St. Pope John Paul II's Christifideles Laici #24).

Dr. Mary Healy - *Healing*

In God's Presence Consider ...

Do I tend to put a straightjacket on the Holy Spirit with my own agenda or through my fears of not being in control? Do I find it hard to accept the free, spontaneous manifestations of the Holy Spirit? Do I over structure my prayer life and stifle the Holy Spirit's freedom?

Closing Prayer

Lord Jesus, help me never to stifle, or control the movement of Your Spirit within me. Help me to discern His presence and movements within me and then to generously follow Him.

Charisms are often times seen as extraordinary gifts which marked the beginning of the Church's life. St. Pope John Paul II called our attention to charisms as gifts belonging to the ordinary life of the Church with their principal aim not personal sanctification but the service to others, and the Church's welfare.

"... these charisms result from the free choice and gift of the Holy Spirit, in whose property as the first and substantial Gift within Trinitarian life they share. In a special way the Triune God shows his sovereign power in his gifts. This power is not subject to any antecedent rule, to any particular disciple or to a plan of interventions established once and for all; according to St. Paul he distributes his gifts to each 'as he wills' (1 Cor. 12:11)....

"We cannot but admire the great wealth of gifts bestowed by the Holy Spirit on lay people as members of the Church in our age as well. Each of them has the necessary ability to carry out the tasks to which he is called for the welfare of the Christian people and the world's salvation, if he is open, docile and faithful to the Holy Spirit's action."

Fr. O'Carroll, CSSp, - *John Paul II*

In God's Presence Consider ...

Do I accept the charisms and give the Holy Spirit thanks for the gifts He bestows? Do I see myself carrying out the various tasks in my life for the welfare of the People of God as something I can handle and do by my own natural abilities, or as being open, docile, and faithful to the Holy Spirit and cooperating with His actions?

Closing Prayer

Come, Holy Spirit, Gift of all gifts, and make me open, docile, and faithful to Your actions in my life. May the gifts You lavish upon me serve the welfare of my neighbor. St. Pope John Paul II, pray for me.

To live in Christ is to live in the Spirit who sanctifies and brings about our sanctification and leads us to imitate His life.

"But the glorified Christ has sent the Holy Spirit, who is his Spirit (Rom. 8:9). In the ages to come and in the Church it is he who will communicate to us the life of God (1 Cor. 6:11). It can truly be said then that the Spirit brings us God's gifts.... The action of the Holy Spirit is placed alongside that of Father and Son. All three work together for our salvation, but each in his own way (1 Cor. 12:4–11).

"... charismata, or extraordinary spiritual favors.... They knew that these favors were a gift of the Spirit.... But these gifts are not attributed to the Holy Spirit alone, but also to the Father and the Son, though in different ways. Coming from the Holy Spirit, they are charismata or spiritual gifts, an enduring possession, a kind of spiritual riches. But seen in relation to the Lord, these gifts are kinds of service, that is, tasks apportioned by Christ to assist in building the Church.... The Holy Spirit bestows on us ... a task which is the continuation of Christ (Eph. 4:11–12) ... in relation to the Father, these gifts or manifestations of power, activities bearing fruit in the Church.... The Father is at the origin of all things, the source of all effective activity, the One whose action is all in all."

Bernard Piault - *What is the Trinity*

In God's Presence Consider ...

Do I ever ponder salvation as a work of the Father, Son, and Holy Spirit? Do I seek spiritual gifts (charismata) or the spiritual riches to assist in building up the Church? Do I trust that God knows what He is doing in sending me His extraordinary spiritual favors and give Him thanks for sending them?

Closing Prayer

Come, Holy Spirit, and communicate to me the life of God, helping me to continue the work of Christ and assist in the building up of the Church.

Not Static, Living **Day 306**

A charism is a living gift that the Holy Spirit uses through a person to minister to a person. It is the Spirit's gift that He initiates through human vessels. We are not entitled to them nor are we to possess them as our own.

"It would be easy to say, 'I know what charisms I have. I don't need or want more.' But what we want or think we need is not the point. The charisms do not belong to me. They are not just one more thing to add to my possessions. In fact, since the word 'gift' often refers to an item, a thing, it could be easy to think about a charism or gift of the Holy Spirit as a static thing. If I have it, I have all of it.

"Is it not possible, rather, that a charism is a living gift, a way in which the Holy Spirit ministers through a person in a particular way, in a particular context, at a particular time?

"Is it also possible that since the Spirit fills the earth and is all embracing that instead of thinking in terms of We have the Spirit we might realize that The Spirit has us? This means that it is the Holy Spirit of Jesus who initiates the activity of the charisms through us. Our part is to be open, to be willing to be used, and to always give credit to God."

Sr. Mary Anne Schaenzer, SSND – *Charisms*

In God's Presence Consider …

There is a danger that I might think I don't need the Holy Spirit or His charisms. To reject the gifts is to reject the Giver. How do I respond to the reality that the Spirit has me, dwells in me, and is initiating the activity of the charisms through me? Am I willing and open to be used by Him?

Closing Prayer

May the power of the Holy Spirit come to us, we pray, O Lord, that we may keep your will faithfully in mind and express it in a devout way of life. Through our Lord Jesus Christ, your Son who lives and reigns with you in the unity of the Holy Spirit, God, forever and ever.

Collect from Monday of the 7th Week of Easter

"Make love your aim; but be eager, too, for spiritual gifts." (1 Cor. 14:1) Charisms are concrete manifestations of the action of the Holy Spirit that are oriented towards service and building up of the community.

"… Love motivates the charisms, it ignites our desire for the gifts. Why? Because the more we love Jesus, the more we desire to let him use us to bring others to know and love him. And the more we desire to be used, the more we recognize our need to be equipped with the gifts of the Spirit. We cannot do it without the empowerment of the Spirit.

"The charisms do not come automatically. Four times in chapters 12–14 of 1 Corinthians, Paul uses a Greek word, zealote, which suggests a passionate desire and an active seeking of gifts. It implies that the charisms must be yearned for and prayed for…. The charisms are the means the Spirit gives us to express the love of Christ in concrete and practical ways…. The charisms are an integral part of the mission of evangelization. Paul uses three words for the charisms: gifts, services, and workings of power … stressing that the gifts are for the work of building up the Church. Without the charisms there is no power in evangelization.

"We need to pray for a fresh outpouring of all the gifts of the Spirit in their great variety. Don't limit God's activity to only those things that seem supernatural…. Charisms are for our ongoing growth and they should not diminish as we mature but become stronger…. Our job is to learn how to use the charisms with a discipline that can release their fullest power and at the same time, fulfill their true purpose."

Sr. Nancy Kellar, SC – *Charisms*

In God's Presence Consider …

The charisms must be yearned for and prayed for. Do I yearn and pray for the charisms? The charisms are the means the Holy Spirit gives us to express our love for Christ in concrete and practical ways. Are they a part of how I show Jesus love?

Closing Prayer

Come, Holy Spirit, and pour out afresh all Your gifts in all their great variety and renew the face of the earth.

Charisms, or charisma in Greek, means a gift freely given. It is based on the word for grace, charis. Grace is the foundation of the Christian life; a favor we don't deserve, but one that God freely bestows on us in Christ as His musical instrument.

"A charism is what might be called a 'gracelet,' a droplet of the vast ocean of God's grace. It is a tangible expression of God's grace in a person's life in the form of a capacity to act in a way that surpasses human power.... They are given by the Holy Spirit. They are charisms because they are given freely ... it is the Holy Spirit Himself that is working through us. They are manifestations of the Spirit because they make the presence of the Holy Spirit evident to others ... a charism is dependent on the operation of the Holy Spirit, and therefore it has an efficacy that surpasses merely human talent.... We can grow in the use of these gifts, but they always remain dependent on the Holy Spirit ... you cannot pull that gift out of your pocket whenever you feel like it. Rather, you are a musical instrument on which the Holy Spirit plays according to His purpose and His timing. The more yielded you are to Him, the more freely He will play."

Randy Clark & Mary Healy - *The Spiritual Gifts Handbook*

In God's Presence Consider ...

Do I see my gifts and talents as God's expression of love for the Body of Christ? Do I know what charisms the Holy Spirit is manifesting in me? Do I yield to Him and allow Him to play me as His musical instrument?

Closing Prayer

Breathe on me, O Breath of God; helping me to more fully yield as a musical instrument in Your hands. Help me to recognize the charisms You have given me, and the humility to realize they come from You. Help me to grow in the use of these gifts always remaining dependent on You to use them as You intend.

The charisms are given to build up the Body of Christ. Each member, diversified as we are, has a part to play. Not knowing the charisms the Holy Spirit has given us and not using them is a great loss to the Body.

"The charisms are gifts not only in the sense that God gives them to people, but that their very purpose is to be used for others. They are by definition gifts to be given away, to be used for the common good (1 Cor. 12:7). They are a means by which God's grace circulates among the members of the Church and overflows beyond its boundaries.... The charisms teach us to receive and give away God's grace, so that the Body of Christ functions as a living organism, each part contributing in a unique way to the whole.... God's idea of unity is a marvelous unity in diversity, each person contributing to the flourishing of the whole by using his or her unique God given gifts.... Scripture therefore emphasizes that exercising our gifts is not optional; it is a sacred responsibility.... Many Christians do not exercise charisms because they have no idea how to use them and grow in them; they may not even know what they are. This is a great loss to the Body of Christ."

Randy Clark & Mary Healy - *The Spiritual Gifts Handbook*

In God's Presence Consider ...

Do I use the gifts and charisms the Holy Spirit is giving me for the common good? Is grace circulating through me to others through the Holy Spirit's charisms? Do I ever ponder that the use of these special gifts of grace is not optional but a sacred responsibility?

Closing Prayer

Come, Holy Spirit, with the Fire of Your Love. Teach me to receive and give away God's graces so that the Body of Christ may function as a living, healthy organism.

In examining the Book of Acts, we are introduced not only to the Gift that the Holy Spirit is, but also to various manifestations and gifts He bestows.

"First of all, the Apostles received a much greater enlightenment from the Holy Spirit regarding the price of the Blood of the Savior; regarding the mystery of Redemption.... They received the fullness of the contemplation of this mystery which they were now to preach to humanity for the salvation of men.

"In this enumeration of the graces of Pentecost we must notice chiefly, not the gift of tongues or other powers of this kind, but rather that special illumination which enabled the Apostles to enter into the depths of the mystery of the incarnation, and more particularly of the Passion of Christ."

Rev. Garrigou Lagrange, O.P. - *The Three Ways of the Spiritual Life*

In God's Presence Consider ...

Have I reflected on the mystery of Redemption by asking the help of the Holy Spirit? Have I ever thought of insight or illumination I have on the mysteries of our Faith as coming from the Holy Spirit?

Closing Prayer

Come, Holy Spirit, enlighten and illumine my mind that I may come to a deeper understanding and reflection of the mysteries of our Faith.

One Beam of His Rays **Day 311**

In speaking to catechumens of the Holy Spirit, St. Cyril of Alexandria tells them how the Spirit knows the hearts and minds of all and distributes to everyone, in their various states of life, His charisms thus illuminating their eyes to see His work.

"O grandeur of the Holy Spirit, admirable, omnipotent lavisher of charisms! Think of those here seated, souls in which he is present and works. He is observing the dispositions of everyone, scrutinizing thoughts and consciences, words, and works.... Throughout the world we can see bishops, priests, deacons, monks, virgins, and lay faithful. At the head of all these is the Spirit who presides and distributes to each one his or her charisms. Throughout the world he gives one purity. Another perpetual virginity, another the gift of mercy, and another love for the poor or the power to chase out demons. As a light makes everything bright with one beam of its rays, so does the Holy Spirit illuminate all those who have eyes to see."

St. Cyril of Alexandria - *Catechesis XVI*

In God's Presence Consider ...

The Holy Spirit lavishes His charisms on us. How do I receive such lavish love? Do I think I can hide things or myself from the Holy Spirit and the work He desires to do within me? Or do I block the working of the Holy Spirit within my soul? Do I allow the light of the Holy Spirit to illuminate my heart and mind with the love of God?

Closing Prayer

Come, O Holy Spirit, the Omnipotent Lavisher of Charisms, preside and distribute Your desired charisms on me. Illuminate me to Your presence and Your work that I may have eyes to see and a heart of faith to respond. St. Cyril of Alexandria, pray for me.

Consolation Carries Pain **Day 312**

The seeds of grace planted in our souls are the gifts, charisms, acts of love, communications with God, and virtues of the Spirit. When the seed that the divine Sower planted in the fertile field of our heart, develops under His gentle operation, they reach in us a certain maturity and then produces its fruit, mild and delicious.

"Consolation is the happiness that carries pain with it. It springs from the very heart of grief: therefore, the Holy Spirit is called 'the Paraclete,' 'the Consoler,' because he gives souls in exile a happiness that is not incompatible with grief, but rather supposes it.

"Jesus does something greater than to suppress pain; He enclosed it (pain) in joy and arranged it so that perfect joy would blossom from its depths. The joy that enfolds grief that is the blossoming flower of suffering is called in Sacred Scripture and in the liturgy, consolation, the consolation poured into our heart by the Paraclete … happiness that is born of pain is the consolation that the Holy Spirit gives to souls…. The Holy Spirit is the Consoler because he is infinite Love … the only thing that can console us is love.

"When our heart is torn to pieces … Love alone possesses the heavenly secret of drawing forth happiness from profound sorrow and pain."

SOG Archbishop Louis Martinez - *The Sanctifier*

In God's Presence Consider …

Have I ever struggled with accepting pain and suffering? Do I see them as the loving means God provides to purify and sanctify my soul? Do I see joy as the blooming flower stemming from suffering? Do I cry out and rely on the Holy Spirit as my Consoler in my brokenness and pain?

Closing Prayer

Jesus, You embraced suffering and pain and raised them to new heights. Send Your Paraclete, Your Consoler that my soul, which is torn to pieces with bitterness, pain, and grief, may experience the love and happiness that is born in pain. Send me Your infinite Love to cultivate and bear the fruit of consolation.

The life of the spirit demands solace, for solace expands the heart, and when the heart is expanded, it runs in the way of the Lord.

"God willed to put delight and comfort in the most essential things of life in order that we should do them not only for duty's sake but also with pleasure and facility, so in the supernatural order he willed to give a ray of happiness, a drop of comfort, that we might fulfill our duties with greater ease.

"… perfection and sweetness … are the two marks of the consolations that the Holy Spirit pours into our souls…. In the Sacred Scriptures the soul is often compared to an orchard…. The soul is a garden into which the Holy Spirit has poured precious, divine seed—the name given by that Apostle St. John to grace. Grace, with its royal retinue of virtues and gifts, is the seed which the Spirit has planted in our souls.

"The fruits are spiritual joys that accompany our works when these have attained a degree of maturity…. Celestial joy comes from the achievement of perfection, even of a relative perfection…. The fruits are found in all the stages of the spiritual life…. Each level of the spiritual life has its corresponding fruits. The work of the Spirit in us is a work of order because the spiritual life consists in the perfect ordering of our being … if we are docile to the Spirit's inspirations, we shall find all along our road not only thorns that torture us, but flowers that breathe forth sweet perfumes and fruits that are delicious to our spiritual palate."

SOG Archbishop Louis Martinez - *The Sanctifier*

In God's Presence Consider …

Do I see grace as the seeds the Holy Spirit plants in my soul? If I lack joy in my life, could it be because I lack order, docility to the Spirit's inspirations, and allowing the Spirit to work in my life? Do I breathe the sweet perfumes or eat the delicious sweetness of the mature fruit of the Spirit in my life?

Closing Prayer

O Holy Spirit, Great Sower of God's seeds, sow within my heart Your seeds of grace that they may attain to a maturity that bears the perfect ordering of my being and the fruits of joy and sweetness.

Holy Spirit, What Must I Do?

The Beatitudes are a call to personal conversion, interior transformation, and an openness to the working of the Holy Spirit. They describe the conditions necessary for a person to be fully open to the Holy Spirit's action of interior transformation; of a happiness that only God can give.

"Even more deeply than a code of conduct, the Beatitudes are a path toward the happiness of the Kingdom, an itinerary for union with God and personal interior renewal.... It proposes an openness to the Holy Spirit. Only the Spirit can give us true understanding of the Beatitudes, and only the Spirit makes it possible for us to apply them in our lives....

"The Beatitudes are the description of this 'new heart' (Jer. 31:31–33) that the Holy Spirit fashions in us, which is the very heart of Christ ... a grace of interior transformation by the Holy Spirit.

"St. Thomas Aquinas following St. Augustine, pointed to the link between the Beatitudes and the seven gifts of the Spirit.... In living the Beatitudes we are open to the gifts of the Spirit, while, inversely, only the Holy Spirit can give us the understanding to practice the Beatitudes fully.

"The happiness promised by the Beatitudes is .... a visitation of the Holy Spirit, a divine consolation.... Only the work of the Spirit can transform us and enable us to fulfill our vocations.... "We can say that the Beatitudes are both fruits of the Holy Spirit and conditions for receiving the Spirit. This is no contradiction."

Fr. Jacques Philippe - *The Eight Doors of the Kingdom*

In God's Presence Consider ...

How can I make myself more fully open to the Holy Spirit and the action of divine grace? Have I considered the Beatitudes as a visitation and divine consolation of the Holy Spirit? Are the Beatitudes the way I live my Christian life?

Closing Prayer

Come, Holy Spirit, and visit me. Give me a new heart and write Your law upon it. Transform me to live the Beatitudes by being fully open to Your action in my life.

Pentecost is Not Over

Day 315

The mystery of Pentecost is to be an everlasting thriller as we open ourselves to seek Him as the source of what our souls and hearts truly desire. We need to make a spot for Him in order for Him to return to us.

"Pentecost is not over. In fact, it is continually going on in every time and in every place, because the Holy Spirit desired to give himself to all men and all who want him can always receive him, so we do not have to envy the apostles and the first believers; we only have to dispose ourselves like them to receive him well, and He will come to us as he did to them.

"The mystery of Pentecost is a permanent mystery. The Spirit continues to come to all souls who truly desire Him.... If they only want Him ... if they only invoke Him ... if they only prepare a place for Him in their hearts.... Who is hungry enough? Who is thirsty enough? Who is humble enough? Who is zealous enough?.... It is necessary that we return to the Holy Spirit so that the Holy Spirit may return to us.

Blessed Elena Guerra - *Renewal Ministries*

In God's Presence Consider ...

Is there a need for the Holy Spirit in my life? Do I dispose myself to the desires the Holy Spirit has for me? Do I truly desire Him? Do I invoke Him and prepare a place for Him in my heart?

Closing Prayer

Blessed Elena Guerra, please pray for me that I will have an ever-growing desire and continually prepare a place for the Holy Spirit in my heart.

A body without a soul is a corpse. A city without inhabitants is a dead city. Evangelization without the wind of Pentecost is lifeless. The work of the Holy Spirit is to bring life, animate the soul, and to bring about renewal. Without the Spirit, we cannot give others the Word of Life.

"The soul gives life to the body, and without the soul the body—whatever its size—is a corpse. A home or city without the strength of its inhabitants breathing "a soul," so to speak, into it is also dead. Without such a soul even a popular tourist site, regardless its famous sight and spectacular monuments, remains a dead city. Lord, my life, my activities, and the society in which I live must have a soul breathed into them.

"This is the work of the Holy Spirit. Am I animated by the Holy Spirit, the Spirit of Christ, or by the spirit of 'the devil, the flesh, and the world?' To evangelize is to give life, and to let the wind of Pentecost renew the face of the earth. The Lord has sent me to proclaim the Good News to the poor. Thank you, Lord.

"I fear for those who evangelize without the breath of the Holy Spirit, without the Virgin Mary, without the apostles, without the Passion and the Resurrection of Christ, for they cannot give the Word of life. If it has been a long time since I led another to the faith, perhaps my preaching of the Gospel is not animated by the breath of the Holy Spirit."

Venerable Francis Xavier Nguyen Van Thuan -
Prayers of Hope, Words of Courage

In God's Presence Consider …

Is my soul animated by the devil, the flesh, and the world, or by the Holy Spirit? When I evangelize, is it with or without the breath of the Holy Spirit, the wind of Pentecost? How long has it been since I led someone to faith?

Closing Prayer

Holy and divine Spirit! Through the intercession of the Blessed Virgin Mary, Your beloved spouse, breathe Your life into my very being, my activities, and the society in which I live. Help me not to be a spiritual corpse or a dead city. I seek You, the wind of Pentecost, to renew me and the face of the earth. Venerable Nguyen Van Thuan, pray for me.

Only God Makes a Pentecost **Day 317**

At Pentecost the Holy Spirit humbled Himself, taking on lowly signs like fire, wind, and tongues. He humbles Himself to dwell in needy creatures of flesh, making them His temples. Fr. Cantalamessa says that humility is the best preparation for receiving the Holy Spirit.

"Pentecost is an important event for the whole Church. What can we ourselves do to make Pentecost happen? Absolutely nothing! Only God makes a Pentecost. The power descends from on high, and nothing on earth can stop it. All that is positive and all that is a gift in Pentecost comes from God. It is the Father who decides the manner, the time and the measure of the Spirit for everyone.

"What can we do, then, to experience our own Pentecost if we can't do anything positive? We can make ourselves empty to allow the Holy Spirit to come! Making ourselves empty means having an attitude of profound, sincere humility before God.... This is how Mary prepared the apostles to receive the first Pentecost. She helped them make themselves lowly, humble, and docile.... Humility, then, seems to be the best preparation for receiving the Holy Spirit."

Raniero Cantalamessa, O.F.M. Cap. - *Sober Intoxication of the Spirit*

In God's Presence Consider ...

Nothing can stop the power of the Holy Spirit descending from God on high. Do I ignore or avoid that power, convincing myself this power is not meant for me? Do I trust the Father to know the manner, time and measure of the Holy Spirit for me? Do I seek Mary's help in emptying myself to become lowly, humble, and docile, to allow the Holy Spirit to come as a new Pentecost upon me?

Closing Prayer

O Lord, my heart is not lifted up, my eyes are not raised too high; I do not occupy myself with things too great and too marvelous for me. But I have calmed and quieted my soul, like a weaned child with its mother. Come, Holy Spirit, and make me share in Your humility.

Based on Ps. 131:1–2.

St. Angela of Foligno was on a pilgrimage when she prayed to St. Francis and asked for his help to love Jesus more deeply and to live her Franciscan life more fervently. The Spirit's answer was tender and was simply to love Him.

"Angela was deeply moved to hear the Holy Spirit speak these tender words to her soul: 'Love me, because you are very much loved by me, much more than you could love me.' What an exquisite pledge of love; what a tender request for the return of that love! May the Holy Spirit's beautiful words to Angela be seared into our own souls, for the Holy Spirit speaks them to each of us.

"Let us pray for the grace to realize and appreciate now the countless gifts that, in the Trinity's plan of love, the Holy Spirit has brought to us: the joys of loving and being loved; the blessings of a cherished family and good health; the treasure of our gifts and accomplishments; the joy of knowing and loving the Trinity; the gift of cherishing … the sacrament of the Eucharist; the treasured strength and comfort of our faith.

"… what the Holy Spirit desires from us in return for the manifold blessings He has bestowed on us is simply our love."

Sr. Mary Ann Fatula, O.P. - *Drawing Close to the Holy Spirit*

In God's Presence Consider …

Do I feel or have I experienced the Holy Spirit speaking to my heart? Have I felt His love? Do I recognize and appreciate the countless gifts of love that the Holy Spirit gives me? Do I love the Holy Spirit in return, "the easiest and sweetest gift to give?"

Closing Prayer

St. Angela of Foligno, pray with me for the grace to realize and appreciate the countless gifts of love that God sends me through the Holy Spirit. Then help me to love the Holy Spirit who desires my love.

To know is to love, thus the doctrines on the Holy Spirit, like all doctrine, are to shed light on the mysteries of the Divine Giver leading to a deeper love and devotion to Him.

"These sublime truths, which so clearly show forth the infinite goodness of the Holy Ghost towards us, certainly demand that we should direct towards Him the highest homage of our love and devotion. Christians may do this most effectually if they will daily strive to know Him, to love Him, and to implore Him more earnestly.

"All preachers and those having care of souls should remember that it is their duty to instruct their people more diligently and more fully about the Holy Ghost.... What should be chiefly dwelt upon and clearly explained is the multitude and greatness of the benefits which have been bestowed, and are constantly bestowed, upon us by this Divine Giver, so that errors and ignorance concerning matters of such moment may be entirely dispelled, as unworthy of the 'children of light.' We urge this, not only because it affects a mystery by which we are directly guided to eternal life, and which must therefore be firmly believed; but also because the more clearly and fully the good is known the earnestly it is loved."

Pope Leo XIII, - *Divinum Illud Munus*

In God's Presence Consider ...

Do I strive to know, love, and implore the Holy Spirit on a daily basis? Do I reflect on the infinite goodness the Holy Spirit bestows in my life? How can I more earnestly love the Holy Spirit?

Closing Prayer

Come, Holy Spirit, Divine Giver, and help me to know, love, and implore You more earnestly in my life.

Our love for the Holy Spirit is not to consist of dry speculations or external observances, but rather is to run forward toward action and especially to flee from sin.

"Now we owe to the Holy Ghost, love, because He is God…. He is also to be loved because He is the substantial, eternal, primal Love, and nothing is more lovable than love…. This love has a twofold and most conspicuous utility. In the first place it will excite us to acquire daily a clearer knowledge about the Holy Ghost. In the second place it will obtain for us a still more abundant supply of heavenly gifts…. For whatever we are, that we are by the divine goodness; and this goodness is specially attributed to the Holy Ghost…. Since He is the Spirit of Truth, whosoever faileth by weakness or ignorance may perhaps have some excuse before Almighty God; but he who resists the truth through malice and turns away from it, sins most grievously against the Holy Ghost.

"Lastly, we ought to pray to and invoke the Holy Ghost, for each one of us greatly needs His protection and His help. The more a man is deficient in wisdom, weak in strength, borne down with trouble, prone to sin, so ought he the more to fly to Him who is the never-ceasing fount of light, strength, consolation, and holiness. And chiefly that first requisite of man, the forgiveness of sins, must be sought for from Him."

Pope Leo XIII - *Divinum Illud Munus*

In God's Presence Consider …

Do I see my goodness as the work and gift of the Holy Spirit? Do I ignore and resist the Holy Spirit by turning away from Him out of fear or deficient wisdom? Have I considered that my lack of pursuit to know more about the Holy Spirit can be a sin that grieves the Holy Spirit?

Closing Prayer

Come, Holy Spirit, enlighten my soul, that I may belong only to You, and seek Your protection and help in all things.

"Truly, I say to you, if you have faith as a grain of mustard seed, you will say to this mountain, 'Move from here to there,' and it will move; and nothing will be impossible to you." Matthew 17:20

"… Faith opens us to God's power, whereas unbelief closes us to it…. Faith is the Lord's door into human hearts, and it can only be opened from within…. Scripture shows us that in fact Christian faith has an active, dynamic quality. It is a personal relationship with the Lord in which we are drawing near to him and entrusting ourselves to him. Faith therefore takes risks, it puts itself forward; it strives against obstacles…. Faith is communal. It is not a purely individual matter but something that belongs to the body of Christ…. Whenever people of faith are gathered together in Jesus' name, their faith is not added but multiplied; the faith of each stirs up the faith of others….

"We should never yield to a spirit of hopelessness but rather, as Paul counseled, 'pray without ceasing, give thanks in all circumstances' (1 Thes. 5:17–18) … faith is a gift of God to which we yield. It is a relationship of trust and surrender to the Father, Son and Holy Spirit. It cannot be conjured up. Rather, faith grows as we come to understand more deeply who God is and who we are in him…. Each one of us has a part in Christ's mission to dismantle the kingdom of darkness and make the kingdom of God present wherever we are…. Our faith is strengthened by prayer, which leads us into deeper heart-to-heart knowledge of the Lord and his ways…. As we grow in faith through prayer and fasting, we are able to speak and act in closer and closer alignment with what the Father is already doing, just as Jesus did (Jn. 5:19)."

Dr. Mary Healy - *Healing*

In God's Presence Consider …

Does my faith lead to and enhance a heart-to-heart personal relationship with Jesus Christ? Do I give in to discouragement or a spirit of hopelessness? Am I about dismantling the kingdom of darkness and making the kingdom of God present?

Closing Prayer

Lord, I believe. Help my unbelief.

St. John Chrysostom speaks of the true nature of evangelization. He says it is to announce the Person of Jesus which is to flow from a life of communion with Him and animated by grace.

"The apostles did not come down from the mountain like Moses, their hands holding stone tablets. They left the Upper Room carrying the Holy Spirit in their hearts and offering to everyone the treasures of wisdom, grace, and spiritual gifts as if they were coming from a gushing spring. They went … animated by the grace of the Holy Spirit.

"Evangelization does not mean announcing abstract truth but the Truth, the person of Christ with whom people are invited to come into communion. It is the Spirit alone who can allow this to happen until the wedding union. The evangelizer is thus called to collaborate with the Spirit so that this miracle can take place. The more receptive the evangelizer's collaboration is with the Paraclete, the more effective will be the evangelization."

THC - *The Holy Spirit, Lord and Giver of Life*

In God's Presence Consider …

Am I animated to the grace of the Holy Spirit dwelling in me? Do I collaborate with the Holy Spirit bringing others to the Person of Jesus? Do I carry stone tablets or the treasure of the Holy Spirit?

Closing Prayer

Come, Holy Spirit, and animate my whole being with Your love, that I may announce the Good News of Jesus with the example of my life. Help me to be more receptive to You.

The Agent of Renewal **Day 323**

God is about the business of renewing souls with His instrument, His agent the Holy Spirit. Renewal is really about an interior conformity to Christ; a striving for a new heart.

"… the baptism, or outpouring in the Spirit … is not an event in and of itself but rather the beginning of a journey whose aim is the profound renewal of life in the Church.

"… the heart … that part of ourselves that needs to be renewed in order for us to resemble Christ, the New Man par excellence. 'Renewing ourselves' means striving to have the same attitude that Christ Jesus had (Phil. 2:5), striving for a new heart…. The renewal should be, above all, an interior one, one of the heart.

"… the Holy Spirit is the instrument, the agent of renewal. The name we give to our experience signifies, then, something very exact: renewal by the work of the Holy Spirit, a renewal in which God, not man, is the principal author, the protagonist. 'I [not you]' says God, 'am making all things new' (Rev. 21:5); 'My Spirit [and only He] can renew the face of the earth' (Ps. 104:30)…. Without the Holy Spirit we can do nothing."

Fr. Raniero Cantalamessa, O.F.M. Cap. - *Sober Intoxication of the Spirit*

In God's Presence Consider …

Do I consider the reception of the Holy Spirit in the sacraments of initiation as the beginning of my journey? Do I seek to have the same attitude of Jesus? Do I allow God to make me new by His instrument, the Holy Spirit?

Closing Prayer

Jesus, send upon me Your instrument and agent of renewal: the Holy Spirit. May Your Spirit help me to have Your mind and attitude. May He aid me in my journey in the profound renewal You desire in the life of Your Body, the Church.

The Later Awakening of an Earlier Gift **Day 324**

A lack of understanding or misunderstanding with "Baptized in the Holy Spirit" could be a real turn off to people. It is rooted in the sacraments of initiation.

"Did you receive the Holy Spirit when you became believers?' (Acts 19:2). To this question of St. Paul, we, as Catholic Christians, give a wholehearted 'yes,' for in the sacraments of initiation we have truly received the Holy Spirit. Just as Timothy was urged to 'fan into flame' an earlier gift (2 Tim. 1:6), so we are challenged to awaken the baptismal gift through an ever-deepening conversion to Jesus Christ.

"... what some early Christian authors called the 'baptism in the Holy Spirit' is a key to living the Christian life to the fullest ... 'baptism in the Holy Spirit' refers to Christian initiation and to its reawakening in Christian experience.... Using this phrase today for the later awakening of the original sacramental grace by no means signifies a second baptism. While not suggesting that the 'baptism in the Holy Spirit' happens only in the charismatic renewal, our pastoral experience and theological reflection lead us to believe that this grace of the 'baptism in the Holy Spirit' is meant for the whole church.

"... we believe that this gift of baptism in the Holy Spirit belongs to the Christian inheritance of all those sacramentally initiated into the church."

McDonnell and Montague - *Fanning the Flame*

In God's Presence Consider ...

If I am fully initiated into the Catholic Church, I have received the fullness of the Holy Spirit. Do I believe this? Do I ask the Holy Spirit to fan into flame my conversion and His love? Am I in need of a reawakening of my Christian experience? Do I fear the "baptism in the Holy Spirit" because I see it as Charismatic or a second baptism?

Closing Prayer

Come, Holy Spirit, and fan into flame Your love within me. Fan into flame Your virtues and gifts. Awaken in me the baptismal gifts through an ever-deepening conversion and relationship with Jesus. Help me to live as fully initiated in the Church.

Baptism in the Spirit must not be reduced either to a formula or to a theological position that has no correspondence to lived experience. God is God and He does whatever He wants. Our response is to allow Him to move and not box Him in with our desires and principles.

"Baptism in the Spirit can have one effect or purpose in one person's life and another in another person's life.... There is no one method or formula for receiving this grace, since it involves a personal relationship with the living God, who always acts freely as He wills ... to be filled, you must belong to God. You must be a believer who has given your life to Christ ... deep-rooted misconceptions about God and about ourselves can block us from fully receiving what God has for us ... we must not let the grace of God be hemmed in by our conditions. We must always be open to the grace of God coming upon someone who is not seeking the baptism in the Spirit, even an unbeliever—even though it is not the normal operation of the Spirit, nor is it the normal order of salvation (Acts 2:38). God is God, He is sovereign, and He can do what pleases Him.... We must be careful not to turn God's gift into a work of man, but must allow the grace of God in Jesus to be the bedrock upon which we approach the throne of God in our time of need."

Randy Clark & Mary Healy - *The Spiritual Gifts Handbook*

In God's Presence Consider ...

Do I belong to God? Do I have a personal relationship with this living God that allows Him to act as He wills? Have I given my life to Christ? Am I open to the grace of God coming upon me?

Closing Prayer

Father, I give You permission to act freely in my life as You will. Help me to give my life totally to Jesus and the Holy Spirit, that I will be totally Yours and not hem You in, preventing Your sovereignty to reign in my life. Let Your Son, Jesus, be the bedrock of my relationship with You.

St. Pope John Paul II continually proclaimed the dignity of every human person reminding us that all are equally created in the image and likeness of God and are equally redeemed by Christ. We are not to hide behind closed doors through fear, but open wide the doors of our hearts to receive the movements of God's love.

"When we Christians make Jesus Christ the center of our feelings and thoughts, we do not turn away from people and their needs. On the contrary, we are caught up in the eternal movement of God's love that comes to meet us; we are caught up in the movement of the Son, who came among us, who became one of us; we are caught up in the movement of the Holy Spirit, who visits the poor, calms fevered hearts, binds up wounded hearts, warms cold hearts, and gives us the fullness of his gifts.... The Church looks at the world through the very eyes of Christ; Jesus is the principle of her solicitude for man....

"Brothers and sisters in Christ, with deep conviction and affection I repeat to you the words that I addressed to the world when I took up my apostolic ministry in the service of all men and women: Do not be afraid. Open wide the doors for Christ.

St. Pope John Paul II -
Homily from a Mass during his first papal visit to U.S., 1979

In God's Presence Consider ...

Do I take time to ponder being taken up into the movement of God? Do I open wide the doors of my heart to the Holy Spirit allowing Him to calm my fevered heart, bind up my heart's wounds, warm my cold and hardened heart, and give me the fullness of His gifts?

Closing Prayer

Come, Holy Spirit, Movement of God's Love, and remove all the fears that cause me to close myself up to You so I may open wide the doors of my heart and receive the fullness of love and life You desire to bestow upon me.

Stirring Up and Rekindling **Day 327**

A personal relationship and openness to the Holy Spirit fits into the Christian life and offers possible solutions to our challenges by looking at the importance of conversion to Christ and living one's life in the Spirit.

"We believe that the solution to these problems lies in a deep personal conversion to Christ, in sanctification and in fuller life in the Holy Spirit.

"… All the charisms bring a new docility to the Spirit, and expectant faith in God's saving intervention in human affairs, and enhanced zeal for the gospel, and a respect for authority in the church.

"Baptism in the Holy Spirit converts many to Christ, committing themselves to service in the church … to an experience of Christian community that transcends anything they have previously known … charismatic empowerment has transformed many by a converted … and touched people of all ages and background.

"The effects of this reception of the Spirit are manifold: sanctification, a new and experiential relationship to God who is called Abba! Father!, to a proclamation that Jesus is Lord, union in the bond of love, the fruits of the Spirit, new insight into the mysteries of God, a taste for the word of God, courageous boldness, a new outpouring and use of the Spirit's gifts…. This life in the Holy Spirit is not, therefore, one spirituality among others…. It is the spirituality of the church. The gift of the Spirit … must be sought repeatedly through prayer, stirred up or rekindled … pray for the full release of the Holy Spirit…."

McDonnell and Montague - *Fanning the Flame*

In God's Presence Consider …

Does my knowledge of Jesus involve head knowledge, or a heartfelt experience? Do I fear the stirring up and rekindling of the Holy Spirit within me? Do I want to live the full Christian life? Can I live this life apart from the Holy Spirit?

Closing Prayer

Come, Holy Spirit, and rekindle in me the Fire of Your Love. Sanctify me in Your Fire that I may have a fuller release of You within me. Help me to live the spirituality of the Church.

The Holy Spirit is in us, for every soul in a state of grace is a living tabernacle. St. Augustine of Hippo said, "The fact that we believe and act belongs to the free choice of our will. And yet both are given by the Spirit in faith and charity." Retractationes, I, 23, 2

"The first all-important fact that we must fully understand is that the Holy Ghost is really, truly and personally in our souls even as He is in Heaven. He loves us with a most tender and infinite love and earnestly desires to pour out on us His Gifts and graces. This He cannot do if we do not correspond to His love, if we do not know Him, love Him, and pray to Him.

"Our most grave obligation, then, is to bear clearly in mind and fully realize that the Holy Ghost is in us, and not merely by His graces and Gifts, but personally and as really as Jesus Christ is in the Tabernacle, though in a different way."

Fr. Paul O' Sullivan, O.P. - *The Holy Ghost Our Greatest Friend*

In God's Presence Consider …

Do I know, love, and pray to the Holy Spirit seeking His help from He who dwells within me? Do I see that my fully realizing the Holy Spirit as a real Person living is me is a grave obligation I have? How am I cultivating the virtue of faith in my life and relationship with the Holy Spirit?

Closing Prayer

Holy Spirit, God of Light and Truth, really and truly in my soul, give me Your blessed light that I may see things clearly especially to see You are a real Person dwelling in me as in a tabernacle.

The Supreme End **Day 329**

Our God is a jealous God who not merely lives with us but desires to live in us, to possess us, and give to us the Gift of Himself according to His pleasure so that our joy may be complete and we may enjoy the happiness of the Gift.

"God gives himself to us with ardor and vehemence, with the deep truth of his infinite love. He does not live with us, but in us. He does not wish to come only at our call to satisfy our desires, like those who love each other on earth. He gives himself to us, delivers himself to us, and makes us the Gift of himself, that we may use it according to our pleasure.

"To use that Gift is to enjoy it because it is the supreme end of our being, our life's happiness; and no other use can be made of happiness than to enjoy it."

SOG Archbishop Louis M. Martinez - *The Sanctifier*

In God's Presence Consider …

Do I experience being on the receiving end of God's infinite love? Do I allow God to deliver Himself to me? Do I see God as a "Big Sugar Daddy" who is sought after to satisfy my desires or do I live for God's desires?

Closing Prayer

O God, You love me with an infinite love according to Your pleasure. Help me to use the Gift of the Holy Spirit in such a way that I may enjoy the happiness of possessing and being possessed by Your Love.

Satisfaction of All Desires **Day 330**

One of the most basic uses of water is for drinking. We must drink water because we need it to sustain our bodily functions. In a similar way, the Holy Spirit gives us supernatural life as the Living Water of our souls.

"On our part, there must be a corresponding desire or thirst for the Living Water of the Holy Spirit in our hearts.... One kind of thirst is caused by deprivation. An example of this is the thirst people suffer during a time of drought. Drought often brings a scorching of the earth and leads to a lack of crops and then of food in general, thereby threatening people with death by starvation. Similarly, a drought of the Spirit means we do not possess Him Who is the Source of all life within us. Our life in Christ is then in danger of dying for lack of the 'Living Water' that we all need.

"On the other hand, there is a thirst or desire ... that is created by a definite longing. On a very hot day, a person can long to drink his or her favorite cold beverage.... Likewise, our thirst for the Spirit makes us seek Him more ardently and constantly. When we drink of the 'Living Water,' our soul experiences joy and refreshment. In this thirst, the soul yearns for God as the satisfaction of all its desires."

Fr. Andrew Apostoli, C.F.R. - *The Gift of God: The Holy Spirit*

In God's Presence Consider ...

What does my soul thirst for? Am I in a spiritual drought right now? Do I thirst and long for the Holy Spirit? Is God the satisfaction of all my desires?

Closing Prayer

As a deer longs for running waters, I ask You Lord, that I may long and thirst for the Holy Spirit in my soul. Help me to drink of Your Life Giving Water so that I may be filled with joy and be refreshed.

The Day of the Fight **Day 331**

The mission of the Holy Spirit is to transform the disciples into witnesses to Christ. The Church Fathers taught that the highest degree of witness is seen in the martyrs. Martyrdom is the pinnacle of holiness and has always been considered the supreme gift that the Holy Spirit gives to believers. Tertullian saw the Spirit as the 'trainer' of martyrs.

"You are about to face quite a fight, where the spectators and judges are God alone. The Holy Spirit is our trainer. The prize, an eternal crown. Our manager Jesus Christ, who has anointed you with the Holy Spirit and who has made you descend into the arena for the day of the fight, has taken you from the world of a comfortable life for a tough apprenticeship in order to train you more tenaciously.

Tertullian - *To the Martyrs*

In God's Presence Consider …

Do I ever consider the eternal crown that awaits me in heaven as my prize for running the good race and fighting the good fight here on earth? Do I see myself anointed in the Holy Spirit by Jesus? Am I too caught up in my comfortable life and seek to avoid a tough apprenticeship and training?

Closing Prayer

Holy Spirit, You are the great trainer sent by the Son to prepare me for the day of battle. Help me to forsake my comfortable life and to seek the tenacious training You desire me to undergo. Prepare me to descend into the arena for the fight with Your anointing.

Our Remarkable Resistance **Day 332**

Fr. Dubay makes two important points on the Holy Spirit in his book of conversion and prayer. The thrust of his book is that we need deep conversion to not only move away from mortal sin but all venial sin and bad habits that tend to make us lackadaisical in seeking to live holy and saintly lives.

"There is a gap for most people between prayer and performance.... We are to be perfect as God himself is perfect. We are to be transformed from one glory to another into the very divine image.... We should be so intimate with the indwelling Trinity that we live a life of love; everything we do becomes an act of loving.... We cannot even imagine what splendors await us if we actually love God and neighbor as we ought.... We are not only to be possessed by the Holy Spirit, but to be filled with him—yes, filled....

"What we know has very little effect on how we live.... Our immediate purpose at this point is to focus on the remarkable resistance most people place before significant moral change happening in their lives.... The logical reaction at this point for any sincere reader understandably may be: 'Help! I can't do this by myself.' And of course, that is perfectly true. The Lord took care of this problem too. Without his Holy Spirit, he told us, we can do nothing (1 Cor. 12:3). Surely no one can become a saint without his aid. But the fact is that his help and grace are always present. It is up to us to use what he offers but never forces."

Fr. Thomas Dubay, S.M. - *Deep Conversion Deep Prayer*

In God's Presence Consider ...

Do I live with a gap between my prayer and the performance of my life? Am I merely possessed by the Holy Spirit or filled with Him? Do I use the graces and helps the Holy Spirit offers me?

Closing Prayer

As I look at my life and the various gaps between my prayer and my performances, and my remarkable resistance to becoming a saint and holy, I cry out to You, O Holy Spirit, HELP! I can't do this myself. I can do nothing without You. Come with Your aid, Your help, and Your transforming grace, that I may use what You offer for the glory of God.

St. Pope John Paul II is talking about the judgment at the end of time. During this judgment, the Holy Spirit, who is truth and love, will help us to see ourselves in the light of Truth and Love which is God. The Holy Spirit will be the source of our final perseverance.

"... Even if the soul in its passage to heaven is purified of its last dregs in purgatory, this soul is already filled with light, certainty, and joy because it knows that it belongs to God forever. At that culminating point the soul is guided to the Holy Spirit, author and giver not only of the justifying 'first grace' and of sanctifying grace, throughout earthly life, but also the glorifying grace in hora mortis. It is the grace of final perseverance.

"One could say that Christian life on earth is like an initiation into full participation in the glory of God. It is the Holy Spirit who constitutes the guarantee for achieving the fullness of eternal life, when by the effect of the redemption like pain and death, the rest of sins will be overcome."

St. Pope John Paul II - *The Holy Spirit, Guarantee of Eschatological Hope and Source of Final Perseverance*

In God's Presence Consider ...

If the Holy Spirit is the guarantee for achieving the fullness of eternal life, and initiates me into full participation in the glory of God, why do I hesitate and hold back from an intimate relationship with the Holy Spirit?

Closing Prayer

O Holy Spirit, true God, guarantee of eternal life and the means of initiation into full participation in the glory of God, come upon me and effect the means of my redemption that I may spend all eternity with You.

Holy Among the Holy **Day 334**

The Christian, according to St. Clement of Alexandria, is one who is guided by the Holy Spirit to become a witness of Christ in their daily life, knowing that to be Christian means to be ready to die for Christ at any moment. In this way, martyrdom extends throughout life.

"… will give witness (martyresei) at night, and give witness during the day. In word, life, and conduct the Christian will give witness. In living together with the Lord he will remain his confidant and table companion according to the Spirit. The Christian will remain pure in the flesh, pure in heart, sanctified in the word. 'The world has been crucified to me (Christ),' says the Scripture, and he is crucified 'to the world' (Gal. 6:14). The Christian, carrying everywhere the cross of the Savior, following in the footsteps of the Lord and becomes, like God, holy among the holy."

St. Clement of Alexandria – *Stromata*

In God's Presence Consider …

Do I give witness to Jesus Christ in my life and in all my conduct? Do I seek the Holy Spirit to help me remain in Jesus and to be His confidant and table companion? Do I follow in the footsteps of Jesus, carrying my cross in a way that purifies and sanctifies me?

Closing Prayer

St. Clement of Alexandria, help me, and pray for me, that working with the Holy Spirit, I may live in union with Jesus so as to remain His confidant and table companion. Help me to be crucified to the world and the world to me, that I may carry everywhere the Cross of my Savior.

St. Pope Paul VI gives Scriptural examples of the Holy Spirit descending, anointing, and manifesting in the life of Jesus and the Apostles. Then he turns to address the Church's need to cooperate with that same Holy Spirit.

"Evangelization will never be possible without the action of the Holy Spirit.... It is in the 'consolation of the Holy Spirit' that the Church increases (Acts 10:44). The Holy Spirit is the soul of the Church. It is he who explains to the faithful the deep meaning of the teaching of Jesus and of His mystery. It is the Holy Spirit who, today just as at the beginning of the Church, acts in every evangelizer and allows himself to be possessed and led my Him. The Holy Spirit places on his lips the words which he could not find by himself, and at the same time the Holy Spirit predisposes the soul of the hearer to be open and receptive to the Good News and to the kingdom being proclaimed.

"Techniques of evangelization are good, but even the most advanced ones could not replace the gentle action of the Spirit. The most perfect preparation of the evangelizer has no effect without the Holy Spirit. Without the Holy Spirit the most convincing dialectic has no power over the heart of man. Without Him the most highly developed schemas resting on a sociological or psychological basis are quickly seen to be quite valueless."

St. Pope Paul VI - *Evangelii Nuntiandi*

In God's Presence Consider ...

Am I open to receive the consolations of the Holy Spirit? Do I allow the Holy Spirit to place on my lips words others need to hear? Have I allowed the Good News to truly sink into and be lived in my heart? Do I sidestep the gentle action of the Spirit and seek to rely more on the sociological or psychological sciences to explain Jesus?

Closing Prayer

Come O Soul of the Church, and in Your gentle action prepare me to be an evangelizer by first helping me to hear the Good News, to repent, and to have Jesus Lord of my life. St. Pope Paul VI, pray for me.

The experience of the baptism in the Holy Spirit is more real than most experiences because it leads to lasting changes in one's life.

"I write of this experience many years after it happened. It hasn't always been glorious by any means.... Prayer has sometimes been difficult, even painful. I have faced obstinate problems that haven't budged at all despite intense prayer. I still sin. I continue to make mistakes. The baptism in the Spirit is a foretaste of eternal life with God, something that hints at what is to come and then diminishes in intensity.

"I know the baptism of the Spirit is real because it brought about lasting changes in me. It has also brought about changes in hundreds of men and women I know well enough to be certain that they are different people because of what God has done for them.

"What are these changes? The first lasting change was in my prayer life.... Up until that time, I had been controlling my prayer time. Afterward, the Lord was running it; the Spirit was praying in me. I learned that living in the power of the Spirit is an experience of being immersed in the life of the Spirit.

"I also noticed an immediate difference in the way I read Scripture ... the words seemed to leap off the page when I read Scripture.... I also received spiritual gifts ... manifestations of the Holy Spirit, given primarily to equip the community of Christians with all the tools they need to be the body of Christ."

Fr. Michael Scanlan, T.O.R. - *Let the Fire Fall*

In God's Presence Consider ...

Do I shy away from thinking or pursuing the baptism in the Spirit? Do I view the baptism of the Holy Spirit as something belonging to the past or as a means of equipping me and the Church with the tools we need to carry out the mission Jesus entrusted to us?

Closing Prayer

Holy Spirit, I do not know how to pray as I ought. Please, give me the utterances that I may seek from the Father and the Son through You, all the gifts and tools needed to help me be formed into the Body of Christ and to effectively carry out my mission.

An Act of Love **Day 337**

God gives the spiritual gifts freely. We can pray for them, learn about them, stir them up, put them into practice, and grow in their exercise. Although the Holy Spirit distributes them as He wills, He works most fully through open and generous hearts.

"Every Christian has an irreplaceable role to play in the Church's mission; each is given charisms that perfectly correspond to his or her unique role. The use of our charisms is therefore not optional. God's gifts bring a corresponding responsibility to use them. Many people do not exercise charisms because they have no idea that they even have them. But this is a great loss to the body of Christ. It is a major reason for the weakness of many efforts at evangelization and parish renewal.... The gifts grow in power and purity as we grow in our relationship with God.

"The risen Lord is waiting for his disciples, filled with the Holy Spirit, to act in the power they have already been given and to ask for more heavenly power to meet the needs of those among them.... You just need a heart filled with simple, childlike faith in the Lord Jesus.... God has given us charisms for the sake of love, and exercising a charism must always be an act of love."

Dr. Mary Healy - *Healing*

In God's Presence Consider ...

Do I try to recognize the charisms that correspond to my unique role in the mission of the Church? Have I ever thought of the corresponding responsibility I have to use the charisms the Holy Spirit has given me? Is my heart filled with a simple, childlike faith in Jesus?

Closing Prayer

O Holy Spirit, You have given me various charisms for the sake of love. Help me to exercise those charisms as acts of love to meet the needs of those around me.

In order to fully know Jesus and to be witnesses to Him, sharing Him with others, we need the Holy Spirit. Jn. 15:26–27

"The supreme and most complete revelation of God to humanity is Jesus Christ himself, and the witness of the Spirit inspires, guarantees and convalidates the faithful transmission of this revelation in the preaching and writing of the Apostles, while the witness of the Apostles ensures its human expression in the Church and in the history of humanity.

"'When the Spirit of truth comes, he will guide you into all the truth; for he will not speak on his own authority, but whatever he hears he will speak, and he will declare to you the things that are to come… He will guide you into all truth….' (Jn. 16:13) For the mystery of Christ, taken as a whole, demands faith, since it is faith that adequately introduces man into the reality of the revealed mystery. The guiding into all the truth is therefore achieved in faith and through faith: and this is the work of the Spirit of truth and the result of his action in man. Here the Holy Spirit is to be man's supreme guide and the light of the human spirit."

St. Pope John Paul II - *Dominum et Vivicantem*

In God's Presence Consider …

How can the Holy Spirit help me develop and grow in my relationship with Jesus? Do I regularly exercise the virtue of faith to enter more fully into the revealed mysteries of Christ? Do I allow the Holy Spirit to be my supreme guide and light?

Closing Prayer

Come, Holy Spirit, increase and perfect the gift of faith in me, that I may see, hear, look upon, and touch Jesus. Be the Light shining in me, guiding me into all truth.

Disposed to Give Everything **Day 339**

There are three obstacles that prevent us from making space for God to love us on His terms and to fill us with His peace. These are: lack of confidence in God, not trusting God's Providence, and fear of suffering. To counter these obstacles, he says we need meditative prayer and to seek the gift of abandonment.

"To preserve peace in the midst of the hazards of human existence, we have only one solution: We must rely on God alone, with total trust in Him.

"Abandonment inevitably requires an element of renunciation and it is this that is most difficult for us. We have a natural tendency to cling to a whole host of things: material goods, affections, desires, projects, etc. and it costs us terribly to let go of our grip, because we have the impression that we will lose ourselves in the process, that we will die.

"This is the way to happiness, because if we leave God free to act in His way, He is infinitely more capable of rendering us happy than we ourselves are … the devil, causes us to imagine that if we put everything in God's hands God will effectively take everything and ruin everything in our lives! On the contrary, the Lord asks only an attitude of disposition to give Him everything.… Abandonment is not natural; it is a grace to be asked of God.… Abandonment is a fruit of the Holy Spirit … who ask with faith (Luke 11:13)."

Fr. Jacques Philippe - *Searching for and Maintaining Peace*

In God's Presence Consider …

Where is my level of trust and confidence in God? Do I shy away from intimacy with God because I fear what He might ask of me? Because abandonment is not natural, do I ask the Holy Spirit for the grace and the fruit to be disposed to detach and give God everything?

Closing Prayer

Lord, I often shrink back from intimacy with You because of my lack of confidence in You, my not trusting Your Providence, and fearing what You might ask. Send Your Holy Spirit that my heart may be disposed to trust You for all and to abandon myself completely into Your hands.

Do Everything with Great Perfection **Day 340**

Blessed Clelia speaks of the Holy Spirit's holy light that illuminates our intellect and spirit with Christian wisdom, that is beautiful in God's eyes, teaches us innocence of life, inspires upright and honest intentions, and inspires eternal joys. She says it is to the Holy Spirit we must pray to for His help.

"If you invoke the Holy Spirit who is divine wisdom, he will come into you and fill you with his light. When his holy light has illumined your intellect and your spirit, you will feel stimulated and eager to travel the road to holiness.... You must pray to the Holy Spirit to teach you Christian wisdom; beg him often to inspire in you the love and practice of it. This wisdom, which is that of the saints, is the life and peace of the soul, the teacher, the guardian and the directress of virtue. It consists in intending to have as the prime and principal goal of all your actions the glory of God and your eternal salvation; you must regard all creatures and all events as means designed to attain this goal.

"No created intelligence will ever understand all the holy and perfect work of the Holy Spirit in Mary's soul, which was so well disposed, so solicitous for perfection, so pure and gentle. Let us thus glorify the Holy Spirit and let us beg him to show us all the beauty of this magnificent scene and to give us the grace to find some trace of it in ourselves. 'Do everything you do with great perfection,' the Holy Spirit tells us."

Blessed Clelia Merloni - *Spiritual Anthology*

In God's Presence Consider ...

Do I seek and invoke the Holy Spirit's wisdom to fill me with His divine light? Do I beg the Holy Spirit to inspire in me the love and practice of wisdom? Is the prime and principal goal of all my actions the glory of God and my eternal salvation?

Closing Prayer

Come, O Divine Wisdom, with Your illuminating light. Fill my intellect and spirit with the desire to travel the road to holiness doing everything with great perfection and that all my actions will be for the glory of God and my eternal salvation. Blessed Clelia Merloni, pray for me.

God is an Earthquake **Day 341**

We cannot get the Holy Spirit; we can only let Him get us. He is God and only God can give Him. Jesus and the Father give Him. They pour Him into our hearts. We simply need to ask and believe.

"The Spirit is free. He is God's gift. There is nothing we can do to get him, we must simply ask, in faith, like a child trusting his father's love. The same is true of the Spirit's gifts, such as wisdom: we get them simply by asking and believing: 'If any of you lacks wisdom, let him ask God, who gives to all men generously and without reproaching, and it will be given him. But let him ask in faith.' (Jas. 1:5–6).

"But be careful what you ask for, because God will take you at your word. The Spirit's work is to sanctify, to make saints, and saints are not safe! They are like the One who makes them. God is not safe. Rabbi Abraham Heschel says: 'God is not nice. God is not an uncle. God is an earthquake.'"

Peter Kreeft - *The Holy Spirit*

In God's Presence Consider …

The Holy Spirit is God's free gift to me. Do I ask God for His Gift, the Holy Spirit, with faith? How much do I really trust God to cover all my bases? Does my life reflect the truth that I am called to be a saint? Do I ask the Holy Spirit to fill up in me what is lacking?

Closing Prayer

Father, I ask You to remove all obstacles that prevent me from asking for Your Holy Spirit. Enkindle within me the Fire of Your Love, and thus consumed in Your Flames, may my faith and trust in You increase and be perfected.

In Galatians 2:20, St. Paul writes, "It is no longer I who live, but it is Christ who lives in me." This melding of the self with Jesus is intimate communion; a communion that God wills, but very few attain because we aren't prepared. Sr. Burrows writes that we must cooperate with the Holy Spirit in order for this communion to be affected in us.

"St. John of the Cross says we are not prepared to take the trouble to do all that we possibly can to prepare for the Holy Spirit's sanctifying activity, nor are we ready to accept the inevitable difficulty and suffering that are its effects: 'this highest union cannot be wrought in a soul that is not fortified by trials and temptations, and purified by tribulations, darkness, and distress….' (St. John of the Cross, Living Flame of Love, 2.25)

"Too readily such expressions seem to let us off the hook. 'That sort of suffering belongs to very special souls, not to an ordinary person like myself.' Pure fallacy … all the ups and downs of the 'ordinary' person—contains everything that the Holy Spirit needs with which to purify us of our selfishness…. But we must allow the Holy Spirit to use it all. This is where we fail to 'take trouble', to make the effort of faith to rise above the level of our senses…. We cannot rid ourselves of this deeply rooted pride and self-possession by our own strength. Only the Holy Spirit of the Crucified and Risen One can effect it…."

Sr. Ruth Burrows O.C.D. - *Essence of Prayer*

In God's Presence Consider …

Do I do all that I possibly can to prepare for the Holy Spirit and to cooperate with Him? What does the Holy Spirit do in me? How can I truly be ready for the communion of prayer?

Closing Prayer

Thank You, O Holy Spirit, for coming to me in the ordinary ups and downs of my life. Purify me of my selfishness, pride, and ego. Help me to rise above my senses and feelings to become one with Jesus and You.

Fr. Philippe encourages us to be alert to recognize, welcome, and put into practice the inspirations of the Holy Spirit for perfection comes by an inner faithfulness to God's inspirations.

"The Spirit of God is a spirit of peace, and he speaks and acts in peace and gentleness, never in tumult and agitation. What's more, the motions of the Spirit are delicate touches that don't make a great noise and can penetrate our spiritual consciousness only if we have within ourselves a sort of calm zone of silence and peace. If our inner world is noisy and agitated, the gentle voice of the Holy Spirit will find it very difficult to be heard.

"If we want to recognize and follow the Spirit's motions, it is of the greatest importance to maintain a peaceful heart in all circumstances.

"The greatest harm that upsetting ourselves does to us is that it makes us incapable of following the impulses of the Holy Spirit."

Fr. Jacques Philippe - *In the School of the Holy Spirit*

In God's Presence Consider …

Have I ever felt the gentle motion and delicate touch of the Holy Spirit in my life? Do I maintain a peaceful heart even amidst tumult and agitation? Why is inner peace so important in my relationship with the Holy Spirit?

Closing Prayer

Come, Holy Spirit, as a gentle breeze and fill my heart with Your peace, that I may recognize and follow Your movements; Your motions in my life; Your impulses.

Cardinal Sarah, in looking at the work of Henri Nouwen, comments that the closer we are to the Holy Spirit, the more silent we are; and the farther we are from the Spirit, the more garrulous we are. The lack of respect for silence is a form of blasphemy against the Holy Spirit.

"We need to cultivate silence and to surround it with an interior dike. In my prayer and in my interior life, I have always felt the need for a deeper, more complete silence. I am talking about a kind of discretion that amounts to not even thinking about myself but, rather, turning my attention, my being, and my soul toward God.... Silence and the development of interior life are absolutely necessary ... we must never forget it.

"In The Way of the Heart, Henri Nouwen writes: 'As ministers our greatest temptation is toward too many words. They weaken our faith and make us lukewarm. Silence is a sacred discipline, a guard of the Holy Spirit'.... After the Ascension, Christ did not leave mankind orphaned. As at the beginning of creation, like a gentle breeze, 'the Spirit of God was moving over the face of the waters': so the Son of God entrusted humanity into the hands of the Holy Spirit, who spreads the love of the Father and silently distributes his light and wisdom. This is why it is scarcely possible to let oneself be guided by the Holy Spirit in the noise and agitation of the world."

Robert Cardinal Sarah - *The Power of Silence*

In God's Presence Consider ...

Do I cultivate silence in my life? Do I see silence in the development of my interior life as absolutely necessary? How do I feel about Jesus entrusting me into the hands of the Holy Spirit? Do I take steps to be guided by the Holy Spirit by creating times of silence?

Closing Prayer

Come, Holy Spirit, and help me to build an interior life around Your great gift of silence. Help me to not only realize the need of silence in my prayer life, but to desire it and cultivate it. Turn my whole attention, my being, and my soul towards God.

Cardinal Sarah says that God's language, speech, and work is silence. If one is to truly enter into prayer and conformity to Jesus, he must be filled with the Holy Spirit. To pray is to be able to hear the ineffable moaning of the Holy Spirit who dwells in us and cries out silently.

"Thus it is important to stay in the presence of the Lord so that he can find us available and introduce us into the great silence within that enables him to become incarnate in us, to transform us into himself. And in this silence, which is not emptiness but is filled with the Holy Spirit, the soul will be able to hear rising from his heart like a murmur: 'Abba! Father!' (Rom.8:15) Prayer is successfully being quiet, listening to God, and being able to hear the ineffable moaning of the Holy Spirit, who dwells in us and cries out silently.

"It is important to create the interior room where man finds God in a genuine face-to-face encounter. This spiritual work demands effort in order to avoid all distraction … the search for interior silence is a path to perfection that demands repeated attempts…. It is necessary to hide in the Spirit in order to divert and escape the senses. The Holy Spirit is the first condition for silence…. It is important to let the Holy Spirit penetrate the innermost regions of the soul. For in that secret space God lives and acts. He works so as to achieve our union with him…. In the school of the Holy Spirit, we learn to listen to God, in the silence that is the language of true love, which he alone can hear…."

Robert Cardinal Sarah - *The Power of Silence*

In God's Presence Consider …

Do I struggle with silence? Have I ever thought of silence being filled with the Holy Spirit who is raising my heart to the Father in prayer? Do I let the Holy Spirit penetrate the innermost regions of my soul in the secret space of silence? Have I created the interior room where I can find God in a genuine face-to-face encounter through prayer?

Closing Prayer

Father, You who examine the secret space where You live and act within me, send Your Spirit that I may learn Your language of silence, and in listening to You come to express the language of true love.

To Die of Pleasure **Day 346**

St. John Vianney was a simple man and used simple illustrations to make his point among the simple living people of his day.

"Worldly people have not the Holy Ghost, or if they have, it is only for a moment. He does not remain with them; the noise of the world drives Him away. A Christian who is led by the Holy Ghost has no difficulty in leaving the goods of this world, to run after those of Heaven; he knows the difference between them. The eyes of the world see no further than this life, as mine see no further than this wall when the church door is shut. The eyes of the Christian see deep into eternity. To the man who gives himself up to the guidance of the Holy Ghost, there seems to be no world; to the world there seems to be no God.... We must therefore find out by whom we are led. If it is not by the Holy Ghost, we labor in vain; there is no substance nor savour in anything we do. If it is by the Holy Ghost, we taste a delicious sweetness ... it is enough to make us die of pleasure!"

St. John Vianney - *Catechism on the Holy Spirit,* Chapter 3

In God's Presence Consider ...

How attached am I to the goods of this world or those things around me? Are my eyes fixed on this life or the life hereafter? Who or what influences and leads my spiritual life?

Closing Prayer

Come, Holy Spirit, dwell in my heart. Lead me to separate myself from the noise and lures of earthly goods, to focus me towards eternity and the sweetness of Your presence. St. John Vianney, pray for me.

A Soft Whisper **Day 347**

To die as a martyr raises many questions within a soul. St. Cyril tells us how the Holy Spirit is present, comforting, encouraging, reminding us of God's promises, giving us strength, and showing us the paradise of delight, despite the hardships in front of us.

"And the Spirit is called the Comforter, because he comforts us, and encourages us.

"Often a man is outraged, dishonored, and hurt for Christ's sake. Tortures on every side – fire and sword – savage beasts – the deep pit. But the Holy Spirit softly whispers to him, 'Wait for the Lord. What is happening to you now is trivial; what you're being given is great. Suffer a little while, and be with angels forever. The sufferings of the present time are not worth comparing with the glory that is to be revealed to us' (Rom. 8:18).

"He portrays the kingdom of Heaven to the man; he almost shows him the paradise of delight. And the martyrs, whose faces must necessarily be turned toward their judges, but whose spirits are already in paradise, despise the hardships they see in front of them."

St. Cyril of Jerusalem - *Catechetical Lecture 16, 20*

In God's Presence Consider ...

Do I ponder the comfort that the Holy Spirit can exercise in me when I am faced with extreme hardships and possible martyrdom? Do I still myself and cultivate silence so that I may hear the Holy Spirit's whisper?

Closing Prayer

Help me, Holy Spirit, to listen to Your whispering in my heart. May Your love direct me and help me to always act in accordance with Your will, strengthening me to face hardship, and keeping my eyes fixed on Jesus and the delights of paradise that await me.

A Second Pentecost **Day 348**

A heart in union with God prays words that reflect the intimacy of friendship between the one who prays and God. The following prayer was written by St. Pope John XXIII in 1959. Note the personalism of his words denoting the knowledge of the One he addresses this prayer to at the beginning of the Second Vatican Council.

"O divine Spirit, sent by the Father in the Name of Jesus, give your aid and infallible guidance to your Church and pour out on the Ecumenical Council the fullness of your gifts.... O gentle Teacher and Consoler, enlighten the hearts of our prelates who ... will gather here in solemn conclave....

"O gentle Guest of our souls, confirm our minds in truth and dispose our hearts to obedience, that the deliberations of the Council may find in us generous consent and prompt obedience.

"Renew in our own days your miracles as of a second Pentecost; and grant that Holy Church, reunited in one prayer, more fervent than before, around Mary the Mother of Jesus, and under the leadership of Peter, may extend the kingdom of the divine Savior, a kingdom of truth, justice, love and peace. Amen."

St. Pope John XXIII - *Journal of a Soul*

In God's Presence Consider ...

How do I direct my prayers to the Holy Spirit? Am I generous and prompt in obedience to the Holy Spirit's guidance? Do I seek the Holy Spirit's help for the extending of the Kingdom?

Closing Prayer

Come, Gentle Guest of my soul. Come and conform my mind in truth, dispose my heart to obedience, and help me to give generous consent and prompt response to Your movement within me. Come upon me as a New Pentecost. St. Pope John XXIII, pray for me.

St. Pope John Paul II's Magisterium called all Christians to be witnesses to the Gospel with their own lives even if this did not necessarily require the martyrdom of blood, but rather that of difficulties in life.

"At the end of the second millennium, the Church has once again become a Church of martyrs.... In our own century the martyrs have returned, many of them nameless, 'unknown soldiers' as it were of God's great cause.

"This revelation of freedom, and hence of man's true dignity, acquires a particular eloquence for Christians and for the Church in a state of persecution—both in ancient times and in the present—because the witnesses to divine truth then become a living proof of the action the Spirit of truth, present in the hearts and minds of the faithful, they often mark with their own death by martyrdom, the supreme glorification of human dignity."

St. Pope John Paul II - *Tertio Millennio Adveniente*

In God's Presence Consider ...

Do I become frightened and shrink back when I think of the possibility of becoming a martyr? How can my bloody or unbloody martyrdom be a living proof of the action of the Holy Spirit in my life? Do I see martyrdom as the supreme glorification of human dignity?

Closing Prayer

Jesus, send Your Holy Spirit, that I may not seek great rewards and recognition for following You, but that I would be living proof of Your action in my life. May I humbly seek to be one of Your unknown soldiers.

Absence Creates Division **Day 350**

Lack of being attentive to the Holy Spirit leads to division, hatred, wars, and sects. We become gravediggers of the divine nature of the Church. To reject the Holy Spirit is the sin of blasphemy against Him.

"Today, the world is not sufficiently attentive to the Holy Spirit. Without attention to the Spirit, men are divided; they scatter, hate one another, and are divided as at Babel. Then wars are started, and sects abound. Without the Spirit, unbelief advances; with the Spirit, God comes close.

"I am sad to see how much we abuse the Holy Spirit. In their imagination and in disregard of the will that intends that we be one, some men, on their own initiative, create their own churches, their own theologies, and their own beliefs, which in fact are only petty subjective opinions. The Holy Spirit has no opinions. He only repeats what Christ taught us in order to lead to the whole truth.

"I say this in all seriousness: The absence of the Holy Spirit in the Church creates all the divisions.... When we are docile to the Holy Spirit, we are sure to be walking toward the truth because we are entirely subject to his inspirations. If we thwart the Holy Spirit by miserable, petty human calculations, secret meetings, and media consultations, we run headlong into tragedy and we are gravediggers of the divine nature of the Church.... The rejection of the Spirit is a blasphemy and a mortal sin because it is a matter of rejecting the truth."

Robert Cardinal Sarah - *The Power of Silence*

In God's Presence Consider ...

Am I attentive to the presence of the Holy Spirit? Is my belief of the Holy Spirit based upon relying on my own initiatives and opinions? Am I blaspheming the Holy Spirit by my lack of docility to Him and His inspirations? Am I unknowingly thwarting His work?

Closing Prayer

Holy Spirit, make me attentive to Your presence and working in my life. Help me to grow in the wisdom and knowledge of You. Increase and perfect my faith in You that I may grow closer to God. Help me to be more docile to You and entirely subject to Your inspirations.

If there is one thing we can learn from the Acts of the Apostles, it is that the Holy Spirit changed the Apostles lives greatly. From timid and fearful men, they were emboldened to face all their difficulties with faith, hope, and love and ultimately gave their lives as martyrs for the Lord.

"We can see from these experiences of the Apostles, which occurred shortly after Pentecost, that the Holy Spirit had brought about a profound change in them. All their fear had been driven out; ardent love now motivated them. With the Holy Spirit's help, they possessed the courage to conquer all obstacles. With the Holy Spirit's help, we too, can overcome all obstacles. As a retreat director once said, 'No matter what difficulties you face, if God is with you, you are always in the majority!' The Holy Spirit is our majority!"

Fr. Andrew Apostoli, C.F.R. - *The Gift of God: The Holy Spirit*

In God's Presence Consider …

Do I live in fear? Do I seek the Holy Spirit's help to have courage to conquer all my obstacles and fears? Is the Holy Spirit my majority?

Closing Prayer

O God, send forth Your Spirit and stir within me a new Pentecost. Grant me the gifts I need to overcome the obstacles that face me and to trust that You are my majority.

All the saints were filled with the Holy Spirit. Their souls overflowed with joy and consolations. They did all the wonders we read of in their lives by His help.

"St. Ignatius of Antioch was insulted by the Emperor Trajan because he was a Christian. The Saint's reply, 'Do not insult Ignatius the God-bearer.' Trajan demanded, 'Why do you say that you are the God-bearer?' The saint responded, 'Because it is true, God is in me.'

"Origen used to say, 'Our souls are little heavens because God is really in them.'

"One of the Holy Fathers once said, 'The Holy Ghost is not in our souls as a guest. He is there as a bridegroom, for His union with us is a marriage; it is a most intimate and loving union.'

"One time the Holy Ghost said to St. Angela: 'I am the Holy Ghost who has come to thee and will give thee such a joy as thou never yet tasted. I accompany thee, I am present in thee. Thou are My spouse, I will never leave thee.' The Saint responded, 'I cannot describe the joy I then felt.'

"St. Teresa of Jesus says, 'Our soul is a little heaven in which the Creator of Heaven and Earth takes up His abode. Is there anything so grand as to see Him, whose grandeur would fill a thousand worlds, hiding Himself in such a little dwelling as our soul!'"

Fr. Paul O'Sullivan, O.P. - *The Holy Ghost Our Greatest Friend*

In God's Presence Consider …

Am I a God-bearer? How is it that I am? If not, how could I become one? Do I see myself wedded to the Holy Spirit as His bride?

Closing Prayer

Glory be to the Father, and to the Son, and to the Holy Spirit. As it was in the beginning, is now, and ever shall be, world without end.

What is Essential Day 353

We can have the greatest programs and best Liturgy in the world, but if we don't have the Holy Spirit working in us, we will not be able to carry out our mission to make disciples and bring them to Christ.

"… we must admire the prophetic rational wisdom of every pope from St. Pope John XXIII up to and including Pope Francis, who have fervently prayed for, and exhorted us to pray for, a new Pentecost for the Church. Orthodoxy isn't enough, however essential it is; correct Liturgy is not enough, however essential it is; chastity isn't enough, however essential it is. What is needed in addition is the power of the Holy Spirit to bring all these wonderful dimensions of Catholic life into a living flame of love that urges on all of us with prophetic zeal….

"We simply cannot carry out the mission without boldly praying for a new Pentecost and courageously removing any limits on what the Holy Spirit is permitted to do. We must not be timid about asking the Holy Spirit to 'fall on us.' May the Holy Spirit 'fall on us' and ignite the fire of prophetic zeal in us all!"

Ralph Martin - *A Church in Crisis*

In God's Presence Consider …

What are the limits I have placed on the Holy Spirit, not permitting Him to do what He desires to do in my life? Am I timid or afraid to ask the Holy Spirit to fall on me and ignite the fire of His divine love?

Closing Prayer

Come, Holy Spirit, into my heart. Descend upon me as on the day of Pentecost when You filled Your first disciples with power from on high. Grant that I may fully participate in all Your gifts that You bestow with such great generosity.

Prayer of Robert Abel

When the Spirit is Lacking **Day 354**

Lack of being attentive to the Holy Spirit, leads to a cold heart, ultimately destroying all life within us. The warmth from the fire of the Holy Spirit in our soul is good and nourishes all living things. It is meant to be a source of warmth for others.

"The power of fire overcomes all things and is not itself subdued; it imparts its action to the things it encompasses, renews everything that comes near it, and does not decrease as it spreads itself. So too does the Holy Spirit pervade all things by his power, for he is ineffable in his might. When he enters a soul, he fills it with his fire and lets it enkindle others. All things that draw near him feel his renewing warmth. He leads all hearts upward to heaven….

"When it is cold, the leaves drop off the tree and one looks in vain for fruit; a proof that warmth is the good and nourishment, so to speak, of all living things. In us, that warmth is the grace of the Holy Spirit. When it is lacking the heart of a man grows cold and ceases to bear fruit, and soon the frost of sin destroys all the life that was in him. 'Wisdom will not abide in a person that is in debt to sin (Wis. 1:14).'"

St. Anthony of Padua - *St. Anthony of Padua: Wisdom for Today*

In God's Presence Consider …

Do I sense a coldness in my heart towards spiritual things? Am I growing in virtues, the gifts of the Holy Spirit, and His fruits? Do I have the fire of the Holy Spirit filling my heart with His ineffable might? Does the fire imparted to me by the Spirit enkindle others or do I hoard His warmth for myself? What must I do to enkindle the fire of God's love within my heart?

Closing Prayer

Holy Spirit, make me attentive to Your presence, and fill my heart with Your fire. Help me to grow in the wisdom and knowledge of You. Increase and perfect my faith in You, that the warmth of Your fire will melt the frost of sin that has grown and caused my heart to grow cold. Lead me upward to heaven. St. Anthony of Padua, pray for me.

All are invited by Jesus to be the source of healing, hope, and joy to everyone we encounter. There are many challenges, being His disciples on mission, in blazing a trail to Jesus. We are encouraged "to be open to the Holy Spirit acting not a minute sooner nor a minute later than the Spirit wills it."

"To be filled with the Holy Spirit and sent on a mission to bring others closer to Jesus Christ and the Kingdom of God is not just something that sounds nice and noble as an idea, or as a program that we want to emphasize or as the goals and objectives of a five-year plan. Jesus proclaimed, 'I came to cast fire upon the earth; and would that it was already ablaze!' (Lk.12:49). The tongues of fire that came to rest on the heads of the apostles set their hearts on fire and they burst forth from the upper room into the world to blaze a trail to Jesus Christ.

"... we must pray to the Holy Spirit to make the impossible happen, to let go of everything and everyone but Jesus.... But we must remember, our prayer and witness as disciples ... are the actions of the Holy Spirit working through us.... Missionary discipleship is not about us, but rather what the Holy Spirit of Jesus wants to do in and through us!"

Bishop Daniel Felton - *Healing, Hope and Joy in Jesus*

In God's Presence Consider ...

Do I become frightened and shrink back when I think of the possibility of becoming a disciple on mission? Do I blaze a trail to Jesus for others to come to know Him? Is my faith in a Someone or a structure and plan? Do I pray asking the Holy Spirit to make the impossible happen?

Closing Prayer

Jesus, help me to listen to others for the voice of the Holy Spirit speaking to me through them. Help me cooperate with His work and become an agent of healing, hope, and joy for those around me. Please Holy Spirit, make the impossible happen and help me to let go of everything and everyone but Jesus.

The Need for the Greater **Day 356**

The growth of the Church did not progress smoothly. It encountered many forms of opposition, human and spiritual: persecutions, arrests, death sentences, and authorities demanding a privatized faith and silence in publicly speaking about Jesus and His message. How the believers responded can teach us how to respond in our times.

"The believers' response is instructive. They gathered to pray, realizing that intercessory prayer is essential for the success of the Church's mission. Surprisingly, they did not pray for the Lord to overthrow their persecutors, or even for themselves to be kept safe. Rather, they prayed for even more confidence to preach the gospel accompanied by supernatural signs. 'Lord, look upon their threats, and grant to your servants to speak your word with all boldness, while you stretch out your hand to heal, and signs and wonders are performed through the name of your holy Servant Jesus' (Acts. 4:29–30).

"Times of greater trouble require a greater release of the Holy Spirit: greater zeal for the gospel, greater faith to move mountains, more healings, more joy, more courage in the face of persecution."

Dr. Mary Healy – *Healing*

In God's Presence Consider …

If the Church felt external pressures against its evangelistic mission and boldly prayed for signs and wonders, then how can I not do so today? What can I learn from the early believers? Do I seek a greater release of the Holy Spirit in my life?

Closing Prayer

O Lord, just as You emboldened and taught Your disciples by the power of Your Holy Spirit, by that same Spirit fill me with more confidence and trust in You. Grant me a boldness to speak Your word, and stretch out Your hand to work signs, wonders and healings in our midst.

Ten years after the Council ended, St. Pope Paul VI, encouraged all people numerous times, to seek a new Pentecost, a new stirring and release of the power of the Holy Spirit in their lives.

"Paul VI thought that the hopes of John XXIII for the Second Vatican Council could really be fulfilled only through the experience of a new Pentecost. We have seen signs of this new Pentecost in a number of spiritual renewal movements following the Council, most notably and literally in the charismatic renewal. And it is noteworthy that perhaps the most widely utilized and effective evangelization going on in the Church today—movements and programs such as Catholic Alpha, Christ Life, and Encounter Ministries—all place strong emphasis on the need for every Catholic to experience the release of the power of the Holy Spirit in their lives, even though they don't consider themselves members of a particular movement dedicated to such. If the Church is to be truly equipped to carry out its mission in the world, it seems that a greater and deeper outpouring of the Spirit is needed—and not just among a few or on the periphery.... We too have wished to place our self in the same perspective and in the same attitude of expectation. Not that Pentecost has ever ceased to be an actuality during the whole history of the Church, but so great are the needs and perils of the present age, so vast the horizon of mankind drawn towards world coexistence and powerless to achieve it, that there is no salvation for it except in a new outpouring of the gifts of God. Let Him come, then, the Creating Spirit, to renew the face of the earth!?'"

Ralph Martin - *A Church in Crisis*

In God's Presence Consider ...

Have I ever sought a new Pentecost in my life asking God to release the power of the Holy Spirit within me? Have I ever thought that Pentecost never ceased to be an actuality in the Church and in my life even today? Am I open to a deeper outpouring of the Holy Spirit in my life to equip me to carry out the Church's mission in the world?

Closing Prayer

Come, Holy Spirit, enkindle in my heart the fire of Your love. Send forth Your Spirit, O Lord, and renew the face of the earth.

Tsunami of the Holy Spirit **Day 358**

The absence of God in our society has left an inner void that people seek to fill with all kinds of counterfeits. There is a growing culture of narcissism that has led to vast empty pursuits, broken lives and relationships, and a development of a consumer spirituality that St. Pope John Paul II summed up as "the culture of death." Things have gotten so out of hand it will take a tsunami of the Holy Spirit to set things right, to bring healing, and to bring people back to God.

"In this age when so many have wandered far from God, the Lord is once more clothing his followers with power from on high (Lk. 24:49). He is calling us to go out and proclaim the gospel not only in words, but also in signs and wonders that bear witness to the truth of the words….

"The world has become a war zone, where countless people are spiritually wounded and in dire need of help. A fierce battle is going on for the hearts and souls and minds of this generation. The stakes are high. What is going to meet the challenge of our times?

"No human strategy or plan or program will suffice. It is God alone who holds the answer. 'Not by might, nor by power, but by my Spirit, says the Lord of hosts' (Zech. 4:6). The answer to the 'tsunami of secularism' is nothing less than a tsunami of the Spirit—a proclamation of the gospel in the supernatural power of the Holy Spirit, accompanied by healing, signs, and wonders that tangibly demonstrate God's love and convince people that Jesus Christ is truly alive."

Dr. Mary Healy - *Healing*

In God's Presence Consider …

What are the war zones in my life? What gospel do I proclaim with my life? God tells us that it will not be by human power, strategies, plans, or power but by His Holy Spirit. How do I avail myself to be clothed with the power from on high?

Closing Prayer

Father, sweep me away in the tsunami of Your Love. Fill me with the supernatural power of Your Holy Spirit. Work in me and through me, Your signs and wonders that I may boldly proclaim Jesus Christ with my life.

Cardinal Ratzinger (Pope Benedict XVI) reminds us that the origin of the Church is not based on a decision of men or a product of man willing it; rather it is a creature of the Holy Spirit. He refers to the "gift" and the "pure light from above" as being the Holy Spirit.

"The more men themselves decide and do in the Church, the more cramped it becomes for us all. What is great and liberating about the Church is not something self-made but the gift that is given to us all. This gift is not the product of our own will and invention but precedes us and comes to meet us as the incomprehensible reality that is 'greater than our heart' (1 Jn. 3:20). The reform that is needed at all times does not consist in constantly remodeling 'our' Church according to our taste, or in inventing her ourselves, but in ceaselessly clearing away our subsidiary constructions to let in the pure light that comes from above and that is also the dawning of pure freedom.

"Let me express what I mean using a metaphor borrowed from Michelangelo.... With the eye of the artist, Michelangelo already saw in the stone that lay before him the pure image that, hidden within, was simply waiting to be uncovered. The artist's only task—so it seemed to him—was to remove what covered the statue. Michelangelo considered the proper activity of the artist to be an act of uncovering, or releasing—not of making ... his work is 'ablatio'—the removal of what is not really part of the sculpture. In this way, that is, by means of ablatio, the nobilis forma—the noble form—takes shape.

Joseph Cardinal Ratzinger - *Called to Communion*

In God's Presence Consider ...

Do I see myself as self-made or as a "gift" from the "pure light," the Holy Spirit, from above? Am I allowing God to do continual ablatio—removing and clearing away—anything that cramps and prevents His image within me from being renewed, released, and made visible?

Closing Prayer

Come, Holy Spirit, Master Artist, and do Your ablatio with me. Remove from me all that hinders my "noble form" from taking shape through Your work of renewal and regeneration.

A New Heart **Day 360**

God is prophesying to His people that He is about to act and do something in their midst, not for their sake but for His holy name, which the House of Israel has profaned. The new covenant that God speaks to us through His prophet Ezekiel is one of hope.

"For I will take you from the nations, and gather you from all the countries and bring you into your own land. I will sprinkle clean water upon you, and you shall be clean from all your uncleannesses, and from all your idols I will cleanse you. A new heart I will give you, and a new spirit I will put within you; and I will take out of your flesh the heart of stone and give you a heart of flesh. And I will put my spirit within you, and cause you to walk in my statutes and be careful to observe my ordinances. You shall dwell in the land which I gave to your fathers; and you shall be my people, and I will be your God. And I will deliver you from all your uncleannesses; and I will summon the grain and make it abundant and lay no famine upon you. I will make the fruit of the tree and the increase of the field abundant, that you may never again suffer the disgrace of famine among the nations. Then you will remember your evil ways, and your deeds that were not good; and you will loath yourselves for your iniquities and your abominable deeds."

Ezekiel 36:24–32

In God's Presence Consider …

God wants to give you a new heart and put His Holy Spirit in you so you can walk in His ways and dwell in His land. Do I confess my sins that prevent me from receiving this great blessing? Do I seek the Holy Spirit's help in walking in God's statutes and observing His ordinances carefully?

Closing Prayer

Come, Holy Spirit, and make me loath my evil ways, abominable deeds, and iniquities; turning to God for forgiveness. Give me again a new heart and help me to walk in His statutes and ordinances.

Openness to Dynamic Union **Day 361**

The Holy Spirit calls each of us, and the Church as a whole, to pattern ourselves after Mary and the Apostles in the Upper Room who accepted and embraced the baptism in the Holy Spirit as the power of transformation with all the graces and charisms needed to fulfill our mission as Church.

"A life baptized in the Spirit is marked both by an experience of dynamic union with God and by an experience of charisms given by the Spirit. These enable us to serve God in praise and worship, to serve one another in love … and to empower our participation in the church's ministry and society. These charisms belong to the church today.

"A renewed parish is a community worshiping in vibrant liturgy, bonded together by the Holy Spirit, serving one another, committed to ongoing conversion and growth, reaching out to the inactive, the unchurched and to the poor…. In these communities, the charisms of the Holy Spirit are identified and welcomed.

"God freely gives this grace, but it requires a personal response of ongoing conversion to the Lordship of Jesus Christ and openness to the transforming presence and power of the Holy Spirit. Only in the Holy Spirit will we be able to respond to its pastoral needs and those of the world."

McDonnell and Montague - *Fanning the Flame*

In God's Presence Consider …

Am I alive and vibrant in the Spirit where others notice the Spirit's fruits in my life? Am I a hallmark of Christian community by my self-sacrificing mutual love and in communion with my brothers and sisters? Am I seeking ongoing conversion to the Lordship of Jesus Christ? Am I open to the transforming presence and power of the Holy Spirit in my life?

Closing Prayer

Father, please, pour out Your Spirit upon me, that transformed by the power and love of the Holy Spirit, I will seek ongoing conversion, openness to Your presence. Lead me to a fuller participation in the Body of Christ.

Giving Adequate Recognition **Day 362**

Fr. Hauser speaks of two models of spirituality. One is a Scriptural model where God initiates and man responds or the Western model where man initiates and God rewards.

"If there is any Christian truth that has gone unappreciated, it is the presence of the Holy Spirit in our activities. The fact of the presence is clear; the problem is that we don't recognize it. There are many reasons for this. The main reason, I believe, is that we live in a secular society which explains all truth, including its understanding of human behavior in secular terms.... Human nature for a secular mentality is not the self-in-God (Scriptural model).

"... much of spirituality has been dominated by a Self-outside-of-God model. We see ourselves as the sole initiator and power behind all good acts. If God has any role, it is in rewarding us for our good deeds after we have done them.... This Western approach to spirituality is our current version of the old heresy of Pelagianism.... I believe that the combination of secularism and an implicit Pelagianism have kept us from giving adequate recognition to the all-pervasive presence and power of the Holy Spirit in our daily lives.... God's Spirit joins our spirit; it does not replace it.... The Holy Spirit is indeed active in us at all times drawing us toward greater love and service of God and others, but the Spirit does not control our response. That flows from our freedom.... In examining the work of the Spirit in us according to the New Testament, it is well to recall that we refer to a gentle prompting rather than an overriding compulsion."

Fr. Richard Hauser, S.J. - *In His Spirit*

In God's Presence Consider ...

Do I have difficulty recognizing the presence of the Holy Spirit in my day to day activities? Is my spirituality based upon Self-in-God or the Self-outside-of-God model? Am I being drawn toward and freely choosing a greater love and service of God and others? Do I recognize the gentle promptings of the Holy Spirit or am I awaiting an overriding compulsion?

Closing Prayer

Come, Holy Spirit, with Your gentle promptings and draw me to a greater love and service of God and others.

Taking on the Character of Christ **Day 363**

We can't become more Christ-like or holier without God's help. The more that we grow in Christ's grace the more we take on the Character of Christ.

"The hardest part about growing in virtue is perhaps learning to rely not on oneself but on God's grace.... Jesus' words apply to all of us: 'Apart from me you can do nothing,' (Jn. 15:5).

"When an iron rod is put into a flame of fire, it begins to change and take on the properties of fire. It becomes hot. It starts to glow, taking on the color of the fire. And it emits smoke, like the fire itself. The rod of iron doesn't become fire. But it takes on the characteristics of fire. Similarly, when our human nature is infused with sanctifying grace though the fire of the Holy Spirit, it starts to change. It is gradually transformed by God so that it begins to take on the characteristics of Christ himself. The soul exhibits more peace, joy, patience, generosity, and love. The soul does not become God, but takes on more of the characteristics of God as it is being transformed by the fire of his love."

Dr. Edward Sri - *The Art of Living*

In God's Presence Consider ...

Does my life reflect the truth that apart from Jesus I can do nothing? What are some ways that I rely on myself more than God? What are characteristics in my life that show I am being transformed and taking on the characteristics of God?

Closing Prayer

O Holy Spirit, I entrust myself to You. Take away my self-sufficiency and fears. Place me into the flames of God's burning love. Change me, transform me, so I will take on the properties of Your fire and the characteristics of Christ Jesus Himself. Complete the good work You have begun within me.

There has been a shift from a Christian world view to an Apostolic Mission world view. What are we facing at this "end of the age"? How are we to cooperate with the Holy Spirit in order to make a difference?

"The modern progressive vision is all around us, incessantly hammered home with all the pervasive power of electronic imagery and consumer affluence, but compared to the one given us by God, it is a weak and anemic vision. From its beginnings its claims have been unreal, and it has been so weakened by generations of dismal human experience that it can now be sustained only by economic prosperity and the apparent lack of a good alternative. The hope that mankind would be made better has in practice been replaced by the hope that we can build yet faster and more powerful phones and screens; the dreams of a perfected world of justice and freedom are ebbing into vague hopes of biotechnological enhancement of physical powers. Much of the current strength of the modern vision is in its immediacy: it appeals with great skill to the human propensity to be distracted by the sensual and the seen … it is intellectually bankrupt and spiritually impoverished.

"The Holy Spirit is at work in every age, ours included.... Our task is to understand the age we have been given, to trace out how the Holy Spirit is working in it, and to seize the adventure of cooperating with him … to prove the liberating life given us by Jesus."

Monsignor James Shea - *From Christendom to Apostolic Mission*

In God's Presence Consider …

Given the current time we live in, do I expect an abundant action of the Holy Spirit? Am I proving myself as a faithful steward of God's message and work? Am I willing to seek the guidance of the Holy Spirit and to seize the opportunity of cooperating with Him in this new apostolic age? Do I witness with my life the freedom and joy of knowing Jesus Christ?

Closing Prayer

O Holy Spirit, help me to understand this age I am living in and to look for You in my everyday circumstances and choices. Help me to be a witness to gift of salvation and the joy of living as one of Your disciples.

In order to be a Christian disciple of Jesus Christ, there needs to be an empowering and guiding action of the Holy Spirit, a new Pentecost.

"… the empowering … guiding action of the Holy Spirit is uniquely important. Only the Spirit of God knows the depths of God, the depths of our own soul, and the real situation of the world and guides us along the only truly wise course…. Seeking God directly for his guidance and developing a sensitivity to the leading of the Holy Spirit is crucial for adequate Christian life and action today.

"One of the great sins … is our neglect of actively seeking God's guidance for the situations we face as individuals and as a people…. One of our great problems as a Church is that we have too many 'natural' men and women … and not enough … 'spiritual' men and women led by the Spirit in their life and work. This failure to submit our plans to God's Word and to the leading of his Spirit is one of the main causes for the emptiness and lack of fruit of so much 'renewal'.

"We simply cannot carry out the mission without boldly praying for a new Pentecost and courageously removing any limits on what the Holy Spirit is permitted to do. We must not be timid about asking the Holy Spirit to 'fall on us.' May the Holy Spirit 'fall on us' and ignite the fire of prophetic zeal in us all."

Ralph Martin - *A Church in Crisis*

In God's Presence Consider …

Do I neglect to actively seek God's guidance for the situations I face and submitting my plans to Him? Am I well-formed and ready to be a missionary disciple? Do I boldly and courageously pray for a new Pentecost seeking the Holy Spirit to stir into flame a prophetic zeal, or am I rather timid, unsure, and place limits on what I allow the Holy Spirit to do in my life?

Closing Prayer

Come Holy Spirit with a new Pentecost. Stir into flame the prophetic zeal within me. Set me aflame with your love that I may become an apostle of the last days, filled with zeal to preach the Gospel with my life of holiness. All for the glory of God and salvation of souls.

Acknowledgments

There are a lot of people that go into making a book possible, especially to get it to a point of publishing. I first want to thank the late Charlie Neff, who encouraged me to write and publish the various teachings and teaching tools I used 30 years ago. A personal thank you to Candace Simar, who has been my writing mentor and encourager through this whole process. To Chrysa and Kay for being the extra set of eyes going over and over the text. Douglas Bushman, S.T. L. who gave valuable insights, and Sr. Juliana Gapasin, DLJC, who offered her battle with cancer for this book. Words cannot express my thanks for this great gift of self. I especially want to thank my wife Lori who first planted the seeds of this book in my heart when she said I should write a book on the Holy Spirit—for all the long hours she endured while I researched and wrote, all the times she edited and made sure everything flowed and was clear, for all our re-edits and adjustments to normal living, and for the encouragement she gave during those challenging times with the various little bumps we faced in the road. I literally could not have done this without her.

A big thank you goes out to all those who excitingly agreed to read a rough copy and write a blurb, as well as Springboard for the Arts and Krista Soukup of Blue Cottage Agency for steering us through the vast terrain of publishing; for Kelly the distributor at Story Laboratory; to Cathy Behrens for the book design and layout, and for my website at deaconmikeknuth.com (see Cathy's at cbgraphicdesigns.com); and to Julie Clark for the stunning cover art.

And finally, I want to acknowledge and give my most sincere thanks to the Holy Spirit, and the Saints that I invoked for their intercession. Without this great crowd of witnesses and the inspiration of the Holy Spirit this book would only be a fantasy and hopeful dream. Praise be to You O Lord, who has not given up stirring Your Fire within me.

Appendix

God is infinite love and His charisms are limitless. The Catherine of Siena Institute has a book entitled: *Fruitful Discipleship* by Sherry Anne Weddell. The Institute has identified 23 charisms and makes it clear that this is not an exhaustive list. Below are the charisms they have listed. Their book *The Catholic Spiritual Gifts Resource Guide*, is currently out of print and undergoing revisions. The book does an excellent job in providing Scripture and Resources that can help in discovering and using your charisms. These charisms are printed with permission of the Siena Institute.

Administration
Celebacy
Craftsmanship
Encouragement
Evangelism
Extraordinary Faith
Giving
Healing

Helps
Hospitality
Intercessory Prayer
Knowledge
Leadership
Mercy
Missionary
Music

Pastoring
Prophecy
Service
Teaching
Voluntary
Poverty
Wisdom
Writing

Works Cited

Anthony of Padua, Saint, St. Anthony of Padua: *Wisdom for Today*, Patrick McCloskey, O.F.M. Ed., St Anthony Messenger Press, Cincinnati, OH, 1977.

Apostoli, Fr. Andrew, C.F.R., *The Gift of God: The Holy Spirit*, Tan Books, Charlotte, NC, 2017.

Aquinas, St. Thomas, O.P., *Summa Theologica*, Coyote Canyon Press, Claremont, CA, 2018.

Benedict, Pope XVI, *Address to Participants of the Catholic Fraternity of Charismatic Covenant Communities and Fellowships*, Libreria Editrice Vaticana, Rome Italy, October 31, 2008.

Bonamy, H.M. Manteau, O.P., *The Immaculate Conception and the Holy Spirit*, Franciscan Marytown Press, Libertyville, IL, 1977.

Calloway, Fr. Donald, MIC, *Consecration to St. Joseph*, Marian Press, Stockbridge, MA, 2020.

Cameron, John, O.P., *Benedictus*, Magnificat and Ignatius Press, Yonkers, New York, 2006.

Cantalamessa, Raniero, O.F.M.Cap., *Sober Intoxication of the Spirit*, Servant Books, Cincinnati, OH, 2005.

Catholic Company Magazine, *"The Saints on the Holy Spirit"*, St. Basil's Treatise on the Holy Spirit, May 2013.

Clark, Randy & Mary Healy, *The Spiritual Gifts Handbook*, Chosen Books, Bloomington, Minnesota, 2018.

Clerissac, Fr. Humbert, O.P., *The Mystery of the Church*, Cluny Media, Providence, RI, 2016.

Colins, Ted, *"Titus as Role Model on Death Role"*, Web page carmelnet.org/brandsma/html/med6.html.

St. Cyril of Alexandria, *Commentary on the Gospel of Luke*, translated by R. Payne Smith, Veritas Splendor Publications L.L.C., 2018.

Dubay, Thomas, S.M., *Deep Conversion Deep Prayer*, Ignatius Press, San Francisco, CA, 2006.

Edward, M. Ann, *The Exemplar: Life and Writing of Blessed Henry Suso*, Priory Press, Dubuque, IA; 1962.

Fatula, Sr. Mary Ann, O.P., *Drawing Close to the Holy Spirit*, Sophia Institute Press, Manchester, NH, 2021.

Felton, Bishop Daniel, *Healing, Hope and Joy in Jesus*, Pastoral Letter, Diocese of Duluth, MN, December 25, 2022.

Fr. Gabriel of St. Mary Magdalen, O.C.D., *Divine Intimacy*, Tan Books and Publishers, INC., Rockford, Illinois, 1964.

Francia, St. Hannibal di, *Divine Will Prayer Book*, MHT Inc., 5th edition published in Italy by Rev. Benedict Calvi, 1936.

Francis, Pope, *Christus Vivit (Christ Is Alive)* #115–117, 122, 130–131, 133, Post-Synodal Apostolic Exhortation, Rome, Italy, 2019.

_____. *Gaudete et Exsultate (On The Call To Holiness in Today's World)*, #21–23, Apostoloic Exhortation, Rome, Italy, 2018.

Gaitley, Michael E., MIC, *33 Days to Morning Glory*, Marian Press, Stockbridge MA, 2011.

Garrigou-Lagrange, Fr. Reginald, O.P., *The Three Ways of the Spiritual Life*, Tan Books and Publishing Co., Rockford, IL, 1938.

Hahn, Kimberly, *Life-Giving Love: Embracing God's Beautiful Design for Marriage*, Servant, Franciscan Media, Steubenville, Oh. 2001.

Hampsch, Fr. John H., CMF, *Receiving the Gift of the Holy Spirit*, Queenship Publishing Co., Goleta, CA, 2003.

Hauser, Richard, S.J., *In His Spirit*, Beacon Pub., Singer Island, Florida, 2nd edition, 2011.

Healy, Dr. Mary, *Healing: Bringing the Gift of God's Mercy to the World*, Our Sunday Visitor, Huntington, IN, 2015.

In the End My Immaculate Heart Will Triumph, Queenship Publishing Co., Santa Barbara, CA, 1993.

Jarrett, Fr. Bede, O.P., *Classic Catholic Meditations to Enrich Your Faith and Help You to Pray*, Sophia Institute Press, Manchester, NH, 2004.

_____. *The Abiding Presence of the Holy Ghost in the Soul*, The Newman Bookshop, Westminster, Maryland, 1943.

John XXIII. Saint and Pope, *Journal of a Soul*, McGraw-Hill Book Company, New York, 1965.

John Paul II, Saint and Pope, *Dominum et Vivicantem (Lord and Giver of Life)*, Encyclical Letter, St. Paul Media, Boston, 1986.

_____. *Tertio Millennio Adveniente (Apostolic Letter on the Great Jubilee of the Year 2000)*, St. Paul Media, Boston, 1994.

Khoury, Fr. Tony El, *A Light from the East: Meditations and Icons Illuminate the Life of Christ*, Magnificat, Yonkers, NY, 2018.

Kolbe, St. Maximilian, *The Writings of St. Maximilian Marie Kolbe, Volume II, Various Writings*, Lugano, Italy: Nerbini International, 2017.

Kowalska, St. Maria Faustina, *Diary: Divine Mercy in My Soul*, Marian Press, Stockbridge, MA, 1987.

Leo XIII, Pope, *Divinum Illud Munus (On the Holy Spirit)*, Encyclical Letter, Libreria Editrice Vaticana, Rome Italy, 1897.

Lubich, Chiara, *Servant of God, From Heaven on Earth: Meditations and Reflections*, Jerry Hearne, Tr., New York City Press, Hyde Park, New York, 2000.

MacDonnell, Kilian and George Montague, *Fanning the Flame*, A Michael Glazier Book, Liturgical Press, Collegeville, MN, 1991.

Martin, Ralph, *A Church in Crisis: Pathways Forward*, Emmaus Road Pub., Steubenville, Ohio, 2020.

Martinez, Archbishop Louis M., Servant of God, *The Sanctifier*, Daughters of St. Paul, Boston, MA, 2003.

Mary of Jesus Crucified, St., *Thoughts of Blessed Mary of Jesus Crucified*, Carmel of Bethlehem, 1997.

Merloni, Blessed Clelia, *Spiritual Anthology: Elements in the Spirituality of Mother, Clelia Merloni*, Sr. M. Clare Millea, Tr., Edusc Sacred Heart University Press, Bauru, Sao Paulo, Brazil, 1992.

Minerd, Matthew, *Made by God; Made for God*, Ascension Press, West Chester, PA, 2021.

Moore, Fr. Brian, SJ., *Devotions to the Holy Spirit*, Pauline Press, New York, NY, 1988.

NguyenVan Thuan, Francis Xavier, Venerable Cardinal, *Prayers of Hope, Words of Courage*, Daughters of St. Paul, Pauline Books and Media, Boston, MA, 2012.

O'Carroll, Fr. Michael, CSSp, J*ohn Paul II: A Dictionary of His Life and Teachings*, J.M.J. Publications, Belfast, Ireland, 1994.

Official web site for Blessed Elena Guerra.

Orthodox Church Quotes orthodoxchurchquotes.wordpress.com.

O'Sullivan, Fr. Paul, O.P., *The Holy Ghost Our Greatest Friend*, Tan Books, Rockford, IL, 1991.

Pasquale, Gianluigi, *Padre Pio's Spiritual Direction for Every Day*, Franciscan Media, Cincinnati, Ohio, 2011 (English Translation).

Paul, VI, Saint and Pope, *Ecclesiam Suam (Paths of the Church)*, St. Paul Editions, Boston, Massachusetts, 1964.

_____. *Evangelii Nuntiandi, (Evangelization in the Modern World)*, St. Paul Editions, Boston, Massachusetts, 1975.

Piault, Bernard, *What is the Trinity?*, Hawthorn Books, New York, NY, 1959.

Philippe, Fr. Jacques, *In the School of the Holy Spirit*, Scepter Publications, NY, 2007.

_____. *Searching for and Maintaining Peace*, Society of St. Paul, NY, 2002

_____. *The Eight Doors of the Kingdom*, Scepter Publications, NY, 2018.

Ratzinger, Joseph Cardinal, *Called to Communion*, Ignatius Press, San Francisco, 1996.

Raya, Archbishop Joseph M., *The Face of God: Essays in Byzantine Spirituality*, Dimension Books Inc., Danville, NJ, 1976.

Renewal Ministries, May 24, 2022.

Robets, Alexander, *Ante-Nicene Fathers Volume 1*, Christian Literature Publishing Co., Buffalo, NY, 1885, revised and edited by Kevin Knight for "New Advent", www.newadvent.org/fathers/0134.htm.

Sarah, Robert Cardinal, *The Power of Silence*, Ignatius Press, San Francisco, CA, 2017.

Scanlan, Fr. Michael, T.O.R., *Inner Healing*, Paulist Press, New York, NY, 1974.

Schaenzer, Sr. Mary Anne, SSND, *Charisms*, Catholic Charismatic Renewal Service Committee, Locust Grove, VA, 2009.

Shea, James, Monsignor, *From Christendom to Apostolic Mission Pastoral Strategies for an Apostolic Age*, University of Mary Press, Bismarck, ND, 2020.

Sheed, Frank J., *The Holy Spirit in Action*, Servant Books, Ann Arbor, MI, 1981.

Sheen, Archbishop Fulton, Venerable, *The Quotable Fulton Sheen*, Doubleday, New York, NY, 1989.

Sri, Edward, *The Art of Living*, Ignatius Press San Francisco, CA and Augustine Institute, Greenwood Village, CO, 2021.

Tanquerey, The Most Reverend Adolphe, *The Spiritual Life, A Treatise on Ascetical and Mystical Theology*, Society of St. John the Evangelist, Belgium, American translation 1930.

The Magnificat—June 2022, Vol. 24, No. 4, MAGNIFICAT Inc., Yonkers, NY, 2022.

The Roman Missal, Catholic Book Publishing, Totowa, NJ, 2011.

The Theological-Historical Commission for the Great Jubilee of the Year 2000, *The Holy Spirit, Lord and Giver of Life*, Crossroad Publishing Company, 1999.

Vianney, St. John, *The Blessed Curé of Ars in His Catechetical Instructions*, Patristic Publishing, Omaha, NE, 2019.

Von Speyr, Adrienne, *The Passion from Within*, (Translated by Sister Lucia Wiendenhöver, O.C.D.) Ignatius Press, San Francisco, CA, 1998.

Weddell, Sherry, *Forming Intentional Disciples*, OSV, Huntington, IN, 2012.

Zenit News, November 16, 2006, Vatican City, *Paul's Teaching on the Holy Spirit*, Pope Benedict XVI.

About the Author

Deacon Mike Knuth is an educator, speaker, and author. His work has been published in Chicken Soup for the Soul, Seeds of Faith, Deacon's Corner, Lakes Catholic Magazine, Catholic 365 and various parish and catholic periodicals, newsletters and bulletins, as well as his own blog, Deacon's Cellar. His previous books include: A Celebration of Life: A Study on the words of Pope John Paul II during the Eighth World Youth Day held in Denver, August 11–15, 1993, Pilgrim Primer II: A Journey of Encounter, Leader's and Participant's guides (1999), Pilgrim's Log: World Youth Day, 2002, Toronto Edition, and L'eaf; A Christmas Story (2009).

Ordained a Permanent Deacon for the Diocese of Duluth in 1991, he has served the Church for over 40 years on a parish, deanery, and diocesan level, as a director of religious education from cradle to grave, with an emphasis on sacramental preparation, RCIA, adult education, and a variety of workshops and seminars for catechist formation. He has conducted a variety of retreats and days of reflection on a variety of topics both on a local, state, and national level for laity and religious communities. He is a regular instructor in the diocesan deacon formation programs for both aspirants and candidates. He is a spiritual director, certified through Our Lady of Divine Providence: School of Spirituality in Clearwater, FL, since 2012. He currently serves the parishes of All Saints and St. Francis in the Baxter/Brainerd area of Minnesota.

Deacon Knuth lives in Pequot Lakes, Minnesota with Lori, his wife of 48 years. They have five children, three now married and two in religious and consecrated life. He enjoys road trips with his wife, visiting their adult children and six grandchildren, camping, canoeing in the BWCA, backpacking in the wilderness, gardening, playing cribbage and other family favorite card games, and ministering together.

Notes

Notes